CLASSROOM CONNECT'S
A+ YELLOW PAGES

K-6 Edition

Reviewed by
CHRIS MAUTNER

Classroom Connect's YELLOW PAGES

K-6 Edition

Reviewed by
Chris Mautner

Contributing writers
Cara Bafile
Lisanne M. Bartram
Nancy Hawkins
Kelli Housley
Tara Houston
David Kershaw
Deborah McLain
Timothy McLain

classroom CONNECT®
Internet made easy in the classroom™

1866 Colonial Village Lane
Lancaster, Pennsylvania 17601
URL: http://www.classroom.net
Email: connect@classroom.net
Telephone: (800) 638-1639

Acknowledgments

Senior Editor: **Kathy Housley**

*Cover illustration
& book design:* **Eric Denlinger**

Layout Designers: **Sam Gorgone**
John Svatek
Greg Wirt

Database Designer: **Nathanael Waite**

Copyright © 1997   Classroom Connect, Inc.
1866 Colonial Village Lane
Lancaster, Pennsylvania 17601

Due to the evolving nature of the Internet, addresses published in Classroom Connect's *A+ Yellow Pages* may change after publication. We do our utmost to check their validity before going to press and cannot be responsible for changes or inappropriate material that may appear after publication.

All terms mentioned in this book that are known to be trademarks or service marks have been appropriately capitalized.

All rights reserved. No part of this book may be reproduced or utilized in any form or by any means, electronic or mechanical, including photocopying, recording, or by any information storage and retrieval system without written permission of the publisher.

Printed in the United States of America

10 9 8 7 6 5 4 3 2 1

ISBN 0-932577-74-1

Table of Contents

Introduction vi

Art and Music 1

Health and Physical Education 41

Language Arts/Languages 65

Math 99

Science 127

Social Studies 171

Teacher's Resources 223

Technology/Internet 265

Introduction to Yellow Pages

Welcome to *Classroom Connect's* A+ Yellow Pages! This book gives you a quick and effective guide to the best educational sites currently on the World Wide Web. In addition to this comprehensive collection of *Classroom Connect's* favorite Web sites, you'll find Internet integration ideas to immediately use in your classroom. You'll refer to this book again and again, whenever you need to find quality educational material on the Net for yourself or for your students.

Why the Web anyway?

In a few short years, the World Wide Web has grown into a powerful resource for K-12 education, offering an inexpensive, easily accessible method to communicate and distribute information. Using the Internet, your students can do much more than play games. They can:

- Communicate with educators, scientists, field experts, and other students from around the globe.
- Access an enormous collection of resources, all constantly updated and revised.
- Create multimedia projects and reports.

Students can find virtually anything on the Web — government documents, biographies of scientists or authors, data on space shuttle missions, dictionaries of Shakespearean English, news magazine articles, song lyrics from every musical era, classical art, and more. In the last three or four years, Web usage and the number of Internet sites has grown by an estimated 400 percent. And each day, more users and more sites add to the volume.

Schools all over the world are contributing to this growth. Hundreds of K-12 schools in the United States are reaching to each other and to the rest of the world via the World Wide Web. In buying this book, you've shown you recognize the incredible potential the Net holds for you and your students. But once your computers are hooked up, how do you find the information you need to make good use of this tool in your classroom? Where are the best Web sites to incorporate into your lesson plans and activities? This book will point you and your students to Web sites useful for a range of subjects. Visit these sites, add them to your bookmarks, and perhaps link your school's Web page to them.

A word on addresses in this book.

According to a recent survey, a vast majority of K-12 Internet surfers use Netscape Navigator or a similar Internet browser to do all their online work. As a result, all of the addresses in this

Introduction to Yellow Pages

book are presented as standard URLs, or Uniform Resource Locators. A URL standardizes Internet addresses, and Internauts cite URL addresses when they refer to and access the various types of resources on the Net. URLs don't have to apply to just World Wide Web resources — they point to gopher databases, newsgroups, ftp sites, and email addresses.

A URL consists of three parts. The first part is simply the letters URL, which tell you that this is, in fact, an Internet address. The second part is the URL prefix and shows the access method. In the Classroom Connect address, **URL: http://www.classroom.net**, the URL prefix **http://** tells you it is a Web site.

The third part of the URL gives the specific address for that particular site on the World Wide Web. It consists of a root address, which in this case is **www.classroom.net.** Sometimes the root address is followed by information that points to a specific subdirectory or filename. Those names are separated by forward slashes.

Here's an example of an actual subdirectory or filename added to the Classroom Connect Web address: **www.classroom.net/classroom/search.htm**. The **classroom** part is the subdirectory and **search.htm** is the name of the file in the classroom subdirectory with the Web page about searching the Internet.

How this book is organized

This book is divided into eight chapters arranged by subject matter, so you can find the educational Web sites you need. The Teacher's Resources section contains sites aimed at improving the teacher's professional development and resources for searching the Web for information on a specific subject. Meanwhile, the Technology/Internet section, focuses on sites not specifically dealing with education, but also offering valuable resources for educators.

Next to each listing, you will find the name of the site, its URL address, and a description of the site's value to educators. To help you apply these sites in your classroom, you'll find, on every odd page, an integration idea.

Introduction to Yellow Pages

What you'll find on a typical page

Since each page in this book contains several sites, we've dissected a sample page to help you find what you need quickly.

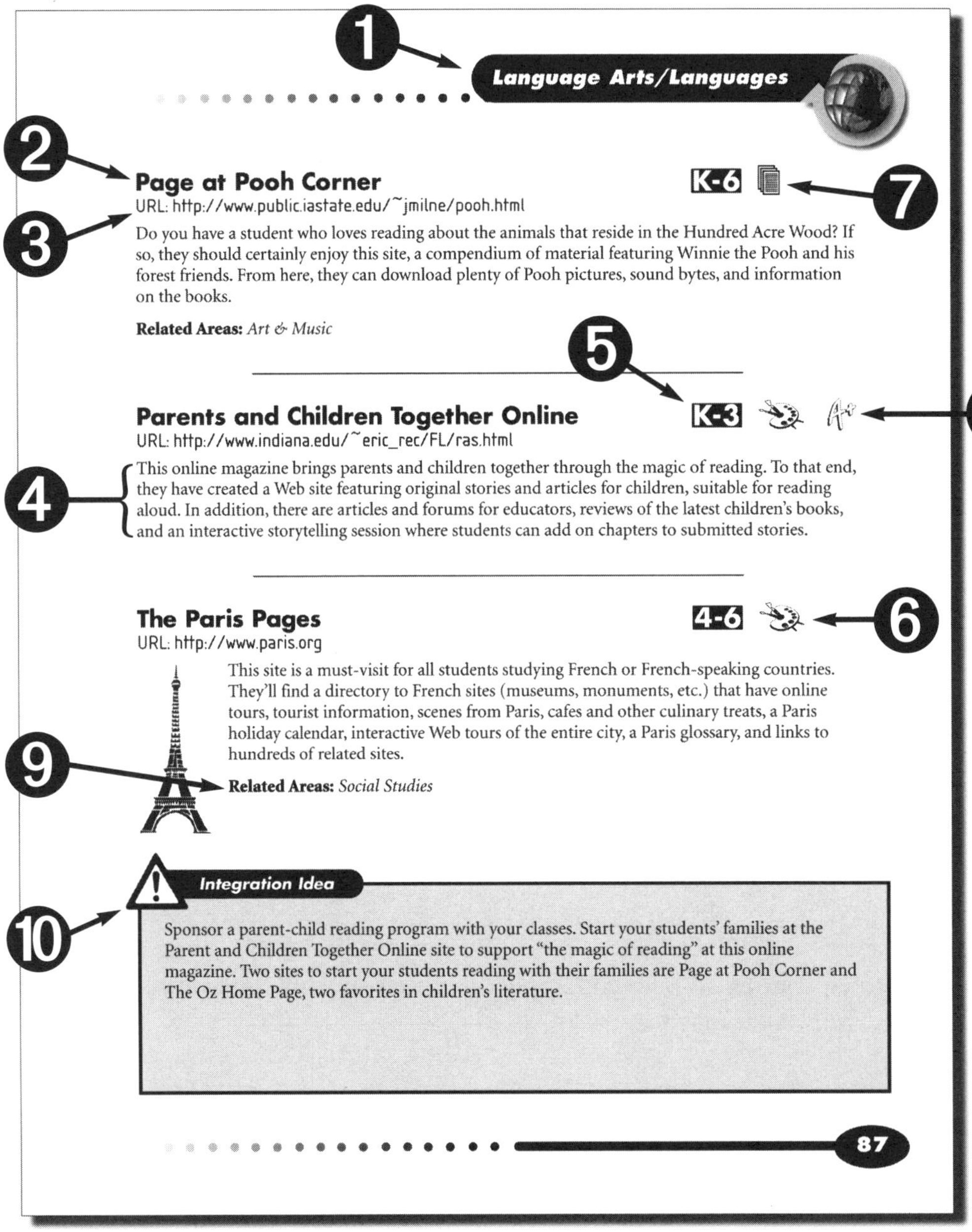

---

① Language Arts/Languages

② Page at Pooh Corner **⑦ K-6** 📋
URL: http://www.public.iastate.edu/~jmilne/pooh.html

③ Do you have a student who loves reading about the animals that reside in the Hundred Acre Wood? If so, they should certainly enjoy this site, a compendium of material featuring Winnie the Pooh and his forest friends. From here, they can download plenty of Pooh pictures, sound bytes, and information on the books.

Related Areas: *Art & Music*

Parents and Children Together Online **⑤ K-3** 🎨 ✏️ **⑧**
URL: http://www.indiana.edu/~eric_rec/FL/ras.html

④ This online magazine brings parents and children together through the magic of reading. To that end, they have created a Web site featuring original stories and articles for children, suitable for reading aloud. In addition, there are articles and forums for educators, reviews of the latest children's books, and an interactive storytelling session where students can add on chapters to submitted stories.

The Paris Pages **4-6** 🎨 **⑥**
URL: http://www.paris.org

This site is a must-visit for all students studying French or French-speaking countries. They'll find a directory to French sites (museums, monuments, etc.) that have online tours, tourist information, scenes from Paris, cafes and other culinary treats, a Paris holiday calendar, interactive Web tours of the entire city, a Paris glossary, and links to hundreds of related sites.

⑨ Related Areas: *Social Studies*

---

⑩ ⚠️ Integration Idea

Sponsor a parent-child reading program with your classes. Start your students' families at the Parent and Children Together Online site to support "the magic of reading" at this online magazine. Two sites to start your students reading with their families are Page at Pooh Corner and The Oz Home Page, two favorites in children's literature.

87

Introduction to Yellow Pages

❶ **Subject Heading** — Name of the chapter/general subject.

❷ **Title** — The name of the Web site or specific topic.

❸ **Uniform Resource Locator (URL)** — Address of the Web site (do not type the letters URL when typing the address into your Internet browser).

❹ **Description** — A brief paragraph describing the value of this site as it applies to educators and students.

❺ **Grade level** — This small icon lets you know the appropriate grade level for this Web site — either K-6, K-3, or 4-6.

❻ **Graphic icon** — This little paint palette ( ) tells you that this Web site is loaded with pictures.

❼ **Text icon** — This paper icon ( ) tells you that this Web site has few if any graphics.

❽ **A+ Icon** (A+) — As a special service, you'll find we've given our favorite sites an A+ award, because we believe these sites offer exceptional content for your classroom. We base their selection on the following criteria: site content, ease of navigation, functional design, and grammar/readability.

❾ **Related Areas** — Other subject areas or chapters related to this site.

❿ **Integration Idea** — One or two ideas to try in your classroom.

Introduction to Yellow Pages

Accuracy of Internet Addresses

The Internet is always evolving. In fact, change is the only certainty on this worldwide "network of networks." We verify the accuracy of addresses as close to press time as possible, but some addresses could change after publication.

Take these steps if an address does not work:

- ◆ Check and retype the address.

- ◆ If you receive a message telling you the site has moved and supplying you with its new address, which is much like the post office notifying you of an address change, copy the new address or add it to your bookmarks. Then try it. It should take you where you want to go.

- ◆ If you don't receive a message and if you typed the correct address, try stripping the address down to what is called the "root directory" and access. (This only works for Web sites.) For example, in the following address for WebElements, you would delete everything after the edu to reach the root directory, or the file where the Web site information resides.

    URL: http://www.cchem.berkeley.edu/Table/index.html

- ◆ If all else fails, go to the Classroom Connect Web site and use one of the six searching tools on the Search page to find your site on the Web.

    URL: http://www.classroom.net/classroom/search.htm

Good luck and happy Web-surfing!

YELLOW PAGES
ART & MUSIC

Art & Music

Africa: the Art of the Continent
URL: http://artnetweb.com/guggenheim/africa/

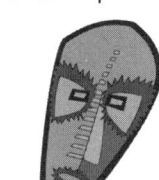 Take your students on a virtual field trip through the art work of deepest Africa. This exhibition includes works ranging from the tools and rock art of early humankind to objects produced well into the twentieth century. A great place to begin learning about the art of a very foreign culture.

Related Areas: *Social Studies*

Annie's Craft Page
URL: http://www.auntannie.com/

Each week, Aunt Annie adds a new craft idea to her already extensive Web site. The projects presented here are explained clearly and include a wide range of fun things to make. There are seasonal projects as well as ideas for making stationery and more. This is a rich source of activites for kids, parents, and teachers.

Related Areas: *Language Arts/Languages*

Ansel Adams
URL: http://www.zpub.com/sf/history/adams.html

 Ansel Adams is one of the world's most famous photographers. His black and white photographs of landscapes set him apart from anyone else who ever fiddled with a camera. Learn about Adams' life and view his breathtaking photographs of the natural world. Students will love the biographical information on this amazing person and the vast array of his beautiful pictures.

Art and Art Appreciation for Young Children
URL: http://www.classroom.net/artlesson.html

Use this lesson plan to challenge young students to create line collages, line printings, and string paintings, all the while paying attention to the most basic of all design elements — the line. This hands-on approach to teaching art appreciation at an early age is truly unique and is only available on the Web.

Related Areas: *Teacher Resources*

Art Laboratory
URL: http://www.artn.nwu.edu/index.html

4-6

Artists around the world are just beginning to use high-end computers and the Internet to create new forms of visual art. The Art Laboratory Web site is your link to the exhibitions of online artists who are using these sophisticated electronic tools to create virtual sculptures, photographs, holograms, and paintings.

Related Areas: *Technology/Internet*

Art Lesson Plans
URL: gopher://ericir.syr.edu:70/77/Lesson/.lesson/lessons?art

K-6

This page from ERIC (Educational Resource Information Center) contains wonderful art lesson plans. Topics range from decorating eggs in the Ukrainian custom, to creating dyes from plants, to making your own comic strips. The lesson plans are clearly written and well organized by title and grade level.

Related Areas: *Teacher Resources*

The Art of Mexican Native Children
URL: http://www.DocuWeb.ca/Mexico/1-engl/kids.html

K-6

 Looking to integrate social studies into your art lesson plans? Your young students will be riveted to their seats as they explore this colorful site, which contains both artwork and short stories written by native Mexican children about their day-to-day lifestyle, celebrations, and the animals that are native to their surroundings.

Related Areas: *Social Studies*

Your students will love creating masks with some help from a few sites here. Show them the art from the collection of Africa: the Art of the Continent. With their ideas in tow, bring them to the recipe for papier mache pulp available at Aunt Annie's Craft Page. If you need some ideas for mask-making, try the "Art History and Creating Masks" lesson at Art Lesson Plans. Masks are so attractive when displayed that you will want to be sure to show them off!

Art & Music

Art Teacher Connection
URL: http://www.primenet.com/~arted/

Are you an art educator looking for information to help introduce students to the visual arts? Look no further than the Art Teacher Connection. Here you'll find links to the latest art-related Web sites as well as Web reviews by K-12 art teachers, lessons to try out in your classroom, and a directory of wired educators and artists interested in connecting and sharing common interests.

Related Areas: *Teacher Resources; Technology/Internet*

Art-Vark
URL: http://home.earthlink.net/~cwolfgang/

Yes, it's another one of those online art galleries you see everywhere on the Net, but this one has a much wider age spectrum: Anyone between the ages of three and 15 can post his or her art work, meaning there's a larger and more varied collection of student art. This site promotes students' interest in art and encourages their imagination and creativity, regardless of whether they've done their work on pen and paper or via a computer, so be sure to have your students contribute!

ArtsEdge
URL: http://artsedge.kennedy-center.org

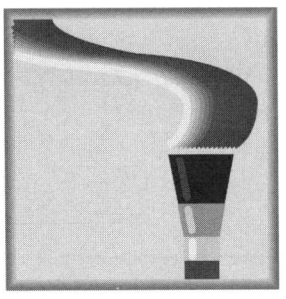

This rich site has a great deal of information for K-12 educators. One entire section is devoted to art education and includes information on arts curriculum design, annotated curriculum materials arranged by grade level, online subject area resource links, and curriculum materials submitted by educators. There is also a For Students page, the latest arts news, and much more.

Related Areas: *Teacher Resources; Language Arts*

ArtsEdNet

URL: http://www.artsednet.getty.edu/

ArtsEdNet, developed by the Getty Center for Education, is an electronic resource designed to support the needs of the K-12 arts education community. In departments such as Currents you'll find art-related articles, news releases, information on the latest teaching trends, and advocacy issues. The site also houses lesson plans, curriculum materials, and excerpts of various art education books.

Related Areas: *Teacher Resources*

ArtServe

URL: http://rubens.anu.edu.au/

Browse through more than 27,000 images of art and architecture, mainly from the Mediterranean Basin, which are not available elsewhere! Contents featured include Western Art, prehistoric megaliths, and classical architecture.

Related Areas: *Social Studies*

Barbara's World Tour

URL: http://www.bway.net/~starlite/

Barbara is an art teacher in the New York City schools. Her site includes links to a world tour of art museums all over the world. She has also included a creative list of art (and science) lesson plans, a scrapbook of her various trips and more. All in all, a fun site for teachers looking for ideas for their classroom.

Related Areas: *Science; Teacher Resources*

⚠ Integration Idea

Introduce your students to the wonderful selection of kid-created works from Art-Vark, and combine this experience with a virtual tour selected from the list of galleries at Barbara's World Tour. Using these galleries as guides, have your students create some paintings and set up their own classroom art gallery. Allow them to devise a tour for visitors, make brochures, and invite another class to visit it. Then you may play classical music over the computer and have your students guide visitors through your "gallery."

Art & Music

Carlos' Interactive Coloring Book
URL: http://www.ravenna.com/coloring/

Your K-3 students will enjoy this interactive coloring book. They can select one of six black and white pictures to color. Then, using the mouse, they can point and click on the area they want to color, filling in the picture section by section. Pictures include a birthday cake, a computer, and an apple. After coloring them in, have your students print them out to be hung on the wall!

Cartoon Corner
URL: http://www.cartooncorner.com/

A site devoted to cartoons which kids will find amusing. In addition to cartoons, there are also illustrated stories, poems to read, and puzzles to solve. The Art Studio area includes sections called How to Draw Cartoons, Drawing Tricks, What Cartoonists Do and Creative Play (which includes great ideas for artistic imaginative play).

Related Areas: *Language Arts/Languages*

The Castles of Wales
URL: http://www.castlewales.com/home.html

Travel to medieval Wales and explore her castles. This site contains rich background information including a time line, material on how the castles were built, and info on what life in the Middle Ages was really like. Pictures of the castles and drawings from the period help make this site come alive.

Related Areas: *Social Studies*

Cello Introduction
URL: http://www.cello.org/Cello_Introduction/Cello_Introduction.html

This Web site is cello heaven. It has samples of songs that you can listen to in 22khz, mono, or 8-bit. There are also ideas for practice sessions. The novice will enjoy the instructions on how to get started playing the cello while the expert will enjoy the practice ideas and list of music schools. There's even a section for those who are completely "clueless" about the cello.

Art & Music

Children's Music Singer/Songwriter Jack Will K-6
URL: http://home.ican.net/~jackw/top.htm

This Web site features some lyrics to songs sung and composed by singer/songwriter Jack Will. It also has other information about karaoke and childrens' concerts. Plus, children can enter contests to name characters.

Related Areas: *Language Arts/Languages*

Children's Music Web
URL: http://www.childrensmusic.org/index.html

A musical treasure for kids including a monthly offering of songs written by students, as well as fun activities and contests. Children's musicians are also featured in a set of linked pages. Kids can join the email forum, find out what music events are happening in their area, and listen to a funny story by loony Maynard Moose.

Related Areas: *Language Arts/Languages*

Chinese Papercuts
URL: http://www.isaacnet.com/culture/papercut.htm

A succinct history of the art of Chinese papercuts, an approximated 2000-year-old tradition, is followed by beautiful examples of papercuts illustrated in black and white. The strong images will delight young kids especially when the technique behind their creation is understood. A simple site for beginners to navigate.

 Integration Idea

> Your students are sure to want to see the Cartoon Corner, and this site will teach them to draw their own creations. After viewing this site, why not have the class make a comic strip and color it? If you have them draw on a strip of paper, creased into sections, you may make a viewfinder. Fold another piece of paper in half and cut two slits in it from the fold. Put the comic strip through the slits to show each picture as you pull it. Another site for artistic expression is Carlos' Interactive Coloring Book, where your students can pick and choose black-and-white pictures to color online.

Art & Music

City Kids by Liz Macklin
URL: http://tmn.com/Community/macklin/home.html

This Web site is the creation of Liz Macklin, a freelance artist. It contains illustrated stories and poems. There are also related links to architecture sites and related literature sites. A section on building treehouses has related activities your students can try out in the classroom.

Related Areas: *Language Arts/Languages*

CitySpace
URL: http://www.cityspace.org/

Navigate CitySpace, a three-dimensional virtual city environment built by kids across the Internet. You and your students can simply tour the city or help build it by sending graphics, sound clips, or anything else you want to digitize and send over the Net. Detailed information is available on the site for the software tools you'll need for building.

Related Areas: *Science; Social Studies*

Classical Insites
URL: http://www.classicalinsites.com/live/home/

A multi-faceted site full of information including a detailed history of classical music. Featured pages include The Bernstein Studio, The Conservatory, The Performance Center, a Hall of Fame with Featured Artists, Corner News, and Fountainside. Very fun and very friendly. A great resource.

Related Areas: *Teacher Resources*

ClassicalNet
URL: http://www.classical.net/

What better introduction to the wide world of classical music than this site on the World Wide Web! Inside you and your students will find brief composer biographies, an overview of the history of classical music, and well-written guides on how to find quality recordings in your local record stores.

Related Areas: *Teacher Resources*

Art & Music

The Claude Monet Home Page
URL: http://www.columbia.edu/~jns16/monet_html/monet.html

`4-6`

This beautifully done site is packed with fascinating information about Claude Monet's life and techniques. Intermediate students will enjoy reading his biography and looking at the steps he took to create his paintings. Many of his paintings and sketches are included here, as well as a bibliography of his works.

Color, Cut, and Fold Village
URL: http://www.wolfenet.com/~por/foldup.html

`4-6`

Kids can use the building patterns found at this company's site to construct their very own town out of paper. Included are ten houses, seven stores, a library and a blank store and house to be designed. The patterns are easy to download and print, after which you simply cut out, color, fold, and connect. Kids can use their creations to experiment with different village set ups to find the best design.

Related Areas: *Language Arts/Languages; Social Studies*

Color Matters
URL: http://www.lava.net/~colorcom/

`K-6`

Color plays a vitally important role in the world in which we live. Color can sway thinking, change actions, and cause reactions. The concept of color can be approached from several disciplines: physiology, psychology, philosophy, and art. This rich Web site provides some starting points for an exploration of color, for students and teachers alike.

Related Areas: *Science*

Integration Idea

To supplement a study of urban areas, you might use these sites with a "city theme." Visit the virtual city created by students at CitySpace, and perhaps add your own landmark to this cyber-town. Then find City Kids by Liz Macklin. Here kids explain how to build a treehouse, a place where any kid will feel like he is in the country even if he or she isn't. Next, construct a class community with the patterns from the Color, Cut, and Fold Village. Have each student take on a different role within this make-believe community. For example, one student could be the mailman, another the mayor, and so on.

Art & Music

Color Me Egypt
URL: http://interoz.com/egypt/kids/

Learn about Egypt from this account which was written for kids and contains some great pictures. Once inspired, kids will want to download Ancient Egyptian images to color or decide to create their own drawing to enter into the drawing contest sponsored here.

Related Areas: *Social Studies*

The Contemporary Recorder
URL: http://handel.pacific.net.sg/~csloh/index2.htm

This site is specially made for music teachers, recorder players, and recorder enthusiasts alike. You will find information on the recorder, the history of the instrument, tips on playing, fingering charts, images, Classical MIDI sound files, and great links to several other Internet sites that cover this rarely-used instrument.

Cora Connection:
The Manding Music Traditions of West Africa
URL: http://www1.drive.net/Kora.htm

This Web site teaches children about the Kora, which is an instrument from West Africa. It tells how the Kora is made and what it sounds like. It also has some very nice pictures so you know what it looks like. A good site for learning about African cultures.

Related Areas: *Social Studies*

Crafts for Kids
URL: http://ucunix.san.uc.edu/~edavis/kids-list/crafts.html

A great list of craft ideas of recipes for play dough, bubbles, finger paint, and more. Seasonal craft directions include some very usual ornament ideas and the Useful Crafts section includes directions for bath salts, centerpieces, vests, and more. There is even a page devoted to crafts made out of baby food jars — including an Advent calender!

Related Areas: *Teacher Resources*

Art & Music

The Crayola Art Education
URL: http://www.crayola.com/art_education/

Packed with interesting and unusual ideas, this site is an art teacher's dream, as it offers interesting uses for crayons, markers, finger paint, watercolors, colored pencils, tempera, and modeling dough. Also included is an Art Educators' Bulletin Board, where you can exchange lesson plans with other art-hungry teachers.

Related Areas: *Language Arts/Languages*

The Cubist Coloring Book
URL: http://www.webdiner.com/cubist/cubist.htm

A different approach to coloring books! This offering of four Cubist images (*Sphinx, Portrait, Landscape,* and *Picture of a Lady*) will interest young kids, especially following a discussion of modern art. Quotes from Pablo Picasso serve as inspiration and are scattered throughout the site.

Related Areas: *Teacher Resources*

Cultural News
URL: http://pathfinder.com/twep/artslink/morfogen/

Planning an art-related field trip? Visit the Morfogen Associates News Web site to preview the latest major museum and gallery exhibitions currently being offered near you. Includes cultural news and related feature stories of interest to art students and educators alike.

Related Areas: *Language Arts/Languages; Social Studies*

 Integration Idea

Your students will love an Egyptian experience. Show them the coloring pages found at Color Me Egypt and discuss the images as they relate to Egyptian culture by reading the captions. They may want to print and color a page or make their own drawing and enter the contest. Incorporate the Cubist style by visiting The Cubist Coloring Book. This site includes a portrait of a Sphinx, so your class may make comparisons between the portraits from both sites.

Art & Music

Cyberjacques Cyber Seas Treasure Hunt
URL: http://www.cyberjacques.com/

An online scavenger hunt hosted by a one-armed, one-eyed, peg-legged little pirate with a French name (he's very friendly, though). Follow Cyberjacques as he takes visitors on one of 12 voyages, each one made up of eight questions, designed to get kids surfing around the Internet. Those who answer all the questions correctly are rewarded with a downloadable animated movie. This site is a great way to have students explore the Net safely. There's also a chat forum to discuss clues and strategies, and a collection of lively shockwave games, such as Connect the Dots, Simon Says, and Hangman.

Related Areas: *Language Arts/Languages; Social Studies; Teacher Resources*

Dinosaur Art and Modeling Home Page
URL: http://www.indyrad.iupui.edu/dinoart.html

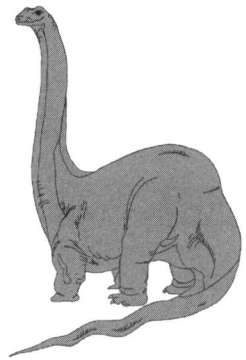

These artists love dinosaurs, and their work, illustrated in this Web site, makes that clear! This site features the best sculptures, paintings, and drawings of dinosaurs on the Internet. Each artist tells a little bit about himself and how his love of dinosaurs has led him to his work. Dinosaurces, a listing of where to find fossil reproductions, kits, dino literature, art, and more, is a valuable resource.

Related Areas: *Science*

Discovering Photography
URL: http://cmp1.ucr.edu/exhibitions/education/vidkids/lessons.html

The invention of photography has allowed historians to use accurate visual records of people, places, and events in their quest to interpret the past. This lesson plan at the California Museum of Photography helps students learn when photography was invented, understand how the medium has changed over the last 150 years, and become acquainted with the types of photographs popular in the nineteenth and early twentieth centuries.

Related Areas: *Teacher Resources*

# Art & Music

Dodoland in Cyberspace
URL: http://www.swifty.com/azatlan/

This multi-faceted Web site offers lots of fun things for kids to do. The Island of Eyes segment introduces visitors to book illustrators and authors. The Giant Flower Islands teaches visitors how to care for our natural environment. You can check out the Dodoland Castle, play games, or enter the Night Bubble Page where kids can share their favorite stories and illustrations.

Related Areas: *Science; Language Arts/Languages*

The Droodles Homepage
URL: http://www.webonly.com/droodles/index.html

What's a droodle? A droodle is a doodle riddle. It's a humerous scribble someone makes, which everyone else tries to decipher. Come see the Droodle of the Week or peruse the archive of droodles past. By the way, clicking on the droodle links you to the answer.

Related Areas: *Language Arts/Languages*

Education at the Met
URL: http://www.operaed.org/

 Education at the Met, a department of the Metropolitan Opera Guild, offers an innovative network of programs designed to help further music and arts education in schools across the United States. By working directly with teachers, parents, and young people, its founders have created programs that make opera, music, theater, dance, and the visual arts accessible and exciting to students of all ages and backgrounds.

 Integration Idea

> If you are looking for interesting problem-solving sites for your students, look no further! Cyberjacques' Cyber Seas Treasure Hunt is the place for you. There are several games at this site to exercise your students' thinking caps. Another fun problem-solving site is the Droodles Homepage. These pictures are open to interpretation, so see how many different solutions your students can suggest.

Art & Music

Eyes on Art
URL: http://www.kn.pacbell.com/wired/art/art.html

There are a lot of good art museums on the Web, but unfortunately, very few of them provide students with a chance to learn about art or art history. Eyes on Art offers activities designed to help students in grades K-12 look at art with a more critical eye.

Free Web Art
URL: http://www.mccannas.com/free/freeart.htm

Looking for free, professionally-created icons and graphics for your Web pages? Artist Laurie McCanna offers free graphics of her own design at this site, plus links to thousands more free art sites on the Internet.

Related Areas: *Technology/Internet; Teacher Resources*

A Gallery of Interactive On-Line Geometry
URL: http://www.geom.umn.edu/apps/gallery.html

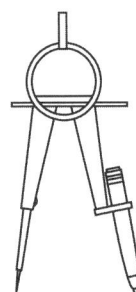

Explore the relationship between art and geometry with this Web site. This site will appeal to gifted students interested in both subjects. The QuasiTiler Page allows kids to experiment with creating different patterns of tilings on a flat plane by changing angles and colors and more. There are many other applications including a look at pinball and geometry.

Related Areas: *Math*

Gallery Walk
URL: http://www.ECNet.Net/users/mfjfg/galwalk.html

Through this site your students can link to more than three dozen online art galleries around the globe — all on the World Wide Web!

Art & Music

Gargoyles & Grotesques
URL: http://www.stonecarver.com/gargoyle.html

Walter S. Arnold is a sculptor who carves in stone. His Web site details his craft by focusing mainly on gargoyles. This site is clearly written with beautiful illustrations, both of Mr. Arnold's work and of the tools and tasks of his craft. Students will be inspired to carve their own unique gargoyles out of clay or paper maché after browsing this site.

Related Areas: *Science*

George Eastman House
URL: http://www.eastman.org

 Students interested in photography will find this site extremely useful. It contains hands-on information about black-and-white photography. Information on George Eastman, the founder of Kodak, is also here, as is a detailed history of photography.

Global Show-N-Tell
URL: http://www.telenaut.com/gst/

This site is a virtual exhibition that lets children show off their favorite projects, possessions, accomplishments, and collections to kids around the world. Each "museum wing" consists of links to kids' artwork on other Web sites all over the world.

 Integration Idea

> Your students will discover the elements of artistic design through the activities found at Eyes on Art. Introduce these elements with the Visual Glossary. The examples of each element will help the group to visualize the concepts. For a real challenge, tour another gallery from Gallery Walk and discuss the art that you find using the terms from the glossary.

Art & Music

The Guitar and Lute Music Page
URL: http://world.std.com/~sdrasky/

`4-6`

This Web site features a collection of scores intended to be played on the classical guitar. Some lute music is also included, with guitar transcriptions. Popular, classical, traditional, folk, and flamenco styles are all included. MIDIs, meant to be used in conjunction with learning the music (or to decide if you even want to learn it), are included.

Gupit-Gupit
URL: http://www.tiac.net/users/gneils/gupit-gupit.html

`K-6`

Mr. Gupit is a sculptor who uses paper to create beautiful shapes. At this Web site, he will show you how to make a sculpture out of one piece of paper. He also shows you the finished results of many other students who have attempted to make this sculpture. Be sure to see other examples of his work and learn about his life.

Related Areas: *Teacher Resources*

Harp Page
URL: http://www.med.virginia.edu/~cam6z/harp.html

`4-6`

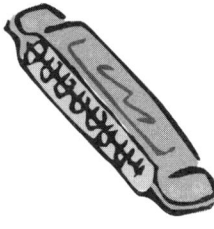
This site contains everything your students will need to understand and play the harmonica. You will find lessons, tips, descriptions, and accompanying audio files. Check out the great collection of sound files available for downloading. Many of these are integrated into the body of the online lessons. There is also a helpful section on popular song keys and information on playing the "cross-harp" style.

The Incredible Art Department
URL: http://www.artswire.org/kenroar/

`K-6`

This multi-faceted site has a great deal to offer elementary students and teachers, including lesson plans, access to elementary school art department Web sites across the U.S., an Art Site of the Week, and the latest art news stories. Older elementary students who are already interested in pursuing art as a career will find the Art Job section very informative.

Related Areas: *Teacher Resources*

Art & Music

Internet Colors Book
URL: http://www.itdc.sbcss.k12.ca.us/projects/patten/

Looking for a place for your students to post their art work on the World Wide Web? Try this site. Students create one-sentence descriptions about the color of an object using a basic paint software program. The combined work is then displayed on the project's Web page. To join the program, simply download the software for free from their site, or email John Patten at **jpatten@deltanet.com**.

Related Areas: *Language Arts/Languages*

The Internet Webseum of Holography
URL: http://www.holoworld.com/

This rich site on holograms includes a section called Holo-Kids which is designed with younger viewers in mind. Frank DeFreitas, the author, presents a detailed but understandable explanation of holograms, lasers, dimensions, and other related terms. View a Hologram Gallery and hologram videos or email the author with your specific questions on holography. This site also contains teacher resources and a chat room.

Related Areas: *Science*

Isfahan Home Page
URL: http://www.anglia.ac.uk/~trochford/isfahan.html

The beautiful buildings of Islamic traditions are featured at this Web site. Take a "taxi ride" to explore some of the most extraordinary examples of mosques, palaces, and minarets. You can also explore links to related topics such as Persian carpets, Iranian food, and more.

Related Areas: *Social Studies*

 Integration Idea

> Young children are especially interested in colors, and most of them are familiar with colors even before they enter kindergarten. Therefore, they will enjoy a reading of the Internet Colors Book. You may even want to make your own book of colors. Older children can deepen their understanding of colors by experiencing the "Warm Colors vs. Cool Colors" lesson that you may borrow from The Incredible Art Department.

Art & Music

Jarea Art Studio—Lessons K-6
URL: http://www.bconnex.net/~jarea/lessons.htm

Search through this resource of imaginative art lessons including Crayon Etching and Magazine Mosaics. This Web site also includes The Fridge, a gallery of "cool art created by cool kids." Educators can also order special art instruction booklets which are age and technique based.

Related Areas: *Teacher Resources*

Jason's Kite Site K-6
URL: http://www.latrobe.edu.au/Glenn/KiteSite/Kites.html

Kite building is an excellent activity for bringing out students' creative talents, physical science knowledge, and cooperative skills. Students can browse dozens of colorful kite photos and read all about single line, double line, or stunt kites, and view some very cool Kite Buggies.

Related Areas: *Science*

Javanese Mask Collection 4-6
URL: http://www.bvis.uic.edu/museum/exhibits/javamask/Javamask.html

This Web site is part of the Field Museum of Chicago's site. The masks are fantastic and will fascinate kids. There are 80 masks, each annotated with a short description. The site contains two interesting and related links, one to the Java Village at the 1893 World's Fair (which has great pictures), and one to a site about the dances of Indonesia which feature these masks.

Related Areas: *Social Studies*

Joseph Wu's Origami Page 4-6
URL: http://www.datt.co.jp/Origami/

Explore the ancient art of origami in detail through this Web site. Included are a list of artists, sources of supplies, and photo galleries. Online diagrams help students create their own origami creatures, like toads, seals, and cranes.

Related Areas: *Social Studies*

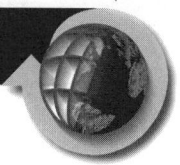

Art & Music

Kaleidoscope Heaven K-6
URL: http://www.ux1.eiu.edu/~csbdb/kr.html

Learn about the beautiful world of kaleidoscopes and the artists who make them! This Web site features a short history of the kaleidoscope and a gallery of the work of current kaleidoscope artists. Included are metal, wood, and stained glass creations.

Related Areas: *Teacher Resources*

Ken Fansler's Online Music Instruction Page 4-6
URL: http://orathost.cfa.ilstu.edu/~kwfansle/

This interactive set of lessons in music theory is a great tool for teaching intermediate kids. The lessons (divided into Beginner, Intermediate, and Advanced levels) begin with the basics, defining the staff, note names, and so on, and progressing through key signatures and major and minor scales. Interactive student tests are also included. Plentiful graphics illustrations and musical sound examples are used to help students understand the material. There is also a resource list of other related links which would be helpful for parents and music educators.

Kendra's Coloring Book
URL: http://www.geocities.com/enchantedforest/7155

A collection of drawings for kids to color online. The drawings include images of frogs, insects, animals, flowers, and geometric shapes. They are very appealing and will delight younger artists. It is also possible to color an image of your own by downloading it onto the Web site. A gallery of drawings completed by young artists is also available for viewing.

 Integration Idea

All children experiment with making paper airplanes, and almost all have played with paper to create a "kite." Jason's Kite Site is a great source of illustrations and ideas for kite-making, and show your class Joseph Wu's Origami Page if paper-folding is what they like. Your students may create paper airplanes and paper kites from the information they gather from these two sites.

Art & Music

Kid's Craft
URL: http://www.ozemail.com.au/~teasdale/craft/craft_ideas.html

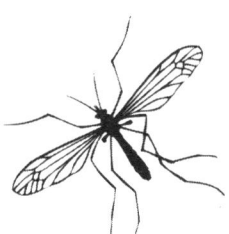

This site features a collection of imaginative craft projects for kids aged 5 to 12 years including candle making, butterfly badges, paper jewelry, and lots more. The directions are clear and easy to follow for all ages. There is also a craft idea exchange section, party games, links to other related sites, and recipes.

Related Areas: *Language Arts/Languages; Teacher Resources*

Kids' Space
URL: http://www.kids-space.org/

At this user-friendly site, your K-3 students can easily maneuver through the activities with a click of a mouse. Students can share their artwork and musical compositions, chat with new friends, and more. Students can also choose to illustrate another student's story, or pick artwork to write a story about.

Related Areas: *Language Arts/Languages*

KidsArt
URL: http://www.merrymac.com/mspage/kidsart/index.html

This Web site is loaded with art activities for children. There are directions for making fun art projects and a wonderful exhibit of artwork created by kids. Students can even send their own artwork to the gallery. They can also get a pen pal in the KidsArt Mail Art exchange.

Related Areas: *Teacher Resources*

Kites, Kids, and Education!
URL: http://www.sound.net/~kiteguy/

Kite making is an art form and so is kite flying. This site tells of the history of kites, includes some safety concerns for inexperienced kite flyers, and offers directions on how to make your own kite. There is also a great list of links to sites about kite art.

Related Areas: *Science*

Art & Music

Learning Through Architecture
URL: http://whyy.org/aie/aie.html

Architecture and the design of surroundings is something you and your students experience every day, both at home and in the classroom. This site is an interactive learning center to help educators integrate architecture concepts in the K-12 classroom.

Related Areas: *Math; Science; Language Arts/Languages; Social Studies*

Leonardo Da Vinci Museum
URL: http://cellini.leonardo.net/museum/main.html#start

The original "Renaissance Man," Leonardo da Vinci was a great painter, scientist, futurist, and thinker. This online museum is divided into several wings and includes his paintings, invention designs, and drawings. The text accompanying each work is full of absorbing details which will fascinate older elementary school students.

Related Areas: *Science; Social Studies*

Lite-Board
URL: http://asylum.cid.com/lb/

This is a fun, colorful way to introduce younger students to the World Wide Web. Teachers will remember using the real-world version of the Lite-Brite toy from their childhood days, pushing colorful, translucent pegs into lighted boxes to create pictures. Now, art students around the world can create their own works using the Lite-Board site.

 Integration Idea

As a teacher, it is always helpful to find a source of excellent art lesson ideas. Two sites with what you are looking for are listed here. Kid's Craft has numerous art projects just waiting for you, and KidsArt includes free sample projects from their art booklets. When you are looking for something new to try with your class, try these Internet resources.

Art & Music

The Little Artist's Gallery
URL: http://nicecom.com/litart/

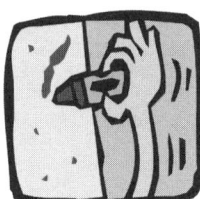 Looking for a place to show off the talents of the young artists in your school? Look no further than The Little Artist Gallery. Your kids will be overwhelmed with pride when they see that their works of art have been made available to the whole world! Now that's motivation!

Lullabies and Other Songs for Children
URL: http://www.stairway.org/kidsongs/

 Find the words to "When I See an Elephant Fly" and "The Bear Went Over the Mountain." This resource contains 319 favorite children's song lyrics.

Marbling for Paper and Fabric
URL: http://members.aol.com/marbling/marbling/index.htm

Learn the basics of the ancient art of paper marbling from the Medieval Marbler! This Web site offers a brief history of the art form, concise directions, and some beautiful examples. There is also information on upcoming workshops and a chance to order supplies.

Related Areas: *Teacher Resources*

Marilyn's Imagination Factory
URL: http://www2.hsonline.net/homepages/kidatart.html

 Make a necklace out of junk mail! This creative site is dedicated to making art out of recycled materials. For background information, there is a section on recycling and why recycling is important. The art lessons and activity directions are detailed, clear, and truly innovative.

Related Areas: *Social Studies; Teacher Resources*

Art & Music

Mark Shepard's Flute Page
URL: http://www.aaronshep.com/Mark/flute/

4-6

This Web site features an online tutorial in eight lessons and a page on how to care for your flute. It also includes some tips on how to approach learning the modern flute and a plan for building a "plumber's pipe," a simple flute made out of PVC pipe from the hardware store.

Related Areas: *Teacher Resources*

Marsalis on Music
URL: http://www.wnet.org/mom/index.html

4-6

This Web site features Wynton Marsalis teaching children about some of the fundamental elements of music such as form, rhythm, and practice. Here your students can send Wynton their comments and listen to a collection of audio clips. This site also has a great music educator's guide with a selection of lesson plans.

Related Areas: *Teacher Resources*

Metropolitan Museum of Art—Education
URL: http://www.metmuseum.org/htmlfile/education/edu.html

K-6

This Education segment of the Metropolitan Museum of Art's Web site is filled with fabulous resources. There are many activities based on the art found in the museum as well as ideas for artistic activities kids can do at home. For example, the Looking At Art segment teaches students to investigate the details of works of art in the museum in order to learn about composition and themes.

Related Areas: *Teacher Resources*

 Integration Idea

One of the most enjoyable forms of art for children is "free art," and the best materials for this type of art are recyclables. Collect junk for a box of art materials and have your students use the suggestions at Marilyn's Imagination Factory to get them going. Then take them to Lullabies and Other Songs for Children and let them choose a character from one of the songs to create with recyclables.

Art & Music

Michael's KidsClub Online
URL: http://www.michaels.com/kids/kid-main.html

This Web site features an online coloring section (the Electric Canvas) which is cheerful and unique. The You Can Make It Too page features over forty fabulous craft ideas such as making paper roses and picture frames. You can also check out the bimonthly newsletter which has great seasonal craft ideas.

Related Areas: *Language Arts/Languages; Teacher Resources*

Mr. Stix's Electronic Treehouse
URL: http://www.interlog.com/~brucem/home.html

This Web site has plenty of things to do such as learn new song lyrics, learn to play the drum using sample sound files, and make instruments by using common things that you could find at home. Children can also write their own songs and submit them. There are also plenty of links to other children's music pages.

Related Areas: *Teacher Resources*

Monty Harper, Children's Musician
URL: http://www.cowboy.net/~mharper/

Monty Harper's home page is full of cool stuff such as his Online Kid's Song Book, which includes the written lyrics and sound files of his humorous and snappy work. Another section, the Looking Glass Gazette, features stories, poems, artwork, book reviews, and other kid productions for preschoolers up to eighth graders. Many of Monty Harper's songs stress the importance of reading and learning but always with a funny twist.

Related Areas: *Language Arts/Languages*

The Mother Goose Pages
URL: http://pubweb.acns.nwu.edu/~pfa/dreamhouse/nursery/rhymes.html

This Web site is an excellent source for song lyrics or the words to specific Mother Goose rhymes. The songs and rhymes are easy to find, sorted both alphabetically and by category. There are food rhymes, rounds and repeaters, and even weather songs. This site is useful as a teacher resource as it has advice on how to read nursery rhymes to young children.

Related Areas: *Teacher Resources*

Art & Music

Muppet Songs
URL: http://www.cs.unc.edu/~arthur/muppet-songs.html

"It's Not Easy Being Green" and other wonderful song lyrics of the Muppets can be found at this Web site. Teachers can copy lyrics and pass them out to students. Over 50 songs from the various Jim Henson TV shows and movies are listed here.

Music 101
URL: http://www.music101.com/

From music theory to basic guitar, anyone interested in music and musical instruments should head over here. There are guitar sessions, an interview with blues guitarists, and sections where you can train your ear to identify relative pitches. Learn about key signatures and improve your reading with the Java Music Quiz.

The Music Educator's Home Page
URL: http://athena.athenet.net/~wslow/index.html

This home page contains music curriculum materials and links to other useful sites. Search through a pool of public domain resources, and find Net links to music-related sites throughout the Internet.

Related Areas: *Teacher Resources*

Integration Idea

What is the epitome of teamwork, camaraderie, and fun? Why a musical band of course! Your class will be thrilled to create a class band and the Net can help them do so. Use the instructions for making instruments at Mr. Stix's Electronic Treehouse. Then let your band members play their instruments with a delightful tune from Monty Harper, Children's Musician.

Art & Music

Music Links
URL: http://www.earthlink.net/music/

This is your launch pad to thousands of sites related to music, including instruments (accordians, pianos, drums, wind instruments, etc.), artists and genres (Blues, Classical, Folk, Jazz), and hundreds of online resources of use to students and professional musicians.

National Art Library
URL: http://www.nal.vam.ac.uk/

A major research library with a searchable database of over one million publications related to the fine and decorative arts, arts history, design, and more. A must visit for any student of the arts young or old!

National Gallery of Art
URL: http://www.nga.gov/

Tour the wonderful collection of paintings, sculptures, decorative art, and graphic art at the National Gallery of Art in Washington, D.C. The site's online exhibit includes historical information, images, and audio sound files discussing many of the works of art in their collection. Search the collections by artist, title, medium, or a combination of attributes.

The National Museum of American Art
URL: http://nmaa-ryder.si.edu/

The National Museum of American Art is the Smithsonian's dedication to the arts and artists of the United States from earliest colonial times to the present day. As a federal institution, the museum serves audiences throughout the land, as well as those who visit its two historic landmark buildings in Washington. The museum presents for a broad Internet public its collections, educational materials, and research resources, which reflect the diversity of the country's citizenry.

Related Areas: *Social Studies*

Art & Music

Native American Indian Art
URL: http://indy4.fdl.cc.mn.us/~isk/art/art.html

This beautiful site is rich with images of Native American art, pottery, beadwork, sculptures, textiles, legend paintings, baskets, and photographs. Each is exhibited along with information about the artist and the techniques and history of the craft. There are also links to related sites such as the Native American Fine Arts Movement and Indigenous Art Resources on the Internet.

Related Areas: *Social Studies*

nFX Living Art Server
URL: http://www.nfx.com/

Your young students will enjoy creating their own original cartoons and artwork at the nFX Living Art Web site. Your students can post their own creation, complete with a humorous caption, in the Gallerie de le Toon and become Web-famous. A free Windows 95-only cartoon maker is also available.

Related Areas: *Language Arts/Languages*

NINA
URL: http://www.washington.edu/bibsys/mattf/nina/

If your students have ever used a Spirograph, they'll find NINA a fitting online replacement! Enter in a set of coordinates and this Web site does the rest. Includes information for retrieving finished NINA images to your computer and then embedding them on your school Web site. Great for young and old students alike!

Related Areas: *Technology/Internet*

 Integration Idea

You may supplement a study of Native Americans with an investigation of their art. Your best source of information is the Native American Indian Art Web site. This site explains the artistic creations with artists' personal accounts and descriptions of how the items are made. The National Gallery of Art also offers some Native American art with a selection of North American Indian paintings.

Art & Music

Ocarinas Are Elementary
URL: http://www.ilstu.edu/depts/labschl/metcalf/suan/

Susan Guess-Hanson, a musician and art teacher, combines her love of art and music in the production and playing of ocarinas. An ocarina is a globular flute originating from Pre-Columbian Central and South America. This Web site gives historical background, links to related sites, and examples of ocarinas her young students have made.

The Official Eric Carle Web Site
URL: http://www.eric-carle.com/index.html

 Meet Eric Carle, the author and illustrator of the famous children's book, *The Very Hungry Caterpillar!* Mr. Carle's cheerful images and charming stories delight kids, and here is a place where they can learn about him. One segment of this page includes answers to frequently asked questions (The answers come with drawings!). There is also a Caterpillar Exchange which serves as a bulletin board for exchanging ideas on how to use his books in the classroom.

Related Areas: *Language Arts/Languages*

OperaWeb
URL: http://www.opera.it/English/OperaWeb.html

All you and your students have ever wanted to know about the world of opera coming to you from the land of opera — Italy — via the Internet! Opera reviews, singers, news, performance schedules, and opera history.

Paper Airplanes
URL: http://pchelp.inc.net/paper_ac.htm

 Kids will love searching through this graphical collection of paper airplanes — complete with instructions for folding their own!

Related Areas: *Science*

Art & Music

The Peace in Pictures Project
URL: http://www.macom.co.il/peace/

Based in the chaotic country of Israel, the Peace in Pictures project invites children of all ages from around the world to draw their impressions of peace and then send them in to the project coordinators. Each picture is added to this Web site, which gives politicians and millions of other Internet users a chance to view, enjoy, and be inspired by them. Drawings can be submitted via email attachments or through the post office.

Related Areas: *Social Studies*

Percussion Education On-Line
URL: http://otto.cmr.fsu.edu/~bula_jo/percussion/index.html

Learn to play the Tympani! This rich resource for parents and students includes clear, step-by-step instructions for playing a wide range of pitched and non-pitched percussion instruments. Other aspects of the site include Interactive Discussions, with topics such as Solo and Ensemble Literature, Questions and Answers, Common Band Director Mistakes, On Line Articles (e.g., How to Practice), and links to related sites.

Related Areas: *Teacher Resources*

 Integration Idea

Peace is a very powerful theme. You can introduce this important idea into your classroom by sharing with your students The Peace in Pictures Project. Have your students create pictures to add to the collection and send them to the site or use them to create a book for your room. To get ideas and advice on how to go about making your book, investigate The Official Eric Carle Web Site to see what themes he chooses for his books. Many of them deal with cooperation and understanding — very "peaceful" ideas.

Art & Music

The Piano Education Page
URL: http://www.unm.edu/~loritaf/pnoedmn.html

4-6

The Piano Education Page is a one-stop resource for teachers, students, and parents, with over 200 pages of free information, updated biweekly. You can get tips on learning to play the piano, including getting the right kind of piano lessons and right piano teacher for you. There is a special page for kids, which teaches children how to have fun playing the piano. Another category is Learning to Play the Piano which explains the different teaching methods, as well as how to find the right piano teacher.

Piano on the Net '97
URL: http://www.artdsm.com/piano/index.html

4-6

This site consists of three groups of piano lessons (Beginning, Intermediate, and Advanced) with 13 to 14 lessons in each group. The detailed lessons are written and illustrated in a clear and easy-to-understand manner. Some lessons include audio examples for the learner. This is an outstanding resource for older elementary students who are interested in learning to play the piano.

Related Areas: *Teacher Resources*

Picture Gallery of Classical Composers
URL: http://spight.physics.unlv.edu/picgalr2.html

4-6

This gallery of composers includes a brief biographical sketch of music-makers from over 28 countries, from the 1400s up until the present day. This site is a great beginning place for older students to start a research project on composers, or on the music from specific countries or time periods.

Platypus Family Playroom
URL: http://www.orst.edu/~dickt/

K-6

This Web site has lyrics of songs in both English and Spanish. It includes Folklores from different countries, a singing game, a silly mnemonic song, and a song about quantities. You'll need a Talker plugin in order to hear these songs, however. This Web site also includes other activities such as stories, puzzles, and other games.

Related Areas: *Language Arts/Languages; Teacher Resources*

Potter's Page

URL: http://www.aztec.co.za/users/theo/potters.htm

4-6

A gallery of ceramics from around the world. This site contains links to artists, ceramics workshops, and factories which produce a wide range of ceramic items including fine arts pottery, tiles, and flower pots. It is a fascinating look at an under-used, multi-faceted craft. Kids will be amazed at the versatility of clay.

Related Areas: *Social Studies*

Professor Bubble's Bubblesphere

URL: http://bubbles.org/

K-6

Do you like bubbles? If you want to visit this page you had better like bubbles, because this page has an awful lot of them. The professor knows bubbles inside and out, and he's more than willing to share his knowledge with curious visitors. They can make their own bubble tools, get the ultimate bubble solution, learn soap bubble history, and more.

Related Areas: *Science*

Quilts, Counterpanes, and Throws

URL: http://www.si.edu/organiza/museums/nmah/docs/quilts/quilt.html

K-6

The earliest existing quilts are from the mid-1700s and you can see them here along with an astonishing collection of other types of quilts. There are examples of pictorial quilts with biblical scenes and family scenes, Amish quilts of beautiful colors and simple geometric shapes, and much, much more.

 **Integration Idea**

Throughout time, some arts have been replaced by mechanical means in an effort to speed production. Your students may glimpse the past with a tour of these sites. Few people now invest hours of love into quilting, but the creations of those who do are lovely. See the beautiful quilts on display at Quilts, Counterpanes, and Throws. By the same token, the Potter's Page will show your students the ancient art of creating pottery with clay. Have the students make a clay pot or figure or draw a quilt pattern to present to the rest of the class. What does this type of art say about the culture that produced it?

Art & Music

Ragtime Home Page
URL: http://www.ragtimers.org/~ragtimers/

This site briefly examines three of Ragtime's pioneers, Scott Joplin, Joseph Lamb, and James Scott. There are brief biographies of these Ragtime fathers, as well as a complete Ragtime discography, MIDI files for your computer, a list of books available on Ragtime music and performers, and a great FAQ on this type of music. Be sure to explore the links to other Ragtime-related Internet sites from this page.

Related Areas: *Social Studies*

Rebecca Golden's Music for Children Page
URL: http://www.albany.net/~justkid/becca/

At this Web site you can read the lyrics to the variety of songs from Rebecca's album "Walk Around the Block." Several of these songs stress good behavior — and they sound good too! Why not have a listen?

Redfrog: The Children's Art Gallery
URL: http://redfrog.norconnect.no/~cag/

This gallery offers free exhibition space to children from various cultures and age groups who wish to present their drawings to the Internet public. Through this, the site's creators hope to create a platform where children, parents, and teachers can meet and share common experiences through their children's drawings. Visitors can view the artwork either through a structured tour, or by creating an exhibition of their own according to the child's name, age, country, teacher, school, or special project.

The Refrigerator Art Contest
URL: http://www.seeusa.com/refrigerator.html

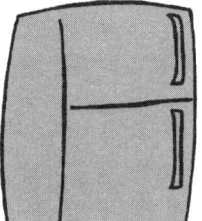

A great site for young artists! Contestants can use a simple, printable form to enter a weekly art contest. Each week, five works of art are chosen from those sent in and are then posted for young people all over the world to vote on. The winner's picture is displayed for a week at the front of the Web site and then joins the Hall of Fame.

Related Areas: *Language Arts/Languages; Technology*

Art & Music

Resources for Music Educators
URL: http://www.ed.uiuc.edu/EdPsy-387/Tina-Scott/project/home.html

This World Wide Web site is a library of printed and online resources for music educators. Its six general categories cover instrumental music, vocal music, general music, special learners, early childhood instruction, and teacher preparation and ongoing education. A directory of related research journals is included.

Related Areas: *Teacher Resources*

SchoolHouse Rock
URL: http://genxtvland.simplenet.com/SchoolHouseRock/

More than 20 years old, SchoolHouse Rock continues to be one of the most popular and educational cartoons ever to grace Saturday morning television. All the songs are listed here, as are the lyrics and pictures of characters like Conjunction Junction and Schoolhouse Rocky.

Related Areas: *Language Arts/Languages; Teacher Resources; Math; Science; Social Studies; Health/PE*

Seven Wonders of the Ancient World
URL: http://pharos.bu.edu/Egypt/Wonders/

Do your students know what the seven wonders of the world are? Do you? If not, here's your chance to bone up on these ancient architectural works that have all but faded into legend. Learn about their history, what they looked like, and the fascinating cultures of yore that created these works. A clickable map, time line, and links to related ancient history sites make this a fun and easy way for students to learn about the cultures that served as the basis for what we call Western Civilization.

Related Areas: *Social Studies*

 Integration Idea

Have you been wondering what to do with all of your students' "refrigerator art?" It doesn't have to keep you from your milk any more! Display a scanned image on the Web, and—Shhh!—throw away the original. You may send your class' art to The Refrigerator Art Contest or set up an exhibit of it at Redfrog: The Children's Art Gallery. What better way could there be to show off the work of your budding artists, since online it has the opportunity to be seen by people from around the globe?

Art & Music

Sharon, Lois, and Bram Club-E
URL: http://207.6.100.1/elephant/home.html

This Web site has many songs from the well-known television show featuring the chanteuses Sharon, Lois, and Bram. There are also photos, song lyrics, activities, and sound clips. Children can join the E-club here to receive information about this popular trio. (E stands for Elephant, just so you know.)

Shrine to Music Museum Virtual Gallery Tour
URL: http://www.usd.edu/smm/galleries.html

See over 750 musical instruments from all over the globe and from many time periods. There are exotic instruments from Tibet such as a serpentine horn, a pipe organ from Pennsylvania, and a jeweled cornet. This exhibition is designed to show online visitors the amazing craftsmanship and variety of instruments throughout the world. Each instrument is accompanied by a short description.

Related Areas: *Social Studies*

Sing a Song of Christmas
URL: http://www.stairway.org/xmas/

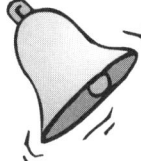

At this Web site you will find a collection of lyrics from popular Christmas songs. Some of these songs have an attached MIDI file. This is a good teacher resource during the holiday season. Just copy the lyrics and pass them out to your students.

The Sistine Chapel
URL: http://www.christusrex.org/www1/sistine/0-Tour.html

This Web site contains more than 300 images of the chapel, paying particular attention to Michelangelo's contributions. A master plan for the chapel and the artwork inside helps viewers understand where each piece appears.

Related Areas: *Language Arts/Languages; Social Studies*

Art & Music

Snowflakes You Can Make

K-6

URL: http://www1.surfsouth.com/~rlogue/snowup.htm

Have your class make beautiful paper snowflakes to hang on your windows or to send in greeting cards. This simple treatment of an oft-attempted activity is easy to follow for young kids and will result in gorgeous, unique six-pointed snowflakes.

Related Areas: *Math*

Stage Hand Puppets

K-6

URL: http://fox.nstn.ca/~puppets/activity.html

From here your young students can retrieve paper puppets and patterns, get performance tips, share ideas on making puppets from scrap materials, and link to other fun spots for kids. Each week during the school year a new paper puppet pattern is placed on the site, along with detailed construction and performance instructions.

Related Areas: *Language Arts/Languages*

TalentZ—A Web of Music and Education

URL: http://www.talentz.com/MusicEd.html

Jeff Brenan, a music educator, has created this Web site to share three areas of musical offerings: a database of lesson plans, an interactive visit to his music classes (K-5), and a musical notation game, Finale, which he invented. Finale is a challenging game with humorous answer choices included along with the right ones. The lesson plans are wide ranging, imaginative and fun, and you can submit your own lessons to add to the collection.

Related Areas: *Teacher Resources*

 Integration Idea

On these two pages you have two sites just perfect for the Christmas season. You will find the words to all of your favorite Christmas carols at Sing a Song of Christmas. While your class is singing, why not have them make some snowflakes? George the Gnome will give them the directions for beautiful snowflakes at Snowflakes You Can Make. Decorate your classroom and fill it with song at the same time!

Art & Music

The Teel Family Web Site—Just the Crafts K-6
URL: http://www.teelfamily.com/activities/crafts.html

This family crafts page contains very unusual ideas for artistic projects, such as making an Athabascan style basket, mixing unique things into paint for painting projects, and lots of snow-related crafts. There is something here for everyone.

Related Areas: *Teacher Resources; Science*

The Thinker K-6
URL: http://www.thinker.org/index.shtml

What is the thinker? Why, the official Web site for the Fine Arts Museums of San Francisco of course! With more than 50,000 images online and growing, this is the largest image database currently on the Web! Visitors can easily get an overview of the various exhibitions and collections at these museums, or do a search for a specific artist or genre, like William Blake. Online teacher's guides help educators incorporate the images found here into their art curriculum. There's even a comic book tour of the museum for young students!

Vellum Gallery of Calligraphy, Illumination, and Letter Arts 4-6
URL: http://catalog.com/gallery/welcome.html

Learn how to carve a bamboo pen to use in your calligraphy projects. This site features The Gallery which includes examples of calligraphy and Illumination. There is also a segment featuring Demonstrations of Technique and A Gallery Shop as well as Links of Interest to Calligraphers.

Violin Making by Hans Johannsson 4-6
URL: http://www.centrum.is/hansi/

The earliest violins date back to the early 16th century in Italy and Mr. Johannsson is carrying on the beautiful craft of making them. This rich site contains fascinating information about the history and construction of violins. The reasons for the uniqueness of each violin's sound is also explained. Sound files of violins and cellos are included for examples. This site can be used by both students of the violin or less serious students of music.

Art & Music

The Virtual Study Tour
URL: http://archpropplan.auckland.ac.nz/virtualtour/front.html

Walk like an Egyptian around the palace of Ramses III! This architectural site lets students "walk through" computer reproductions of ancient buildings and modern structures. Click on direction buttons to move through the buildings as if you were really traveling through them. A very hands-on, fun way to introduce them to not only architecture, but also the next generation in Internet navigation.

Related Areas: *Social Studies; Technology/Internet*

A Wearable Arts Homepage
URL: http://www.geocities.com/SoHo/7212/

View the Tie Dye Primer and find out how to tie dye square and sunburst designs! This wonderful site also includes information on polyclay techniques such as instructions for making beads. Make the beads and then use them to make necklaces and earrings. There is also a gallery of wearable creations.

WebMuseum: Bienvenue!
URL: http://watt.emf.net/wm/

An online museum rich with images of famous paintings and information about art history, art techniques, and artists. The General Exhibition section includes works by hundreds of artists along with biographical information. There is also a Special Exhibition section which houses an exhibit of Paul Cezanne's work and an Auditorium section where one can download classical music selections and take a tour of Paris.

Related Areas: *Teacher Resources; Social Studies*

Integration Idea

You will find a wealth of ideas and instructions for art projects to use in your classroom at the two following sites. A Wearable Arts Homepage has great background information and tips for making jewelry and decorated clothing you can wear. The Teel Family Web Site—Just the Crafts offers all kinds of ideas for projects that your students will love. Young children will enjoy the Binky Polar Bear Puppet, and older students will find the 1910 Paper Doll lots of fun.

Art & Music

World Art Treasures
URL: http://sgwww.epfl.ch/BERGER/index.html

According to its creators, the purpose of this well-stocked Web site is "to promulgate the discovery and love of art." To that end, they have collected photos of art works from around the world covering just about every period of history. The site is divided into a series of programs, each one focusing upon a particular artist or artistic period. Program subjects include Botticelli, Vermeer, gardens of the Renaissance, Roman portraits, and the ancient art of Egypt and China.

Related Areas: *Social Studies; Language Arts/Languages; Teacher Resources*

World Band Project
URL: http://co-nect.bbn.com/WorldBand/CoNECTMusic.html

This online project gives student band members the chance to share their musical talents with their peers from around the globe using the latest in computer technology. World Band consists of participant schools around the world, each equipped with a MIDI synthesizer studio that enables the transmission of music compositions. This music is combined with submissions from other schools, and placed on this Web site for all to explore and enjoy!

Related Areas: *Social Studies*

World of Escher
URL: http://lonestar.texas.net/~escher/

Explore the intriguing world of the artist M.C. Escher. This site features a Reading Room which includes Escher's biography and interesting stories about his life and work. The Art Museum pages contain many of Escher's mind-boggling works, complete with an explanation and description. Kids can also enter a Tessellation Contest through the Contest Page or order Escher-related books, puzzles, socks, and more.

Related Areas: *Math*

Art & Music

World-Wide Webs

 K-6

URL: http://itpubs.ucdavis.edu/richard/string/

The author of this Web site considers the art of string figures a mobile form of art. After browsing through this site and trying out some of the examples, you will agree. The site includes a history of this ancient world-wide art form and illustrated directions for various string figures. A bibliographic page is included if you wish to investigate the history of any of the figures presented.

Related Areas: *Social Studies*

 Integration Idea

> Compare an ancient art form with the more modern work of an unusual artist. Visit the World of Escher and examine the unique creations of the man who "never considered himself a mathematician or an artist" but was respected by both groups. Contrast this experience with the ancient form of art, making string figures. Reproduce some of the designs form World-Wide Webs by following the directions. Do your students consider both of these types "forms of art"? Why or why not? Debate the topics, "What is art?" and "What is not art?"

YELLOW PAGES
HEALTH & PHYSICAL EDUCATION

Health & Physical Education

American Heart Association
URL: http://www.amhrt.org

This is the official site of the American Heart Association. Inside its pages you'll find a lot of information about healthy living, nutrition, and fitness. Of special interest is a section just for kids with exercise activities, healthy recipes, and useful data about the heart.

Related Areas: *Science*

Arbor Nutrition Guide
URL: http://arborcom.com/

This page contains a plethora of links to other Web sites about food and nutrition. Learn about food science and safety, and get info on the latest nutritional and clinical facts via this online index.

Related Areas: *Science*

The Arc Home Page
URL: http://TheArc.org/welcome.html

This site, the home page for one of the largest national organizations on mental retardation, includes an enormous amount of information about the subject. By going online, the folks behind the Arc are hoping to shed some light on one of the most misunderstood disabilities in the world. Learn facts about mental retardation or post a question to the online bulletin board.

Ask the Experts
URL: http://www.druginfonet.com/askprof.htm

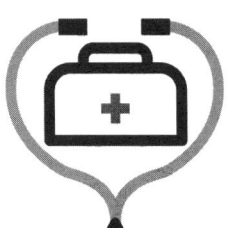

Do your students have a question that only a fully qualified doctor can answer? Do they just want to meet someone in the medical profession? InfoLink offers an Ask a Doctor service through their popular Web site. Previous answers can be viewed here in a searchable archive.

Health & Physical Education

Baseball Coaches Page
URL: http://www.geocities.com/Colosseum/2407/

Baseball coaches, managers, and trainers may want to check out this page to find the "drills and techniques to make your program a success." There's information and discussions on such issues as baseball camps, player discipline, practice drills, and league organization.

Benny Goodsport
URL: http://www.bennygoodsport.com/

At this colorful Web site, children can learn all about the Goodsport Gang and, through them, how to be healthy. There are "worm mazes," games, puzzles, and more. Children can also share their stories with other online visitors or learn about such things as the food pyramid. Good graphics make it easy for primary readers to maneuver around most of these pages.

Related Areas: *Language Arts/Languages*

The BHealthy Gym
URL: http://homepages.enterprise.net/bhealthy

This Web site features ten great stretches for students to try out between lessons, and offers advice on why you should always stretch before and after you exercise.

Integration Idea

To culminate your class' health unit hold a health fair in your school. Invite medical professionals from your area to set up booths and talk to students. Have students complete research so that they can also set up information booths. They can visit the American Heart Association and the BHealthy Gym sites to gather heart and exercise information, and then set up computer booths at the fair so visitors can read about Benny Goodsport or head over to the Ask the Online Experts their medical questions.

Health & Physical Education

Bicycle Helmet Safety Institute
URL: http://www.bhsi.org

Many children often wonder why they are required to wear helmets when bike riding. This site contains a statistics section intended to make children, as well as adults, more aware of the importance of bicycle safety. A consumer guide to good helmets can also be found here.

CEC ERIC Clearinghouse on Disabilities and Gifted Education
URL: http://www.cec.sped.org/er-menu.htm

The CEC ERIC Clearinghouse focuses on the professional literature, information, and resources relating to the education and development of those who have disabilities or are gifted individuals. Here you'll find a searchable database of educational materials, reports, research, and bibliographic information. ERIC also provides digests of information covering topics like ADD, gifted, behavior disorders, early childhood, inclusion, mainstreaming, and learning disabilities.

Related Areas: *Teacher Resources*

Center for the Study of Autism
URL: http://www.autism.org/

The Center for the Study of Autism has produced this site to inform parents and professionals about this horrible disease. There is an overview of autism and on related here. Issues regarding genetics, self injurious behavior, and tunnel vision are also discussed. Teaching tips are available, as well as a sibling center.

Related Areas: *Teacher Resources*

Child Safety Forum
URL: http://www.xmission.com:80/~gastown/safe/safe2.htm

Did you know that more children die in home accidents than from all childhood diseases combined? This Web site, however, seeks to lower that number considerably. It contains guides to safe products, excerpts from books on safety, kitchen safety advice, advice from parents and other experts, and tips on how to reduce child-related accidents.

Health & Physical Education

Children, Stress, and Natural Disasters K-6
URL: http://www.ag.uiuc.edu/~disaster/teacher.html

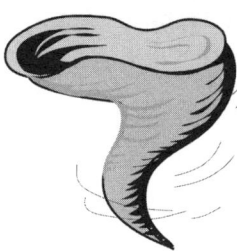

The University of Illinois Cooperative Extension Service hosts this disaster resource for teachers and other child care providers to help them be prepared when working with children who have been through some sort of disaster. Activities, a bibliography of children's literature, and a list of resources available from the American Red Cross are all included here.

Related Areas: *Teacher Resources; Language Arts/Languages*

Children with Diabetes K-6
URL: http://www.castleweb.com/diabetes/

This online community for kids, families, and adults with Type I diabetes has plenty of good content for those either suffering from this disease, or dealing with it through friends and family. There are plenty of databases and ways to contact others who have diabetes, whether through the online chat room, or simply via email. In addition, sections like Ask the Diabetes Team provide useful facts and advice on such topics as what products to purchase, how to maintain a healthy diet, and the latest diabetes news and information.

Children's Medical Center K-6
URL: http://galen.med.virginia.edu/~smb4v/cmchome.html

The Children's Medical Center is the first "hospital without walls." Inside its doors you'll find lots of information about children's health — from clinical case tutorials, pediatric care, prenatal health maintenance and immunizations, to a hypertext index of children's diseases and a primer of molecular genetics.

Related Areas: *Science*

 Integration Idea

Most of the sites located on these two pages can give parents a resource for help in dealing with their child's health, disability, and/or safety, as well as provide them with helpful contacts. If you write a newsletter for parents, be sure to include these sites within its pages.

45

Health & Physical Education

Colgate–Palmolive Kids World
URL: http://www.colgate.com/Kids-world/

Although a commercial company, this Web site has very good information for children regarding maintaining good oral hygiene. There are a lot of activities for children to do such as making charts, playing games (find the healthy snacks), and obtaining a special message from the tooth fairy.

Council on the Education of the Deaf
URL: http://www.educ.kent.edu/deafed

This site is designed to serve as a primary Net location for information concerning the education of deaf and hard-of-hearing students. Particular attention has been given to providing teachers with curriculum materials, instructional strategies, and professional development opportunities.

Related Areas: *Teacher Resources*

Deaf World Web's Deaf Cyberkids
URL: http://dww.deafworldweb.org:80/dww/kids/

Deaf Cyberkids is for school-aged kids from around the world who experience hearing problems. There are available keypals for your students' age groups, a deaf discussion forum, and an "add-a-story" group writers area. Arts and Literature information here also.

Related Areas: *Language Arts/Languages; Art & Music*

Dental Hot Topics
URL: http://www.ada.org/consumer/hottopic/breath.html

Halitosis! Gum disease! It won't be long before your students will be asking you what causes bad breath and how to stop it. Now you will have the answer thanks to this Web site. Your students can also email their own hygiene questions to the American Dental Association and get them answered in no time flat.

Related Areas: *Science*

Health & Physical Education

Dental-Related Internet List of Links (DRILL) **K-6**
URL: http://www.citizen.infi.net/~dmtrop/dental/dental3.html

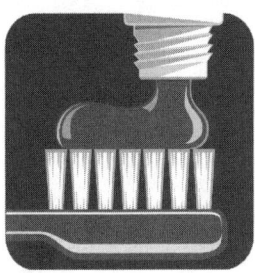

This site contains hundreds of dental-related links. Some of the information is for dental professionals, but much is educational and geared toward the general public.

Related Areas: *Science*

Department of Food Science and Nutrition **4-6**
URL: http://fscn1.fsci.umn.edu/

The Department of Food Science & Nutrition at the University of Minnesota provides information relative to aspects of the study of food science and nutrition in general. This ranges from their K-12 resource page to their Food-Law page (providing information and links to sites relating to food law).

Related Areas: *Science*

The Diabetes Home Page **K-6**
URL: http://www.nd.edu/~hhowisen/diabetes.html

Designed for the lay-person as well as the expert, this is the central Web repository for diabetes information. There's even a virtual diabetic game where you and your students can test your knowledge on this all-too-common disease.

 Integration Idea

> Teachers of students who are deaf or hard-of-hearing will appreciate the site from the Council on the Education of the Deaf for its lesson plans and instructional strategies. The Deaf World Web's Deaf Cyberkids site is another great place to send your hearing-impaired students to read the works by other deaf students or submit their own.

Health & Physical Education

Dole Food's 5 a Day   K-6
URL: http://www.dole5aday.com/

This Web site teaches children excellent nutrition information in a fun and lively manner. Students can browse through the fruit newsroom, get great nutritious recipes, and much more. This site also has a section about how teachers can help their students make wise food choices.

Related Areas: *Teacher Resources*

Dyslexia: The Gift   K-6
URL: http://www.dyslexia.com

Are there any positive effects to having a learning disability such as ADD or Dyslexia? The answer, according to this site, is yes. Visual thinking and "the gift of mastery" are but two positive traits that most dyslexics share. This Web site contains a plentiful amount of valuable data for parents and educators about these disabilities and where to find counselors and groups that provide quality treatment and advice. Hands-on materials can also be ordered through this site.

Electronic Learning Health Lesson Plans   K-6
URL: http://eeunix.ee.usm.maine.edu/smp/mlr/heaL.heaL.conC.3-4.html

Looking for curriculum ideas? This site has ideas covering all sorts of health ideas posted online in the form of ready to be printed lesson plans. Objectives and outcomes are also listed.

Related Areas: *Art & Music; Language Arts/Languages; Math; Science; Social Studies; Teacher Resources*

Emergency!   4-6
URL: http://www.catt.citri.edu.au/emergency/

Students who want to be a doctor, police officer, or fireman when they grow up should get a kick out of this site, a guide to the emergency services around the world.

Related Areas: *Science; Social Studies*

Health & Physical Education

Facilitated Communication
URL: http://soeweb.syr.edu/thefci

The Facilitated Communication Institute was formed in 1992 to get people with disabilities and their families, as well as practicing professionals, to examine, learn about, and share information on facilitated communication. People who cannot speak, whose speech is highly limited, and who cannot point reliably can use this method as an alternative means of expression.

Family Health Home Page
URL: http://www.tcom.ohiou.edu/family-health.html

Students can use this site to listen to the latest health information. Family Health is a daily, online series of 2.5 minute audio programs featuring practical, easy-to-understand answers to some of the most frequently asked questions about health and health care.

First Aid Online
URL: http://www.prairienet.org/~autumn/firstaid/

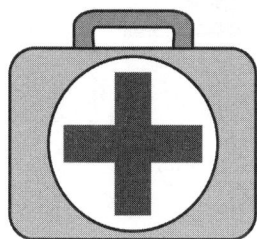

This site provides basic, easy-to-follow information on how to deal with animal bites, food poisoning, burns, frostbite, sprains and fractures, choking, and other health problems that can occur in the classroom as well as out. With links to other handy online medical resources, this Web page also comes with a list of necessary first aid supplies you should keep on hand in case of an emergency

---

Integration Idea

Have your students create and complete a safety guide that also includes occupations dealing with safety. The Emergency! site will help to build interest about safety occupations. In addition incorporate the first aid site and the family health site as resources for collecting information for this guide.

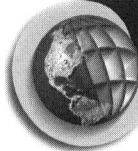

Health & Physical Education

The Fitness Files
URL: http://rcc.webpoint.com/fitness/index.htm

This Web site teaches students the basic fundamentals of how to become healthier. There are four main areas to navigate: Fitness Fundamentals, Get Active, The Injurenet, and Fuel for Fitness. Though aimed at a broad audience, students will especially get a kick out of the InjureNet interactive display which allows them to click on different parts of a stick figure.

Fitness Fundamentals
URL: http://www.hoptechno.com/book11.htm

Guidelines to physical fitness as developed by the President's Council on Physical Fitness and Sports are listed at this site with detailed descriptions. Your students can use it as a study guide or you can use it as a reference for creating an activity or lesson plan.

Related Areas: *Language Arts/Languages; Teacher Resources*

Food and Drug Administration
URL: http://www.fda.gov/

Let this site be your electronic source of information about the U.S. Food and Drug Administration. From here you and your students can obtain the latest FDA news, as well as news on medical devices, drugs, and tobacco. Be sure to stop by the food section, as it has a lot of good nutritional material for educators.

Related Areas: *Teacher Resources*

Food Finder
URL: http://www.olen.com/food/

This Web site provides nutritional information about the fast food items that pervade the globe's towns and highways. It is an excellent resource for teachers as they could have their students find the fat content in their favorite food items and then figure out how much exercise they would have to do to burn off the fat.

Related Areas: *Science; Teacher Resources*

Health & Physical Education

Food Pyramid
URL: http://www.ganesa.com/food/foodpyramid.html

Here's a nice graphic of the food pyramid that will help students understand the importance of good nutrition. Children can click on a food group to get more information on what their daily intake of the foods in that group should be. Simple, but very functional.

Games Kids Play
URL: http://www.corpcomm.net/~gnieboer/gamehome.htm

This Web site offers the "official rules" of all different games for elementary school children to play. In fact, there are 38 games listed, from Duck, Duck, Goose to sorts of Tag. This is an excellent site for Physical Education teachers.

Related Areas: *Teacher Resources*

Gentle Teaching
URL: http://utopia.knoware.nl/users/gentle/

Gentle Teaching is a nonviolent approach for helping people with special needs and sometimes challenging behaviors that focuses on four primary goals of "care giving." This site discusses the psychology of interdependence, companionship, and basic values.

⚠ Integration Idea

Find out how many of the students in your classroom eat fast food and how often. Use the Food Finder site to research the nutritional value of their favorite fast foods and check the food pyramid site to see if they are getting a balanced meal.

Health & Physical Education

Global Health Network
URL: http://info.pitt.edu/HOME/GHNet/GHNet.html

The concept of the Global Health Network is simple: Its organizers hope to network everyone engaged in public health and disease prevention worldwide across the Net! Use this site to have students research the status of infectious diseases, such as Ebola outbreaks and tuberculosis.

Related Areas: *Science*

Health Education Shareware
URL: http://www.ualberta.ca/~jhancock/softwar.html

Looking for multimedia software for your Macintosh or Windows PC? Look no further than the University of Alberta's Health Education Shareware Library. You'll find software focusing on more than a dozen health topics, from various diseases to alcohol use. A gold mine for health educators.

Related Areas: *Technology/Internet*

Health World Online
URL: http://www.healthy.net/

At this Web site, children can walk through a virtual "Health Campus" gathering important and current information on many health issues. Be sure to check out the online library which has a number of "healthy" articles, journals, and audio files.

Health-Net
URL: http://www.health-net.com/

This comprehensive online medical information site covers topics in everything from alternative medicine to nutrition to child behavior and development. Be sure to check out their brand new live forums.

Health & Physical Education

HealthLinks K-6
URL: http://www.hslib.washington.edu/

HealthLinks attempts to consolidate and distribute electronic health information across the Internet. Use this site to learn about public health, heath statistics, and links to related educational resources.

Related Areas: *Science*

Healthtouch K-6
URL: http://www.healthtouch.com/

Accurate, up-to-date information on various health topics and diseases. There's also a pharmacy search that provides a guide to common drug uses, precautions, and side effects.

Hygiene K-6
URL: http://teacherpathfinder.org/School/Subjects/Health/hygiene.html

Download lesson plans, blackline masters, and other activities from this site. From here, you can skip over to the Oral-B Web site, which also helps teach students oral care. You will be able to use this site for grades 3-6.

Related Areas: *Art & Music; Teacher Resources; Technology/Internet; Science*

Integration Idea

Do your students wonder what it's like to be a doctor? Well, they can find out by attempting to diagnose a patient and discover the ailment by using the Interactive Patient site (p. 54). While your students work through the site have them write down words they did not know and research them at Health Touch or the library at Health World On-line.

Health & Physical Education

The Interactive Patient
URL: http://medicus.marshall.edu/medicus.htm

Here's an interactive Web program that allows students to "play doctor" while online. Using the program, students get to examine an imaginary patient who complains of back pain. Your students can ask him questions, take x-rays, make a diagnosis, and prescribe medicine. While this site is mainly designed for older medical students, it's an ideal way to introduce younger students to the world of medicine.

Related Areas: *Science*

International Food Information Council Foundation
URL: http://ificinfo.health.org/

For those teaching or learning about good eating habits, there are few sites better than the International Food Information Council's home on the Web. This site hosts a wealth of information about food safety, nutrition, and good health. Follow the Information for Educators link to find invaluable teaching aids and articles.

Related Areas: *Teacher Resources*

Kid Safety on the Internet
URL: http://www.uoknor.edu/oupd/kidsafe/start.htm

This site for young students uses a question and answer format to help them learn to protect themselves and handle emergencies of all kinds, including any that might occur on the Net.

Related Areas: *Technology/Internet*

Kids Health Organization
URL: http://www.kidshealth.org/

This Web site has excellent information about children's health for parents as well as teachers. Topics include the benefits of different types of vitamins, the food pyramid, healthy children's recipes, how to read food labels, and keeping fit. Children can also submit their own questions. In addition, there are sections for health care professionals.

Related Areas: *Science; Teacher Resources*

Health & Physical Education

KidSource
URL: http://www.kidsource.com

K-6

Geared to parents and teachers, this site offers a wealth of information covering all aspects of a child's health, from newborn to sixth grade. An activities section contains lesson plans for basic fitness.

Related Areas: *Teacher Resources*

KinderGarden
URL: http://aggie-horticulture.tamu.edu/kinder/index.html

K-3

Believe it or not, gardening has proven to be a therapeutic exercise for many—even the very young. This Web site is dedicated to the proposition that gardening as a learning experience and as a hobby can help children cope with the stresses of the world in which we live. There are many opportunities available for children to become involved with plants, gardens, or the outdoors in general, and this site lists several. In here you'll find ideas for starting a garden in your school or community, fun garden-related activities for young children, botanical gardens you and your class can visit, and ways to teach not only science, but also history, economics, poetry, and math using garden plants!

Related Areas: *Science; Art & Music; Social Studies; Math*

Integration Idea

Complete your unit on health with planting a garden of vegetables. Visit the KinderGarden site and get some pointers on your garden and kids' health for recipes. The KidSource site will also compliment this type of lesson with its lesson plans and activities on fitness.

Health & Physical Education

LD Online: Learning Disabilities In-Depth
URL: http://www.ldonline.org/index.html

LD Online offers a tremendous amount of information on many different kinds of Learning Disabilities. The ABCs of LD brings you a number of articles on types, causes, and determining learning disabilities. LD In-Depth has a large variety of topics such as math skills, ADD/ADHD, speech and language, and teaching techniques.

LD Online's Kid Zone
URL: http://www.ldonline.org/kidzone/kidzone.html

A special place on the Web where learning disabled students of all ages can play and learn. Users can browse student creations, or post their own art work, poems, fiction, and articles for Kid Zone magazine. Includes activities that teach students about famous people with learning disabilities, and a reading activity to help students understand what it's like to have a reading disability.

Related Areas: *Art & Music; Language Arts/Languages*

Learning Disabilities Association of America
URL: http://www.ld.ucsf.edu

The LDA is a national, nonprofit organization which advances the education of children of normal or potentially normal intelligence who manifest handicaps of a perceptual, conceptual, or coordinative nature. You'll find articles related to mainstreaming, ADD/ADHD, dyslexia, education standards, literacy, and more.

Related Areas: *Teacher Resources*

The Locker Room: Sports for Kids
URL: http://members.aol.com/msdaizy/sports/locker.html

Do your students play on a school sport's team? Or on a city, town, or organized team? Do they just like to watch sports, or learn about them? By heading over to this site, kids can learn all about their favorite sports, or just post news about their favorite team. They can learn some new ways to practice their skills, brush up on some rules, and test their sports knowledge. There's even a section on how to get along with your coach and teammates.

Health & Physical Education

Mentadent: Word of Mouth
URL: http://www.mentadent.com/index.html

Have your students learn how to brush, floss, and listen to what their teeth are telling them all at this site. You can also have your students compose questions to ask oral professionals who frequently visit this Web page.

Related Areas: *Language Arts/Languages; Teacher Resources*

Muscular Dystrophy Association Australia
URL: http://www.mda.org.au/

This Web site posts valuable papers about Muscular Dystrophy for downloading, with additional information on the disease's history and characteristics. Check out Ryan's Page, a place for young students with MD to meet.

National Center for Health Statistics
URL: http://www.cdc.gov/nchswww/nchshome.htm

The mission of the National Center for Health Statistics (NCHS) is to provide statistical information that will guide actions and policies to improve the health of the American people. As the nation's principal health-statistics agency, NCHS leads the way with accurate, relevant, and timely data.

Related Areas: *Teacher Resources*

Integration Idea

Students who are learning disabled will appreciate submitting writings to the LD Online site while reading stories written by other students dealing with similar disabilities. Have students read the information about LD/ADD, so they can better understand their disability and be better equipped to adapt their work habits if they suffer from it. Kids Health Organization (p. 54) will allow them to submit questions about their problems and receive quick answers.

National Clearinghouse for Alcohol and Drug Information
URL: http://www.health.org/

This Web site offers very good information to children not only about smoking and alcohol abuse, but also about Internet safety! Children can email any questions they may have about these subjects, learn how to say no to drugs, or just try out some of the fun games and activities available here.

National Safekids Website
URL: http://www.safekids.org

Although this site is geared mostly toward adult guardians of children, it does contain some important information that kids should be aware of to avoid injuries. The Fact Sheet section discusses many common and unfortunate accidents that often involve youngsters. In addition, there is a Family Safety Check List that can help make kids more aware of what they should and should not do in order to avoid accidents and injury.

NCADD Youth Messages
URL: http://www.ncadd.org/youdir.html

This site offers two student-oriented, multimedia presentations about the dangers of alcohol and drug abuse. Entitled "Who's Got the Power? You . . . Or Drugs?" and "How are Alcohol and Drugs Affecting Your Life?" these Web-based offerings are colorful and factual, presenting basic information in a student-friendly fashion that's perfect for inclusion in health education classes at any level.

NCSA Mosaic Access Page
URL: http://bucky.aa.uic.edu

The NCSA Mosaic Access Page is a resource for educators and administrators interested in how students with disabilities use the Internet and the World Wide Web. The project's goals are to identify the major barriers people with disabilities encounter while using Internet navigation software. Solutions are being designed and implemented, and this site is your link to these latest developments.

Related Areas: *Technology/Internet*

Health & Physical Education

Net-Doctor
URL: http://www.net-doctor.com/

Whether your students are learning about the circulatory system, allergies, the nervous system, or the stomach, this site will prove to be an extremely helpful online biology reference. Amusing Web animations help explain the various body parts, while the informative text explains the functions of organs like the pituitary gland or the thyroid. A lengthy glossary is also available for those just looking for a quick definition or two.

Related Areas: *Science*

PE Central
URL: http://www.chre.vt.edu/~/pe.central/

A comprehensive Web site designed especially for physical education teachers, students, and parents. You'll find classroom teacher lesson plans with physical education components, assessment ideas, information on equipment purchasing, health lesson ideas, links to PE-related mailing lists, "instant" PE activities, conference information, and "Top" Web site links.

Related Areas: *Teacher Resources*

PE-TV
URL: http://www.pe-tv.com

Filled with knowledge, energy, and variety, PE-TV is a weekly, 12 minute, commercial free television program that's coming to a local computer near you! The shows are designed to be shown in physical education classes, and feature the world's greatest athletes and performing artists to teach kids that fitness is a way of life and an ongoing process for all of us.

Integration Idea

Help your students visualize how the body works by viewing Net-Doctor. The movies at this Web site make it easier for them to appreciate how the body works when you teach about diseases of the body. Include the NCADD site for students to read about drug prevention and gather information to use in performing a skits about saying no to drugs!

Health & Physical Education

Pear Bear Healthy Kids
URL: http://www2.usapears.com/pears/pbbear.htm

Follow Pear Bear as he teaches your students about good nutritional eating through a variety of stories and a collection of healthy recipes (many of them pear-related).

Rainbow Raccoons
URL: http://www.rainbowjoe.com

This colorful Web site packs a lot of good information on health and safety. There are neat little slogans, such as "Make sure your smoke detector gives a beep, so it will warn you of fire, even while you sleep!" It also has some good science and history information. A very good site for the primary grades since it uses a lot of great pictures.

Related Areas: *Science; Social Studies*

Recipe Archive Index
URL: http://www.cs.cmu.edu/people/mjw/recipes/

From appetizers to pasta to special diet dishes, this Web site plays host to a large number of recipies, both easy and complex. Links to other cooking sites can also be found here.

Related Areas: *Teacher Resources*

School Psychology Resources
URL: http://www.bcpl.lib.md.us/~sandyste/school_psych.html

This is your one-step source of links to online resources related to anxiety disorders, ADD, autism, conduct disorders, learning disabilities, stress management, mood disorders, and more. This valuable resource is managed by Sandra Steingart, a school psychologist in Maryland.

Health & Physical Education

Shape Up America
URL: www.shapeup.org/sua/

Shape up America is chaired by Dr. C. Everett Koop and was organized to promote healthy weight and physical activity. This site contains tons of educational information and tips about the benefits of staying in shape. Assess your fitness level and find out about different types of physical activity. Take a health and fitness quiz, or just read about what one must do to stay in shape.

SPARK
URL: http://www.foundation.sdsu.edu/projects/spark/index.html

SPARK (Sports, Play, and Active Recreation for Kids) is an elementary-level physical education curriculum and staff development program that began as a National Institutes of Health funded research project. The primary goal of the research is to design a health program for kids that decreases their risk for heart disease by promoting regular physical activity. You'll find the results of their work here for your perusal and use in your classroom!

Special Education Online
URL: http://www.sped.ukans.edu/

The University of Kansas Department of Special Education hosts this Web site, which is a central clearinghouse for online resources, mostly mailing lists and gopher sites, relating to special education.

Related Areas: *Teacher Resources*

 Integration Idea

K-3 students can interact with the health sites Pear Bear and Rainbow Raccoons on their own or with minimal guidance and learn about nutrition, health, and safety. When students are finished give them a sheet of story paper and have them write and illustrate a story dealing with nutrition or safety involving one of the characters found at these sites.

Health & Physical Education

The Sporting News
URL: http://www.sportingnews.com

This Web site features many professional sports, showing statistics of teams and the players. It's a good way to keep track of your favorite teams. You can also use this site for math lessons because of all the statistics given.

Related Areas: *Math*

Sports Illustrated for Kids
URL: http://pathfinder.com/SIFK

Ideal for the student-athlete, this site is packed with sports information and activities. Your students can test their skills at a tile puzzle. They can also join a fantasy basketball or baseball league. Then they can "draft" their own players and compete with kids around the world.

The Sports Network
URL: http://www.sportsnetwork.com/index.htm

Though a news oriented sports e-zine, this site also offers plenty of statistics and rankings in both amateur and professional worlds. It's a good site to get kids to read, find a sport they like, or to make up math problems.

Related Areas: *Math; Language Arts/Languages*

The Tooth Fairy
URL: http://www.toothfairy.org/

"Be true to your teeth or they'll be false to you!" This colorful, fact-filled site will appeal to both young and older students. There are funny stories about the tooth fairy for elementary-aged students, as well as links to online courses about tooth decay and periodontology for older students.

Health & Physical Education

Tossed Salad Productions
URL: http://www.tossed-salad.com/

Tossed Salad Productions is the home of Healthy Herb, the walnut wacky eggplant ambassador of children's fitness and nutmeg nutrition. Healthy Herb "Starring You" programs air on the PBS affiliate in Orlando, Florida. Their official site boasts an illustrated storybook, cartoons, and an interactive virtual playground, all focused on eating nutritiously.

TurnStep Aerobics
URL: http://www.turnstep.com/

This site is packed with information about nearly a dozen types of aerobic exercises and exercise programs. Included is a searchable database of aerobic exercise patterns your students can access to discover the perfect pattern suited to them! You'll also find tips concerning warm-ups, double aerobics, aquatic activities, slides, and more.

UVA Special Education Web Site
URL: http://curry.edschool.Virginia.EDU/go/specialed/

This site provides a very clear and concise overview of the history of special education, the laws and availability of online medical journals, definitions of disabilities, and other related resources. Links to information and resources are arranged according to categories of disability.

Related Areas: *Teacher Resources*

 Integration Idea

> Incorporate reading comprehension and math into one lesson by using the two sports sites: Sports Illustrated for Kids and The Sports Network. Go into statistics on The Sports Network and have your students figure out the average number of yards used for their favorite team. Have them visit Sports Illustrated for Kids and summarize an article to be presented over the intercom as a sports minute news report.

Health & Physical Education

Virtual Children's Center
URL: http://www.med.jhu.edu/peds/pedspage.html

Sponsored by the Johns Hopkins University, this site has clinical information, research data, and pediatric announcements. What makes this site noteworthy, however, is their Points of Pediatric Interest, a massive selection of links dealing with medicine, pediatrics, parenting, and general child-health concerns.

Wee Willie Wheezie
URL: http://enterprise.newcomm.net/ies/

Wee Willie Wheezie is an educational program produced for children with asthma, to help them better understand their condition and learn certain principles of asthma self-management. It also teaches about different medications through games.

Wellness Web
URL: http://www.wellnessweb.org

What is wellness? How does one stay well? Through the use of puzzles and games, this site strives to promote healthy living and explore what it means to be healthy by explaining the importance of mental, physical, and social wellness.

Related Areas: *Teacher Resources*

What's Up with Down's?
URL: http://www2.pcix.com/~kehler/

This informative site provides parents and teachers with first-hand contributed stories "from families and friends who have had their lives touched by Down's syndrome." There is a portrait of Down's syndrome, a letter to new parents, and research pages. Be sure to check out the coloring pages for your students, and articles like "Teaching People with Down's Syndrome to Understand and Use Numbers."

YELLOW PAGES
LANGUAGE ARTS/ LANGUAGES

Language Arts/Languages

Adam's Fox Box
URL: http://tavi.acomp.usf.edu/foxbox/

Feeling a little foxy? This Web site has a collection of fox-related stories, poems, pictures, and miscellany to keep any fox fan happy for hours. Impressive graphics and links to a variety of other fox sites provide an additional layer of interest

Related Areas: *Social Studies; Science; Art & Music*

American Literary Classics
URL: http://www.mindport.net/~arezis/

Each day a different chapter from a classic American novel is posted here for faithful visitors to read. Past novels include *Little Women, Moby Dick,* and *The Last of the Mohicans.* Visitors also get to vote on what novel should be posted next.

Related Areas: *Social Studies*

American Slanguages
URL: http://www.slanguage.com

Do your students know how to talk like a "New Jerseyian"? How about someone from Minnesota? This site lets your students learn about language within the various areas of the United States by examining the different types of slang people use in their state. See if your own city's or state's "slanguage" is there. If not try to submit it for them. There is also a slanguage quiz and a slang time tunnel.

Related Areas: *Social Studies*

American Verse Project
URL: http://www.hti.umich.edu/english/amverse/

This electronic archive is mostly made up of 19th century poetry, although a few 18th and 20th century texts are also included. Featured authors include Emily Dickinson, Carl Sandburg, and a host of lesser-known, but equally talented, writers.

Language Arts/Languages

An Awesome Site for All Ages! K-3
URL: http://www.marlo.com

The Webmasters at this site are trying very hard to live up to their title — and are succeeding rather well! Follow Marlo Marmalade and JJ Jamm as they help students make chocolate mousse, tell knock-knock jokes, travel to Hong Kong, or tell some of their favorite stories about their friends.

Related Areas: *Art & Music; Social Studies; Teacher Resources*

Anagram Insanity 4-6
URL: http://Infobahn.com/pages/anagram.html

An anagram is a word or phrase formed by reordering the letters from another word or phrase. Just enter your phrase at this interactive site and see the various words or phrases they change into. How many words can you make out of your favorite phrase?

Related Areas: *Technology/Internet*

Antics K-6
URL: http://www.ionet.net/~rdavis/antics.shtml

Students will be very ANThusiastic about this ANTeractive ANThology which explores words in the English language that include the syllable ant. Look at the cartoon and then guess which "ant" word goes with it. Très amusANT!

Related Areas: *Art & Music*

⚠ Integration Idea

Children have always been fascinated by the antics of animals. There has been a lot of literature written detailing the adventures of animals. Use some the resources from Adam's Fox Box, "The Call of the Wild" on American Literary Classics, and the Antics pages to have your students create a fun cartoon about the adventures of a favorite animal. An Awesome Site for All Ages incorporates cartoons and postcards that could help your students animate their cartoons.

Language Arts/Languages

Arthur
URL: http://www.pbs.org/wgbh/pages/arthur/

"Arthur," the famous young aardvark who appears in the book and TV show by Marc Brown, also lives at this Web site. From here, students can download pictures of Arthur to color, or learn to write stories with helpful tips for parents and teachers. Students can also email Arthur or read the latest news about him, his friends, and even Brown.

Related Areas: *Art & Music*

Author Online
URL: http://www.aaronshep.com/

Children's author Aaron Shepard has posted a lot of valuable free information on his Web page for students and educators interested in creative writing to download and use. Visitors will find online stories, writer's resources, tips, and exercises to try out in the classroom, and reader scripts to be read aloud.

Related Areas: *Art & Music*

Author's Pen
URL: http://www.books.com/scripts/authors.exe

When it comes to finding authors on the Internet, let this site be your guide. Here, your students can find links to pages devoted to authors, such as Walt Whitman, and online libraries galore.

Britannica Online
URL: http://www.eb.com/

At 44 million words, the *Encyclopædia Britannica* is recognized as the world's most comprehensive reference. Now, it's online as a fully searchable and browsable collection of authoritative references, including the full encyclopedic database, a dictionary, and more. Visitors may try the site for free, but regular users must pay a small fee to subscribe to the service.

Related Areas: *Social Studies*

Language Arts/Languages

Building Blocks to Reading
URL: http://www.macconnect.com/~jrpotter/Ltrain.spml

K-3

This colorful, friendly site contains hands-on reading readiness ideas to use with primary level children. Includes links to phonics and whole-language teaching methods, activities geared to learning each letter of the alphabet, a parent's guide to reading for kids, and monthly and seasonal activities and word search puzzles. If you are a teacher or parent of a preschool child, then this site is custom-tailored to you!

Related Areas: *Art & Music*

Carnegie Mellon English Server
URL: http://english-server.hss.cmu.edu

4-6

This enormous site contains more than 18,500 files covering just about every area of the arts and humanities and boasts over 200,000 readers per week. Inside are resources and online magazines ranging from such topics as poetry, nonfiction, fiction, history, cultural theory, and more.

Related Areas: *Teacher Resources; Social Studies; Art & Music*

The Canadian Kids Page
URL: http://www.onramp.ca/~lowens/

K-3

Of special interest to Canadian educators, this online index has links to over 300 educational Web sites all specially designed for young students. Sites are constantly added and updated to keep this page from growing stale.

Related Areas: *Art & Music; Social Studies*

Integration Idea

With the following sites your students can become authors! Begin by letting your students write to Arthur about some amazing personal story. Have them compare their works to Aaron Shepard's at Author Online or use Author's Pen as a resource to find other authors' pages to help revise their story. Then lastly go Building Blocks to Reading to have your students follow the step-by-step directions for making their own books in class.

Language Arts/Languages

Carol Hurst's Children's Literature Site
URL: http://www.crocker.com/~rebotis/index.html

Author Carol Hurst has put together an impressive collection of reviews of great books for kids, ideas for ways to use said books in the classroom, and activities about particular subjects, curriculum areas, themes, and professional topics. Books are arranged by title, author, and curriculum interest.

Related Areas: *Social Studies; Math; Teacher Resources*

Children's Literature
URL: http://www.parentsplace.com/readroom/childnew/index.html

This online newsletter is designed to enhance children's literacy by helping adults find the best available children's books. Hundreds of new children's books are reviewed here by highly qualified individuals and educators. Several books are arranged into useful bibliographies, such as holidays, animals, and insects. What's more, there is a rich section featuring reviews of electronic books, CD-ROMs, and other multimedia resources.

The Children's Literature Web Guide
URL: http://www.ucalgary.ca/~dkbrown/

If you're looking for good children's literature—no matter what the grade level—don't pass by this Web site! Categories in the site's List of Recommended Books include "Best Books for Young Adults 1995" (selected by the American Library Association), "Books for Young Adult Reluctant Readers," and "Sure-fire Can't Miss Books for Junior High Students." Other materials include online children's books and resources that help parents teach children to read and use the library.

Related Areas: *Social Studies; Art & Music*

The Christmas Page
URL: http://www.ucalgary.ca/~dkbrown/christmas.html

This site gives you a number of online stories for the holidays. There are original Christmas stories and old favorites like "A Christmas Carol," "The Gift of the Magi," "The Night Before Christmas," "How the Grinch Stole Christmas," and "The Selfish Giant."

Related Areas: *Art & Music; Social Studies*

Language Arts/Languages

The Complete Works of William Shakespeare
URL: http://the-tech.mit.edu/Shakespeare/works.html

The bard would be astounded to find his complete, annotated works available to anyone in the world via computer. Here, you can find an online copy of everything he ever wrote, including his sonnets and lesser-known poems.

Concertina Children's Books
URL: http://www.digimark.net/iatech/books

Concertina is a Canadian-based children's publisher, committed to releasing books simultaneously to print and to the electronic highway. Here your K-3 students will find four complete children's books with colorful, easy-to-read pages, including: *Waking in Jerusalem, I Live on a Raft, My Blue Suitcase,* and *The Song of Moses.*

Related Areas: *Art & Music; Social Studies*

Creation Stories and Traditional Wisdom
URL: http://www.ozemail.com.au:80/~reed/global/mythstor.html

At this Web site, youngsters from around the world can study the literature of indigenous peoples in their own countries, look for common themes, and practice using the Internet to conduct research. Students can write their own myths, legends, or fables and then submit their completed stories to the site's owner via email for publication on the Net. Each story should include the author's name and details about his or her school. The home page for this project explains the details, including specific educational goals and procedures as well as suggested classroom strategies and activities.

Related Areas: *Social Studies*

 Integration Idea

Some of the world's richest stories from generations past are religious in nature. These stories have molded how cultures live, think, and view the world. Take your students on a tour of these types of stories from Christmas stories and *The Song of Moses* at The Christmas Page and Concertina Children's Books to explanations of "creation and the relationship between humans, the environment, and the spirit world" at Creation Stories and Traditional Wisdom.

 **Language Arts/Languages**

Creative Dramatics Lesson Plans
URL: http://www.byu.edu/tmcbucs/arts-ed/StanHome.html

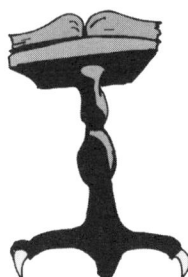 Here is a collection of creative lesson plans aimed at allowing your students to create and perform stories of their own. One lesson, for example, helps them bring the story of the three little pigs to life right in your classroom. Have your students learn creativity of expression, elements of drama, and how to use expressive speech with these lesson plans.

Related Areas: *Teacher Resources; Art & Music*

Critical Thinking Discussion
URL: http://www.smoky.org/~nces/Jane_Jackson/CriticalDiscussion/CritThink.html

The series of seven lesson plans at this site asks students tough questions about race, gender, immigration, and education in order to help them think critically and to engage in responsible and reasoned debates with others. Using the lesson plans, students first view a graph from the National Center of Education Statistics. They then attempt to "answer" the open-ended questions provided. Although designed for high school students, these lessons can be easily adapted for younger children.

Related Areas: *Social Studies*

CyberKids
URL: http://www.mtlake.com/cyberkids

 CyberKids is a free online magazine for kids by kids, created with a little help from their friends at Mountain Lake Software and Woodwind Consulting. It contains colorful stories, artwork, puzzles, and more. The site's creators also host an annual CyberKids International Writing and Art Contest that your class could consider entering.

Related Areas: *Art & Music*

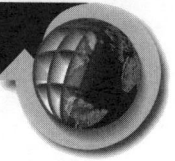

Language Arts/Languages

Dictionaries and Translators
URL: http://rivendel.com/~ric/resources/dictionary.html

Whether you're an elementary student wanting to bone up for the vocabulary test, a foreign language teacher looking for some online aid, or just an online traveler wanting to learn Esperanto, this site is one of the best language references on the Net. Rivendell International Communications, the sponsor of this site, has put up links to translation dictionaries for 37 languages, including Hebrew, Arabic, Latin, and Zulu! In addition, Rivendell has created their own experimental translating dictionary, which can translate words you type into English, Spanish, French, German, or Italian.

Related Areas: *Teacher Resources; Social Studies*

EFLWeb
URL: http://www.u-net.com/eflweb/

Educators and students will find great value in this resource for those learning English as a foreign language. There are plenty of straightforward articles, resources, and answers to questions like: Where do I go to learn English? What are some of the experiences of ESL teachers and students?

Related Areas: *Social Studies; Teacher Resources*

The Electronic Text Archive
URL: http://www.etext.org

A rich Web site, home to thousands of electronic texts (etexts). This site is truly one of the world's first online libraries! You and your students will find the complete text of hundreds of classic books, current e-zines (electronic magazines), philosophic texts, mailing lists, and more.

Related Areas: *Teacher Resources; Technology/Internet; Social Studies*

 Integration Idea

The CyberKids site is host to an International Writing and Art Contest. Bring these worldly experiences into your classroom with a small international project. The Dictionary and Translators site will work well with EFLWeb for communicating with international students. Sponsor a writing contest where your class's writing is judged by a class from across the globe and your class judges their writing, also.

Language Arts/Languages

Elementary Spanish
URL: http://star.ucc.nau.edu/ES/index.html

Although this distance-education learning unit has come to an end, elementary educators can still take advantage of its sample Spanish lesson plans and activities, as well as a number of enrichment projects. Find out what countries speak Spanish, for example, or learn how to make a piñata!

Related Areas: *Art & Music; Social Studies; Teacher Resources*

The Encyclopedia Mythica
URL: http://www.pantheon.org/mythica/

An online encyclopedia of mythology and folklore, this site contains hundreds of definitions of gods and goddesses, supernatural beings, imaginary lands, and legendary creatures and monsters from around the world.

English as a Second Language
URL: http://www.lang.uiuc.edu/r-li5/esl

ESL educators who want to enhance their lessons and projects using the Web should get a kick out of this site, which contains writing instructions, a helpful lab, and online stories to help your students with their English-speaking abilities. Easily indexed.

Related Areas: *Social Studies*

The English Teacher's Web Site
URL: http://www.mlckew.edu.au/english/

Based in Australia, this site is designed to help English teachers find the Internet resources they need for their lesson plans, activities, and projects.

Related Areas: *Art & Music*

Language Arts/Languages

Fake Out

K-6

URL: http://www.eduplace.com/hmco/school/dictionary/index.html

Fake Out is the definition guessing game where visitors must guess the definition of words listed under their grade level (from K-6 and above). There's also an area where you can create fake definitions for words that will be used next week. Lots of fun.

Familiar Quotations

4-6

URL: http://www.columbia.edu/acis/bartleby/bartlett/

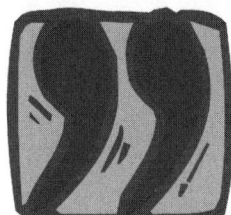

This online version of *Bartlett's Quotations* lets visitors enter a series of keywords to retrieve a lengthy list of familiar quotations. There is also a chronological index of primary authors you can search through that includes Geoffrey Chaucer, William Shakespeare, John Quincy Adams, Ralph Waldo Emerson, and lots more.

Related Areas: *Teacher Resources*

Foreign Language Teaching Forum

K-6

URL: http://www.cortland.edu/www_root/flteach/flteach.html

This Web site features an assortment of foreign language teaching methods including school/college articulation, training of student teachers, classroom activities, curriculum, and syllabus design. The archive of the popular FLTEACH mailing list is also housed here.

Integration Idea

Have your students role-play moving to a different country where the native language is different from English. What kinds of problems will they have? Use the Elementary Spanish Web site to set the language for the students to overcome. Use the English as a Second Language and the Foreign Language Teaching Forum as resources to increase the realism of this exercise. How long can you students handle this new set of problems? Hopefully your students will discover some empathy for other world travelers as well.

Language Arts/Languages

Grammar and Style Notes   4-6
URL: http://www.english.upenn.edu/~jlynch/grammar.html

This alphabetical glossary provides a miscellany of grammatical rules and explanations, comments on style, and suggestions on usage for students to refer to in their essay and creative writing projects.

Hangman   4-6
URL: http://www.allmixedup.com/cgi-bin/hangman/hangman?

Play the game of hangman on the computer! All you need to do is have your students pick letters from the alphabet to solve the puzzle before the poor stick figure ends up on the wrong end of the noose.

Help Your Child Learn to Write Well   K-6
URL: http://www.ed.gov/pubs/parents/Writing/

This U.S. Department of Education site gives pointers on how to help children write well. It describes what writing is for and then what writing "well" means. There are many pointers to be shared with parents and teachers that show how they can help by setting a place for homework, having materials readily available, and praising their child often.

Inkspot: for Young Writers   4-6   A+
URL: http://www.inkspot.com/young/

Young students interested in creative writing will find links to more than 75 online resources, including links to author workshops and writing associations, online contests, publications for student authors, publications seeking young writers, and more. There are also lots of links to school publications as well as school-based electronic magazines, known as e-zines.

Language Arts/Languages

The Internet Classics Archive
URL: http://classics.mit.edu

Aeschylus, Aristotle, Homer, Plato, and Sophocles—they're all here, plus a few of their friends and relations. Whether your students are studying Latin, or are just getting acquainted with some of the great classic works of literature, this site can provide them with access to downloadable copies of such works as *The Odyssey*, *The Aeneid*, and *Antigone*. Visitors are encouraged to leave comments about the works and their authors if they wish to.

Internet Poetry Archive
URL: http://sunsite.unc.edu/dykki/poetry/

Philip Levine, Seamus Heaney, and Czeslaw Milosz are just three of the poets features at this Web site, dedicated to making poetry accessible to new audiences as well as giving teachers and poetry fans new ways of presenting and studying these poets and their texts.

The Internet Public Library
URL: http://ipl.sils.umich.edu

A World Wide Web site designed to furnish answers to reference questions about libraries and librarians. Links to material on public, international, and school libraries, mailing lists, journals, professional organizations, and employment. Perfect for use by students on the lookout for specific information found both online and in public libraries. Students can ask a reference librarian for help with their research questions and get answers within hours!

Related Areas: *Technology/Internet*

 Integration Idea

Here are the largest storehouses of literary resources for your classes. These three sites, the Internet Classics Archive, the Internet Poetry Archive, and the Internet Public Library will provide scores of literary texts for any need which may arise. Bookmark these for your first stop on any literary search.

Language Arts/Languages

Jefferson Elementary's Writing Gallery
URL: http://boe.cabe.k12.wv.us/jefferso/gallery/wgallery/writing.html

Every month, teachers at Jefferson Elementary School choose and post a different writing activity for students to try. The students' work is then displayed the following month. Past writing activities are also available online.

Kaitlyn's Knock-Knock Jokes and Riddles
URL: http://www.bayne.com/wolfBayne/kaitlyn/default.html

An ever-increasing list of knock-knock jokes and riddles for young children. Meet Kaitlyn, a very precocious five-year-old, her pets, Mom and Dad, her toys, and find out what she wants to be when she grows up.

Related Areas: *Art & Music*

Kid Lit Project
URL: http://www.netc.org/web_mod/klp/index.html

Looking for a good way to use the popular KidPix software in your classroom? This site has a number of fantastic project ideas using popular children's books like *Chicken Soup with Rice* and *Dinner at Aunt Connie's House* to have children learn about history, geography, and science. Many of these projects connect students to online resources so your class can continue the project online as an extension. Students can also display their finished work at the Galore, or talk about their creations at the online forum.

Related Areas: *Art & Music; Technology/Internet*

KIDLINK
URL: http://www.kidlink.org/

KIDLINK is a grassroots project aimed at getting as many children as possible in the age group 10-15 involved in a global dialog. The work is supported by 27 public conferences (mailing lists), a private network for interactive dialog (chat), and an online art exhibition site.

Related Areas: *Art & Music*

Language Arts/Languages

KidNews Home Page
URL: http://www.vsa.cape.com/~powens/Kidnews.html

This site might possibly be the best online forum for kids—well-designed, thoughtful, and child-friendly. There are a variety of forums available, with topics ranging from "Why are kids so mean to each other?" to "Why are the Chicago Bulls so good?" Students can submit stories, poems, reviews, essays, or just look for pen pals. Anyone may use stories from the service for educational purposes, and anyone may submit stories. Writing contests are frequently posted as well. A section for grown-ups is included, just so they don't feel left out.

Related Areas: *Social Studies*

Kidopedia
URL: http://wilcox.unibase.com/kidopedia/

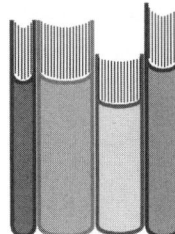

A Kidopedia is an encyclopedia written by children. Schools around the world are making their own Kidopedias, and the best articles from each are collected here, the "Best of Kidopedia!"

Related Areas: *Social Studies*

Kid's Crambo
URL: http://www.primenet.com/~hodges/kids_crambo.html

Kid's Crambo is a children's word game your young students will adore. Check out the rules for the game, see how other people have played the game, and then jump in and try it out yourself. You and your students will have fun playing the other games found here, like ziggy piggy, and doggerel.

 Integration Idea

Enhance your students' writing with a keypal-sharing or an online forum project. The Kid Lit Project, KIDLINK, and the KidNews Home Page have resources for a variety of easy activities for your class. Start with an interesting topic in an online forum which will motivate your students. Students can draft essays on the topic of "What makes a great friend?" Make sure the students go through the proper revision steps before sending the essays to the forum.

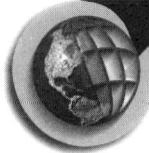

Language Arts/Languages

Kids Page
URL: http://web.aimnet.com/~veeceet/kids/kidzpage.html

A variety of children's poetry and verse are easily accessible at this site. Many of the poems have amusing graphics with them. Section titles include "Verse and Worse," "For Better or Verse," and "Have a Bash with Ogden Nash." Fun reading for children of all ages.

KidsPub
URL: http://www.kidpub.org/kidpub

A Web site devoted to putting student's written work online for the world to read! Geared to K-6 grade level. This is a great way to get your student's work online ASAP. Accepts submissions of artwork, writing, and more.

Related Areas: *Art & Music*

The Kid's Zoo
URL: http://www.ncsa.uiuc.edu/Edu/classroom/kids/e-zoo/

Your primary students will enjoy this easy-to-use site, created by a fourth-grade classroom. There is an animal listed for every letter of the alphabet and a simple description is given of the animal. The larger print is wonderful for beginning readers. Colorful and fun!

Related Areas: *Science*

Kino's Storytime
URL: http://www.pbs.org/kcet/storytime/

"Storytime" is a children's reading program currently on PBS. Dubbed the "coolest show on television," their Web site gives visitors an enormous amount of reviews of quality children's books. There is also a matching game with prizes at each level and some coloring pages. Lots of ideas are given to help care givers help kids learn to love reading.

Related Areas: *Art & Music*

Language Arts/Languages

Knowledge Adventure
URL: http://www.adventure.com/

A publisher of educational CD-ROMs, this company has kept their site from becoming too commercial by providing plenty of good, free, online content. Visit the online library, download history charts, build a dinosaur, go on a scavenger hunt, or create your own superhero.

Related Areas: *Art & Music; Science; Social Studies; Math*

Lamb Chop's Play Along
URL: http://www.pbs.org/lambchop/

Come and visit Lamb Chop, Charlie Horse, and Hush Puppy. See the welcome message from Shari Lewis and then go to the classroom activities to see how to integrate her ideas into your classroom. There's also a broadcast schedule, knock-knock jokes, and coloring activities.

Related Areas: *Art & Music*

The Latin Page
URL: http://www.geocities.com/Athens/Acropolis/3773

This site is designed especially for K–12 Latin teachers. The main feature of the site is the LPOL (Lesson Plans Online) section, which gives resources for Latin lesson plans that can be carried out online. Also contains a section on convenient references and fun stuff like Pig Latin, sound clips, and more.

Related Areas: *Social Studies; Teacher Resources*

 Integration Idea

> Make sure your take advantage of the student fun offered at the following sites. We all know that if we can hide education in games for our students it reduces the motivation we have to supply. Try the online educational games at Kino's Storytime and Knowledge Adventure. Your students can also benefit from the coloring pages at these sites as well as at Lamb Chop's Play Along.

Language Arts/Languages

Latino Bibliography
URL: http://Latino.sscnet.ucla.edu/Latino_Bibliography.html

This online index of Latino children's literature will help your students discover the culture, history, and people of Latin America. There are fiction and nonfiction books listed as well as poetry and picture books. Each book listing provides bibliographic information, a summary of the book, and the appropriate grade level.

Related Areas: *Social Studies*

Lewis Carroll Home Page
URL: http://www.lewiscarroll.org/carroll.html

This site provides useful information for the Carroll enthusiast as well as the novice and all those in-between. Whether you and your students are looking for Lewis Carroll organizations, world events, research articles, graphics, bibliographies, or online texts, you can find them at this online looking-glass.

The Lingua Center Grammar Safari
URL: http://deil.lang.uiuc.edu/web.pages/grammarsafari.html

The phrase "It's a jungle out there" takes a whole new meaning at this Web site! Designed to help students begin experiencing English as it occurs in its natural surroundings (i.e., outside of the classroom), this site allows your students to search for conjunctions, gerunds, infinitives, dangling prepositions, and more in documents on the World Wide Web.

Little Explorers
URL: http://www.EnchantedLearning.com/Dictionary.html

Sponsored by an educational software company, Little Explorers is a fun way for children to learn about computers and the alphabet. Just click on any letter at the top to see a list of words beginning with that letter. Then click on a word to visit a related Web site. Be sure to stop by Zoom School, which focuses on a different country each month.

Related Areas: *Social Studies*

Language Arts/Languages

The Little Planet Times
URL: http://www.littleplanet.com

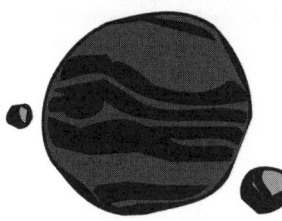

Have you heard the latest about Baldy and Ribbit? No? Well, if you're intrigued, then head on over to the Little Planet Times, an online newspaper designed for students in grades K-5. Instead of learning about current events, students meet hybrid animals such as Owly-Bear, who promotes reading, writing, and communications skills.

Related Areas: *Art & Music; Social Studies; Teacher Resources*

The Looney Bin
URL: http://www.geocities.com/Athens/3843/index.htm

Whether they're just doing homework or preparing for exams, the Looney Bin will help your students learn to improve their study skills. There are helpful sections on passing exams and tests, writing reports and essays, and how to take good notes.

Mad Libs
URL: http://he1.uns.tju.edu/madlib/

Make your students practice their language arts skills while having fun with mad libs. All they need to do is enter nouns, verbs, and adjectives in the appropriate areas to create a crazy story they can print and read.

Integration Idea

Follow the lead of The Lingua Center Grammar Safari by taking your class on a safari hunting for the parts of speech in the online texts from the Lewis Carroll Home Page. This will be an exciting exercise to get your students away from the standard way of diagramming sentences. On the way, make sure they stop at The Looney Bin for inspiration to be better all-around students.

Language Arts/Languages

Manford of Morning Glory Mountain K-6
URL: http://www.manford.com

Your students will love to follow the adventures of Manford the Moose and his friends as they trek across Morning Glory Mountain. The stories are written about a small group of animals and their adventures in the forest. Upbeat, positive, and funny, they are written to educate and entertain. Students can even email the characters if they want.

Mark Twain Resources on the World Wide Web 4-6
URL: http://marktwain.miningco.com/

If there's a Web page that mentions Mark Twain in some way, shape, or form, you can trust the creator of this site to have a link to it. Visitors here will find online exhibits, texts of Twain's works, critical essays, scattered writings, and much more.

Related Areas: *Social Studies*

Merriam-Webster Online K-6
URL: http://www.m-w.com

America's foremost publisher of language-related reference works, Merriam-Webster's site is an excellent place on the Internet to find authoritative information about the English language. Look up a definition, pronunciation, etymology, spelling, or usage point; check the Word of the Day; or enjoy the transcripts of their "Word for the Wise" radio program. Be sure to send your students to the About Merriam-Webster section for an informative essay on the history of the English language, as well as a look at how the company decides which words go into their dictionaries.

Related Areas: *Teacher Resources*

Mr. Men Silly Page K-3
URL: http://www.rucc.net.au/neteffect/mrmen/

From Australia comes this site dedicated to the immensely popular children's book collection collectively known as the Mr. Men and Little Miss series. Kids can vote for their favorite Mr. Men or Little Miss character, write their own Mr. Men adventure, or create a character of their own and have it posted in the gallery. Students who design the most interesting characters can win a free tee-shirt!

Related Areas: *Art & Music*

Language Arts/Languages

Mr. Rogers' Neighborhood
URL: http://www.pbs.org/rogers/

 K-3

Mr. Rogers has brought his whole neighborhood onto the World Wide Web so a whole new generation of Net-savvy youngsters can stop by and visit! Features like Starting School with Mr. Rogers give tips for parents on how to help young children adjust to the world of education. A collection of fun activities teaches children how to put on an opera or deal with their angry feelings. Visitors can also get lyrics to the songs from the show, download some pictures to color, and even email Mr. Rogers himself!

Related Areas: *Art & Music; Teacher Resources; Social Studies*

My *Little House on the Prairie* Homepage of Laura Ingalls Wilder
URL: http://www.pinc.com/~jenslegg/index.htm

 4-6

Head over here for everything you ever wanted to know about Wilder and her family. This site provides a listing of all of Laura Ingalls Wilder's books, with a short summary, personal information, the places and dates of the Ingalls family travels, and assorted trivia.

My Virtual Reference Desk— My Virtual Newspaper
URL: http://www.refdesk.com/paper.html

  K-6

This site can link your class to newspapers around the world. There are links to worldwide forecasts, National Storm Watch, wire services, current events, major newspapers, and Web news sites.

Related Areas: *Science*

 Integration Idea

Here is a great treat for your students. Spend a day doing Mad Libs with a twist at the site on the previous page. Your students can only use words they find from the Mark Twain Resources on the World Wide Web or from *My Little House on the Prairie*. Your students will have fun and be paging through some great literature. Or you can combine Mad Libs with Merriam-Webster Online, where your students can only use words they have never seen before. Of course, they will need to be able to define these new words to the rest of the class.

Language Arts/Languages

Nathaniel Hawthorne
URL: http://www.tiac.net/users/eldred/nh/hawthorne.html

 One of the most influential American authors of the 19th century, Nathaniel Hawthorne is captured in all his glory via this Web page. Here you'll find complete texts of such works as *The Scarlet Letter,* as well as audio files, time lines, and critical essays.

The OnLine Book Page
URL: http://www.cs.cmu.edu/books.html

More than just a resource of online books, this site also has specialty and foreign-language materials, a database of publishers, exhibits on women writers, and the history of banned books.

Online English Grammar
URL: http://www.edunet.com/english/grammar/index.html

Sure, your students know what nouns and verbs are, but are they familiar with reflexive pronouns and interrogative adverbs? This Web grammar guide is an excellent reference tool for students that need to bone up on their English, whether they're learning it for the first time or the fiftieth.

The Oz Home Page
URL: http://seamonkey.ed.asu.edu/oz/

 The Oz Home Page is based on the famous imaginary world created by Frank L. Baum. Young students are encouraged to write letters to the Scarecrow, Toto, and Dorothy. They can also contribute to CyberOz, an ongoing story, post drawings of their favorite characters, or take a tour of the various lands in Oz.

Related Areas: *Art & Music*

Language Arts/Languages

Page at Pooh Corner

URL: http://www.public.iastate.edu/~jmilne/pooh.html

Do you have a student who loves reading about the animals that reside in the Hundred Acre Wood? If so, they should certainly enjoy this site, a compendium of material featuring Winnie the Pooh and his forest friends. From here, they can download plenty of Pooh pictures, sound bytes, and information on the books.

Related Areas: *Art & Music*

Parents and Children Together Online

URL: http://www.indiana.edu/~eric_rec/fl/pcto/menu.html

This online magazine brings parents and children together through the magic of reading. To that end, they have created a Web site featuring original stories and articles for children, suitable for reading aloud. In addition, there are articles and forums for educators, reviews of the latest children's books, and an interactive storytelling session where students can add on chapters to submitted stories.

The Paris Pages

URL: http://www.paris.org

This site is a must-visit for all students studying French or French-speaking countries. They'll find a directory to French sites (museums, monuments, etc.) that have online tours, tourist information, scenes from Paris, cafes and other culinary treats, a Paris holiday calendar, interactive Web tours of the entire city, a Paris glossary, and links to hundreds of related sites.

Related Areas: *Social Studies*

 Integration Idea

Sponsor a parent-child reading program with your classes. Start your students' families at the Parent and Children Together Online site to support "the magic of reading" at this online magazine. Two sites to start your students reading with their families are Page at Pooh Corner and The Oz Home Page, two favorites in children's literature.

Language Arts/Languages

Pony Show's Kids
URL: http://www.ponyshow.com/kidsnet/website.htm

These Web pages are filled with fun things to see and do. Super's Studio has art projects by kids for kids and some for you to try too; Bambozzle's Booknook has lots of books, book reviews, and original stories; Lightfoot's Software Loft has software reviews; and then there's Ragamuffin's Raft and Kudo's Kitchen.

Related Areas: *Art & Music; Science; Social Studies*

Positive Press
URL: http://www.positivepress.com

Are you and your students tired of all of the "bad news" reported in the popular press? Looking for a source of upbeat news? Look no further than *The Positive Press* Web site, which contains a growing collection of nothing but good news as culled from media outlets all over the world. Recently, a new section of the site went live—Positive Kids. It contains positive news stories geared just for younger students.

Related Areas: *Social Studies*

Positively Poetry
URL: http://iquest.com/~e-media/kv/poetry.html

Created by a 14-year-old interested in creating and sharing poetry, this home page is designed for students between the ages of five and 15 to share their artistic abilities by writing poetry with people from around the globe.

Project Gutenberg
URL: http://www.promo.net/pg/

Think of this Web site as your after-hours library, open 24 hours a day, with no library card or late fees! Project Gutenberg has been publishing free electronic texts (or etexts) since 1971. The site has more than 400 books online that can be read, printed out, or downloaded for free. Works include *Aesop's Fables* and *The Wonderful Wizard of Oz*.

Language Arts/Languages

The Purdue University OnLine Writing Lab (OWL)
URL: http://owl.english.purdue.edu/

Hung up by a grammar question? This site offers grammar tips and more than 100 documents on topics ranging from English as a Second Language, to sexist language, to proper MLA style for research paper writers. You can also ask tutors your usage questions by email.

Related Areas: *Teacher Resources*

The Realist Wonder Society
URL: http://www.wondersociety.com/

If only more Web sites were as rich as this one! Anyone interested in children's or young adult literature should bookmark this site as soon as it's downloaded. There are enough stories here to get lost for hours, including an illustrated children's novel, two original screenplays for animated films, more than a dozen fairy tales and fables, excerpts from journals, essays, poems, and scores of artwork. Read about the romance between the Mole and the Owl, examine the woodcuts of Lynd Ward, or find out why C.S. Lewis said: "Nobody does fantasy better than George MacDonald."

Related Areas: *Art & Music*

The Realm of Books and Dreams
URL: http://www.bconnex.net/~mbuchana/realms/page1/index.html

This is a wonderful collection of stories for children. Your students will love the animal fairy tales and fables, adventure stories, and myths and legends. There is also a holiday page, children's poetry, and a coloring book. Your students will find new stories and jokes each time they visit the kids corner too.

Related Areas: *Art & Music*

Integration Idea

The Positive Press is a jumping off station for a wealth of ideas. The concept of looking for "the good" will translate to everything including your classroom. Have your students look at the positive aspects of poetry at Positively Poetry. Or spend hours finding the positive reflections gotten from the novels, screenplays, and short stories at The Realist Wonder Society.

Language Arts/Languages

Researchpaper.com
URL: http://www.researchpaper.com/

Are your students having trouble getting their papers written? If so then send them over to *Researchpaper.com*, the Web's largest collection of topics, ideas, and assistance for school-related research projects. Here you'll find some of the the best information available online, designed eliminate frustration, and help students get better grades. This site also answers email questions and has practice activities in grammar.

Related Areas: *Science; Social Studies; Art & Music; Teacher Resources*

Rigby Heinemann Keypals
URL: http://www.reedbooks.com.au/heinemann/global/global1.html

Rigby Heinemann, an educational publishing company, has put together this list of keypals to give teachers as well as students the chance to find their peers from around the globe to converse with through email. Keypals are divided according to age group and grade level.

Related Areas: *Teacher Resources*

The Riggs Institute
URL: http://www.riggsinst.org/

This site describes, in detail, how to use phonics and whole language to teach young students listening, speaking, spelling, reading comprehension, and penmanship skills. An excellent place to begin finding out about the whole phonics debate currently going on in many schools.

Related Areas: *Teacher Resources*

Roget's Thesaurus
URL: http://www.thesaurus.com/

This official Internet thesaurus is searchable by word or letter. Students can also search for words relating to space, matter, or the intellectual facilities.

Related Areas: *Teacher Resources*

Language Arts/Languages

Scholastic Place
URL: http://scholastic.com

One of the leading publishers of children's books has now gone online with a treasure trove of information that will keep your students busy for hours! Fans of the *Magic School Bus* or *The Babysitters Club* series can look up trivia on their favorite characters and episodes, while teachers can read some of the online magazines or sign up for one of the various Internet projects. Be sure to check out the Scholastic Network section, which is chock full of valuable curriculum materials.

The School Show Page
URL: http://www.schoolshows.demon.co.uk

Planning on putting on a play in your school? This Web site has technical guides, drama articles, plays, reviews, and classroom resources, all available to download directly onto your computer!

Related Areas: *Art & Music*

Seussville
URL: http://www.randomhouse.com/seussville/

The Cat in the Hat, Sam-I-Am, Horton and the Whos, and all the rest of the Seuss characters can be found at this official Seuss-filled playground in cyberspace. Here your students can play games like "Grab the Grinch," chat with the Cat in the Hat, win prizes, find out about new Dr. Seuss books and CD-ROMs, and much, much more! Do you know why snugs wear gloves? Or anything about the real-life Dr. Seuss? Come to this site and find out!

Related Areas: *Art & Music*

 Integration Idea

Here is a great combination. Put on a school play of one chosen story from Seussville. The Seussville site offers a variety of wonderful, even magical, stories. Then spend the rest of your time at The School Show Page for resources to organize your play.

91

Language Arts/Languages

Stone Soup
URL: http://www.stonesoup.com

Stone Soup is the international literary magazine for the home, school, and library. Written and illustrated by students ages 8 to 13, it hopes to inspire young writers and readers everywhere.

Related Areas: *Art & Music*

Storytelling—Flannelboard
URL: http://falcon.jmu.edu/~ramseyil/flannel1.htm

Keep your younger students' attention during storytime by making your stories come into their class with flannelboard. This site gives you guidelines for storytelling, how to create the flannelboard, and suggested books and original stories for flannelboard.

Related Areas: *Teacher Resources*

Syndicate.com
URL: http://syndicate.com/index.html

Do your students love puzzles? If so, then they should adore the weekly and monthly word challenges offered by *Syndicate.com*. Although a commercial company, Syndicate has free puzzle contests that cover a range of language and writing skills.

Related Areas: *Art & Music; Teacher Resources*

Tales of Wonder
URL: http://itpubs.ucdavis.edu/richard/tales/

This site provides an incredibly extensive list of folk and fairy tales from around the world, including English, Scottish, Scandinavian, Russian, Siberian, Middle Eastern, African, Indian, Central Asian, Chinese, Japanese, and Native American tales. (Whew!)

Related Areas: *Social Studies*

Language Arts/Languages

Theater Education Literature Review
URL: http://www.aaae.org/theatre/thfront.html

This online catalog of 60 annotated literature sources on theatre educations offers the answers to important questions like: "Why study theatre?" and "Do the arts make a difference in education?" An excellent guide for those wondering how to incorporate the theatre into their classroom.

Related Areas: *Teacher Resources*

---

thekids.com
URL: http://www.thekids.com

Beautifully illustrated, well-organized, and chock full of quality content, thekids.com promises to keep your students engaged for hours on end. In addition to reading the large collection of adventure stories, students have the opportunity to write their own stories and have them posted online. Online discussion rooms allow students to talk about their favorite stories, while the Kid Stuff section has an interactive connect-the-dots game.

Related Areas: *Art & Music*

Theodore Tugboat
URL: http://www.cochran.com/theodore/

The online activity center for *Theodore Tugboat*—a Canadian TV show about a cheerful little tugboat who likes to make friends and have adventures—will appeal to young students. Your students can help Theodore decide how he should spend his day through an interactive story. If you wish, your class can also download a page from the online coloring book, or receive a postcard from Theodore.

Related Areas: *Art & Music*

 Integration Idea

> Enjoy all of the wonderful stories provided at the Theodore Tugboat site. Then have your students attempt to write their own Tugboat stories. Use **thekids.com** site to publish the stories online. For closure have the students tell their stories orally and with flannelboard. Use the Storytelling-Flannelboard site for advice on how to use this great resource.

Language Arts/Languages

Time Magazine's Pathfinder
URL: http://www.pathfinder.com

Pathfinder is your interactive link to Time Incorporated's publications, including the latest issues of *Time, Sports Illustrated, Money,* and *Vibe.* You'll find full-text stories (and a searchable database of past articles) from more than a dozen other publications as well. This is an excellent site your students will enjoy visiting, both to read up on and gather materials for current events-related activities or assignments.

Related Areas: *Social Studies*

To Kill a Mockingbird
URL: http://www.sonoma.edu/CThink/FResource/9-12/mock.html

The Center for Critical Thinking created this lesson plan. Focusing on the classic novel by Harper Lee, students will have to ask questions about stereotypes and prejudices that may exist in their own schools as well as within the novel. What happens when people make these kinds of assumptions about others? What are the positive and negative consequences of identifying yourself with a particular group and excluding yourself from other groups?

TOWS: The Online Write Stuff
URL: http://www.santacruz.k12.ca.us/~jpost/projects/TOWS/TOWS.html

TOWS (The Online Write Stuff) is a literary magazine publishing the writings of fourth through sixth-grade students across the country. They accept poetry, fiction, memoirs, movie and book reviews, and other appropriate material.

Related Areas: *Social Studies; Art & Music*

Travelers' Japanese with Voice
URL: http://www.ntt.co.jp/japan/japanese/

This Web site uses a collection of audio clips to teach students new to the Japanese language simple words and phrases, such as "Good Morning" and "How much is this?"

Related Areas: *Teacher Resources*

Language Arts/Languages

Treasure Island
URL: http://www.ukoln.ac.uk/treasure/

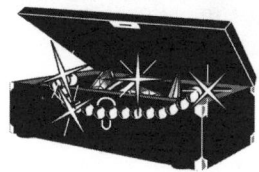

These pages offer just about everything you could ever want to know about the novel *Treasure Island*. Find out about author Robert Louis Stevenson and the history of the book. Then, try some of the interesting online activities.

Related Areas: *Art & Music; Social Studies; Teacher Resources*

UBS for Kids Online
URL: http://www.univbkstr.com/kids/authors/

There are many opportunities at this site—not only to read the latest reviews of childrens books—but also to have your students contribute their own reviews. The Kids Creations Gallery offers them a chance to submit their artwork, while a Meet the Author area gives them the chance to learn about being a writer. There's a section for parents as well.

Related Areas: *Art & Music*

The Virtual English Language Center
URL: http://www.comenius.com/

Any teacher looking to improve their students' English skills will find this site a valuable aid. Inside, you'll find an online resource of materials, services, and products for students and teachers of English around the world. Keypals, writing tips, software, and fairy tale lesson plans are all included here.

Related Areas: *Teacher Resources*

 Integration Idea

Let the Internet be the creative backbone to fantasy for your students. Let your students go off on wild jaunts with *Time* Magazine in their own fantasy adventures. Try letting them take Theodore Tugboat (p93) into the story sites *To Kill a Mockingbird* or *Treasure Island*. If your school has an official Web site, they can then post their stories online for others to read.

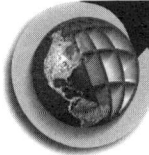

Language Arts/Languages

The Vocal Point
URL: http://bvsd.k12.co.us/cent/Newspaper/Newspaper.html

The Vocal Point is produced by K-12 students in the Boulder Valley School District in Colorado. Each monthly issue contains hyperlinks to color photographs, short video clips produced by the school, and lots of student-written articles on themes such as violence in the media. The staff of the Boulder newspaper is featured on the home page for Vocal Point.

Related Areas: *Social Studies; Science; Art & Music*

Wacky Web Tales
URL: http://www.hmco.com/hmco/school/tales

If your students love Mad Libs, show them this creative and interactive spot in cyberspace geared for students in grades 4 and above. The students pick one of over 20 different tales and fill in the requested information, such as noun, verb, place, name, and so on. They can then see how their submissions were used to create a really wacky story!

Winnie the Pooh and Friends—An Exposition
URL: http://www.worldkids.net/pooh/100aker.html

Travel through the Hundred Acre Wood with Winnie the Pooh, Rabbit, Eeyore, Christopher Robin, and the rest of A.A. Milne's colorful characters. There are twenty places to visit at this site and your students will get a kick out of the activities found at each one.

Word-A-Day
URL: http://www.wordsmith.org/awad/index.html

Available via email and the Web, *Word-A-Day* is an excellent resource for English and foreign language teachers. Anu Garg, the mind behind the service, offers the meaning and pronunciation of a new word each day to more than 15,000 Internet users worldwide.

Language Arts/Languages

World Village Kidz
URL: http://www.worldvillage.com/kidz/

Visit with Billy Bear, Jerry, and Beth at this "KIDZ safe" playground. Here, students can read books online, write their own stories, try out crossword and word search puzzles, explore mazes, and find pen pals. Plenty of activities to keep you and your class occupied.

Related Areas: *Art & Music*

The Young Writers Club
URL: http://www.cs.bilkent.edu.tr/~david/derya/ywc.html

This online club encourages children to make writing a creative pastime. They are invited to share their work and help others improve their writing skills. There is a Global Wave Magazine online with articles written by the club. "Word of the Week" helps them increase their vocabulary, while "Storybooks" add chapters to an ongoing story. Other areas include activities, book reviews, film reviews, research projects, and more.

ZuZu!
URL: http://www.zuzu.org/

ZuZu is an online magazine for kids. It began as a real newspaper distributed free-of-charge to schools, libraries, and theme parks around New York City and later around the world. It's now back online and includes poetry, mysteries, author information, and interviews. Also, there are plenty of opportunities to have your students published here.

 Integration Idea

Increase your students' vocabulary daily with a "word of the day" theme in your class. Students will have fun using special words they learn in a sentence or a short story. You can get help from The Young Writers Club or the Word-A-Day site. Put some international flavor to this exercise with recurring visits to the World Village Kidz site for wonderful new words.

YELLOW PAGES
MATH

Math

A Fractal Lesson
URL: http://cml.rice.edu/~lanius/frac/

Use this site to teach about fractals — thus incorporating geometry, language arts, and computer graphics. Once K-6 students have an understanding of its definition, they can make a fractal of their own and explain step-by-step in writing and orally what they did.

Related Areas: *Language Arts/Languages; Art & Music; Teacher Resources; Technology/Internet*

About Today's Date
URL: http://acorn.educ.nottingham.ac.uk/cgi-bin/daynum

Head to this site each morning to receive interesting facts and figures surrounding today's date. For example, did you know that the nine of diamonds is often called "Curse of Scotland"? In addition to the trivia, there are useful math problems and games for students to try.

AIMS Education Foundation
URL: http://www.aimsedu.org/AIMS.html

Here is an excellent math resource site that includes various lessons, math-related stories, and a monthly puzzle to challenge your students. This site will help you combine math with science, social studies, and language arts.

Related Areas: *Language Arts/Languages; Science; Social Studies; Teacher Resources; Technology/Internet*

AIMS Puzzle Corner
URL: http://http://www.aimsedu.org/Puzzle/PuzzleList.html

Challenge your students with a monthly puzzle that stimulates their interest and imagination. Puzzles like "Leprechaun on the Loose" give students the opportunity to develop their problem-solving skills.

Related Areas: *Science*

Math

Appetizers and Lessons for Mathematics and Reason
4-6
URL: http://www.cam.org/~aselby/lesson.html

This Web site offers suggestions and problems for math lessons as well as reflections on teaching for all disciplines. Logic puzzles, pattern-based reasoning, algebra-building skills, and a guide to studying math are all here.

Related Areas: *Science*

Arithmetic Lesson Plans
K-6
URL: http://forum.swarthmore.edu/arithmetic/arith.sites.html

Don't reinvent the wheel; use already-made lesson plans to supplement your math activities and units. These lessons have been created by other teachers from various states and placed on the site for easy access.

Related Areas: *Teacher Resources*

Ask Dr. Math
K-6
URL: http://forum.swarthmore.edu/dr.math/dr-math.html

Students can use this site to get assistance with their math problems from the experts or discuss math topics with other students. This site is split by grade levels to make navigation more precise.

Related Areas: *Language Arts/Languages; Teacher Resources*

⚠ Integration Idea

One of the best ways to get your students motivated in math is to show them how they will use it in the future, and mind puzzles do this easily. The AIMS Puzzle Corner has fascinating problems for your students to work with, especially in groups. What better way could there be to relate math skills to everyday life than the eternal, bewildering "Cab Conundrum?" If your class struggles with this and other problem-puzzles, send them to Ask Dr. Math for help. Their expert mathematicians can solve any of your students' real-life math questions.

Math

Bamdad's Math Comics
URL: http://www.csun.edu/~hcmth014/comics.html

Math Comics is exactly what every math teacher needs at the end of the day. Take a break from your lesson plans and see what the newest cartoon is. You may want to pace yourself, as they can be a tad addictive.

Related Areas: *Science*

Big Sky Telegraph Math Lesson Plans
URL: gopher://bvsd.k12.co.us:70/11/Educational_Resources/Lesson_Plans/Big%20Sky

Math teachers should have a field day with this site, which features dozens of online lesson plans on a variety of math subjects. Sample lessons include "The Addition and Subtraction Game," "Exploring Base," and "Making Estimations."

Related Areas: *Teacher Resources*

Biographies of Women Mathematicians
URL: http://www.scottlan.edu/lriddle/women/women.htm

What woman was awarded the National Medal of Technology? This site will give you the answer and more. Female students will find a variety of math mentors to research, write about, and inspire them here. This is an excellent site that is constantly being updated.

Related Areas: *Language Arts/Languages; Science; Social Studies*

Blue Dog Can Count!
URL: http://kao.ini.cmu.edu:5550/bdf.html

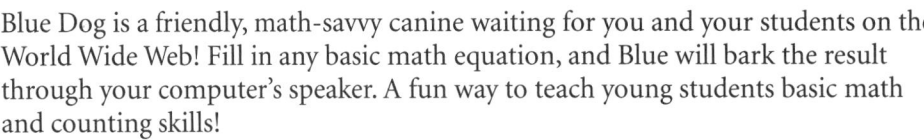

Blue Dog is a friendly, math-savvy canine waiting for you and your students on the World Wide Web! Fill in any basic math equation, and Blue will bark the result through your computer's speaker. A fun way to teach young students basic math and counting skills!

Related Areas: *Technology/Internet*

Brain Teasers   4-6
URL: http://www.eduplace.com/math/brain/index.html

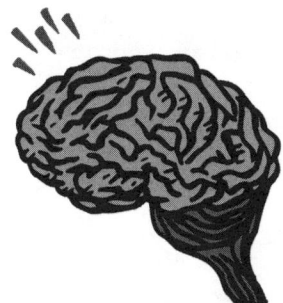

Looking for some fun, quick activities that your students can do during their free time? Send them to this site, a collection of fun teasers and puzzles designed to get kids in grades 3-6 thinking. You don't need to be a math whiz to solve these — all you need is patience.

Related Areas: *Science*

Calculators Online   4-6
URL: http://www-sci.lib.uci.edu/HSG/RefCalculators.html

Need to do some online addition? How about some agricultural calculations? If so, head to this massive index. The creators of this Web site have sought out every single online calculator, converter, and spreadsheet table in existence on the Web and indexed them all on one page. The calculators range from the scholastic (math), to the mundane (taxes), to the somewhat silly (wedding calculators). Typical links include a Morse code translator, a circle distance calculator, financial aid, astronomy, and space physics calculators.

Related Areas: *Science*

 Integration Idea

You can find great problem-solving activities on the Web for your students no matter what grade level you teach! For example, Brain Teasers has activities for elementary grades beginning with third, all of which involve the kind of critical thinking skills your students need to develop. Teachers of younger students will find Blue Dog Can Count! a terrific spot for children to work with missing addends and counting inside one's head, without the help of fingers and toes!

Math

Centre for Innovation in Mathematics Teaching

URL: http://www.ex.ac.uk/cimt/welcome.html

This site is great for challenging students who have mastered all their math skills and are ready to move on to activities that call for higher levels of thinking. Extensions such as tangram activities can also be found here.

Related Areas: *Teacher Resources*

The Chance Database

URL: http://www.geom.umn.edu/docs/education/chance/

If you plan on teaching a unit on probability and statistics, chances are you'll find lots of useful data and teaching tips at this site. Documents include a newsletter, articles, and a number of chance-related activities.

Related Areas: *Science*

Classifying

URL: http://www.eiu.edu/~scienced/3290/science/defineprocesses/classify.html

Introduce patterns and classifying to your K-3 students using this site as your guide. This online lesson plan gives excellent ideas on how to introduce the subjects of this difficult concept in a hands-on manner.

Related Areas: *Teacher Resources; Science*

Clever Games for Clever People

URL: http://www.cs.uidaho.edu/~casey931/conway/games.html

Author and mathematician John Conway turns the table on learning math by showing how games can be used to describe numbers. A number of games are available for your students to try (and get hooked) — including "coin-strip," "snort," and "trafficjam." Lots of number-learning fun.

Cuisenaire Learning Place
URL: http://www.awl.com/www.cuisenaire.com/

K-6

The Cuisenaire company is best known for producing "minds-on" educational materials that help young students learn math and science. Their Web site contains a catalog of their products, but that's not all you'll find here. There's also a nice collection of useful articles, downloadable lesson plans, online forums, and some fun activities for kids — like the "World Wide Pet Survey."

Related Areas: *Science*

Department Stores and Catalogs
URL: http://www.brandpoint.com/depart~1.htm

4-6

Shopping spree! Give your students an allowance to spend at any department store of their choice and tell them their goal is to buy items you have listed as necessary yet still have money left over. When they are done, have them write about the experience and explain in detail changes they might have made. This is an excellent life skill to practice.

Related Areas: *Teacher Resources; Technology/Internet; Language Arts/Languages*

Developing Spatial Sense: Some Fun Tips
URL: http://www.stemnet.nf.ca/~abrother/SPATIAL.HTML

K-3

Here is a small site for K-3 teachers that gives a few ideas on developing spatial sense in your students using manipulatives like shapes, angles, symmetry, and pattern blocks.

Related Areas: *Teacher Resources*

 Integration Idea

Classification is a vital skill for elementary students to master. The Classifying lesson plan will make an ideal introduction to this concept. You may follow it with the activity from the Cuisenaire Learning Place, "World Wide Pet Survey." In this "experience," your class will evaluate the results of a survey of children with pets and submit their own data.

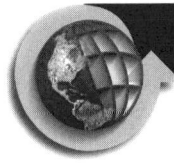

Math

DPI InfoWeb
URL: http://oaktree.dpi.state.nc.us/dpihome.html

Lesson plans, unit ideas, and teacher resources are all available at this site ready for you to print out and use. This site also has a link to the excellent Eric database lesson plan collection.

Related Areas: *Math; Technology/Internet; Science; Social Studies; Health/PE; Art & Music; Language Arts/Languages*

E-Math
URL: http://e-math.ams.org/

This excellent Web site is the home of the American Mathematical Society, and as a result is full of the latest mathematics news and online publications. You'll find a wealth of information pertaining to teaching math, as well as discussions of ethical issues and reviews of recent publications.

Related Areas: *Science*

EDC's Elementary Mathematics Products
URL: http://www.edc.org/LTT/EMP/INDEX.HTML

Educational games that meet the NCTM math standards can be ordered from this site to be used on your classroom computer. Many of these games have won awards for their originality.

Related Areas: *Technology/Internet; Teacher Resources*

ENC for Mathematics and Science Education
URL: http://www.enc.org/

The purpose of the Eisenhower National Clearinghouse Web site is to encourage the use of K-12 curriculum materials and programs that improve teaching in math and science. Here you can get access to a huge catalog of materials from a variety of sources. There are also games for all grade levels that call for predicting, visual thinking, and deductive reasoning.

Related Areas: *Teacher Resources; Science*

Math

Eric's Puzzles of Wonder
URL: http://www.xmission.com/~ericward/puzzle.html

K-6

Your students will love these math word puzzles and story riddles. See if they can get the answers to the tennis ball boggle, or the unusual paragraph. To get the answers from the author you must email him a new, good puzzle to add to the page.

Related Areas: *Language Arts/Languages*

Explorer
URL: http://explorer.scrtec.org/explorer/

K-6

The Explorer is a collection of educational materials for K-12 math and science education, and one of the richest resources for this type of material on the Net. Teachers will find pointers to all sorts of valuable math lesson plans, courseware programs, shareware educational games, and videos covering a wide range of curriculum types and grade levels. Many of these resources are free and can be downloaded directly onto your desktop.

Related Areas: *Science*

Financial Calculators
URL: http://www.centura.com/formulas/whatif.html

4-6

Use the online calculators at this site to teach students about financial planning, saving, and percentages. Types of calculators include ones for auto loans, mortgages, and investments.

Related Areas: *Social Studies; Science*

> ⚠ **Integration Idea**
>
> If you have been searching for a place to begin using professional resources via the Internet, these sites are for you. ENC for Mathematics and Science Education and Explorer have a wealth of information for the educator who wants to improve the teaching of math and science. E-Math, meanwhile, focuses specifically on mathematical news.

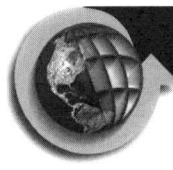

Math

Flash Cards for Kids
URL: http://www.wwinfo.com/edu/flash.html

Have your K-6 students practice multiplication, addition, subtraction, and division at this site. It lets the students know when their answers are correct or incorrect. You can also adapt the difficulty to the students' needs. Have K-3 students use manipulatives to solve incorrect answers; for grades 4-6 students can choose a problem and write a math story about it.

Related Areas: *Teacher Resources*

Fundcraft Recipe Archive
URL: http://www.cookbooks.com/archive.htm

Cook up something good in math with this Web site. Choose one of the easy recipes and teach your students about measurements. They can convert the recipes to accommodate the class and have fun with food. Have students write their own recipes to demonstrate the importance of order of directions.

Related Areas: *Teacher Resources; Health/PE*

The Geometry Center
URL: http://www.geom.umn.edu/

Created by the University of Minnesota, this site has plenty of ideas concerning teaching geometry in the K-6 classroom. Interactive applications, downloadable software, video animation, and math research and visualization are all located here.

Related Areas: *Science*

Math

Good News Bears

URL: http://www.ncsa.uiuc.edu/edu/RSE/RSEyellow/gnb.html

Good News Bears is a Web-based interactive stock market learning project for K-12. Using a variety of lesson plans, online forms, and activities, classmates engage in an interactive stock market competition and apply real-time stock market data from the New York Stock Exchange and NASDAQ. The students play the roles of buyer and seller, deciding what stocks are worth trading.

Related Areas: *Language Arts/Languages; Social Studies; Teacher Resources*

The Guide to Math and Science Reform

URL: http://www.learner.org/content/k12/The_Guide/

This Guide is a database of more than 950 entries that describe projects and groups dedicated to improving K-12 mathematics and science education in America. It can be downloaded for free at this Web site.

Related Areas: *Science*

Helping Your Child Learn Math

URL: http://www.ed.gov/pubs/parents/Math/index.html

Math activities for students ages 5-13 are the focus of this Web site, hosted by the U.S. Department of Education. Topics include things that kids can do at home, at the store, or in transit. It is designed for parents, but could easily be adapted for classroom use.

Related Areas: *Teacher Resources*

 Integration Idea

> The stock market is often perplexing even for adults, but it doesn't need to be a puzzle! You and your students will be wizards of Wall Street after you complete the activities located at Good News Bears. When you are ready, borrow a recipe from the Fundcraft Recipe Archive, and create a product that your class can "market." Design a container and advertising, and set price for your food. Then project its performance on the stock market!

Math

The History of Computing

URL: http://www.ifi.unizh.ch/groups/se/people/hoyle/Lecture/

This online presentation takes visitors on a tour of computing and mathematics, from the Stone Age to the personal computer. In between, you can learn about mathematicians like Pascal, Charles Babbage, and Alan Turning.

Related Areas: *Social Studies; Science*

History of Mathematics

URL: http://aleph0.clarku.edu/~djoyce/mathhist/mathhist.html

A good starting place for those students interested in learning about ancient mathematical discoveries and famous mathematicians. Time lines, chronologies, and a host of links to history oriented sites round out this site.

Related Areas: *Science; Social Studies*

How Far Is It?

URL: http://www.indo.com/distance

Using this site, students can find the distance between cities, their populations, latitude and longitude, elevation, and telephone area code! Visitors type in the names of the cities, like New York and London, in the appropriate areas and click on the "Look it up" button. Within a matter of seconds, the shortest distance between the cities is displayed. You can also link to an online map if you want to view the cities.

Related Areas: *Science; Social Studies*

The Hub

URL: http://ra.terc.edu/HubHome.html

This Web site is tailor-made for K-12 math and science teachers. It features lesson plans and pointers and hyperlinks to other valuable Internet sites — all focusing on math and science. The site also has information about publishing reports, developing curricula, and writing proposals for funding. An excellent repository of math-related links, information, and resources.

Related Areas: *Science*

Math

Interactive Mathematics Miscellany and Puzzles
URL: http://www.cut-the-knot.com/

`4-6`

Lots of intriguing games and puzzles are available here as well as some fun math facts and famous math quotations. Did you know that a sphere has two sides?

Related Areas: *Science*

The Internet Pizza Server
URL: http://www.cs.rice.edu/~sboone/Lessons/Titles/pizza.html

`4-6`

In this online lesson plan, students will create their own pizza using a choice of toppings. They will be able to "order" their creation from the Internet and view it through their Web browser. They will use their order to calculate the area of various size pizzas, determine the "better buy" and cost per topping. Students will also have to use research skills to answer questions pertaining to the Pizza Home Page.

Introduction to Probability
URL: http://www.richland.cc.il.us/james/lecture/m170/ch05-int.html

`K-6`

Probability can be introduced to K-6 students using this site. Older students can read the information on sample spaces, analyze the chart, and try the experiment on their own, in groups of two. Younger students can discuss the chart with the teacher and do the experiment in class.

Related Areas: *Teacher Resources; Science*

 Integration Idea

> Your students are no doubt amazed by lotteries and other games of chance. You can explain probability to your class with a trip to the History of Mathematics. Then you might want to try an experiment of your own based on the Introduction to Probability site. Talk to them about how games of chance work, about sweepstakes, and how special offers on products actually benefit the producer, not the consumer. Your students will be wiser consumers because of your help!

Math

K–12 Statistics
URL: http://www.mste.uiuc.edu/stat/stat.html

Here is a list of resources for the statistical-minded, including lessons and useful data sets. Each activity follows the NCTM Statistics Standards. Be sure to fill out the statistics questionnaire on your way out.

Related Areas: *Science*

M & M Graphing and Probability
URL: http://www.col-ed.org/cur/math/math26.txt

M&Ms can help teach your students how to make decisions. This site is a lesson plan that incorporates graph making, critical thinking, writing, and cooperative learning into a tasty activity. Extension activities are also included.

Related Areas: *Language Arts/Languages; Math; Science; Teacher Resources; Art & Music*

MacTutor History of Mathematics
URL: www.vma.bme.hu/mathhist/index.html

Students and teachers of math history, add this site to your bookmark list right away. This archive contains biographies of thousands of important figures in math history. Be sure to check out the articles on the development of mathematical ideas such as "Pi Through the Ages" and "Babylonian and Egyptian Mathematics."

Related Areas: *Social Studies*

The Maine Mall: Purchase Plus
URL: http://www.mainemall.com/7pp.html

You spent $50.00 for a suit that was 10% off. How many points do you earn? Use these types of questions to design your own game using the rules established at this site. Have your students break into groups and create a board game where they shop the stores and encounter money gains and pitfalls in order to gain the points for the prizes listed.

Related Areas: *Art & Music; Teacher Resources; Language Arts/Languages; Technology/Internet*

Math

Making Sense Online
URL: http://www.makingsense.com/

4-6

Are your students worried about how to save for college? Are they curious about the stock market? Do they have trouble saving money or choosing a career? If so, you may want to send them over to Making Sense, an online magazine that focuses on career choices, mutual funds and stocks, cool companies, and other financial topics that are of interest to kids, such as allowances and earning money. Articles on young investors provide models on how to save and spend, while fun sections like Trivia and Number Crunching help them learn and develop skills that will be of great value outside of school as well as in.

Math Archives
URL: http://archives.math.utk.edu/

K-6

This WWW server has information on software, teaching materials, institutes, journals, contests, and resources, all pertaining to mathematics.

Math Central
URL: http://MathCentral.uregina.ca/index.html

K-6

This simple K-12 math education Web site can be used as a meeting place for teachers to share resources and for confused students and faculty to find answers to their super-tough mathematical questions. Areas of interest include: Teacher Talk, a math-oriented mailing list; the Resource Room, a listing of where to find math Web sites and newsletters; and the Bulletin Board, a database of math-related postings. Use the Quandaries and Queries section to ask questions about the Internet. Be sure to check the archive to see if your question has been asked before!

Related Areas: *Science*

 Integration Idea

Looking for resources to guide you through a tough math lesson? Need another math teacher to bounce some ideas off of? Head over to the archives for math, K-12 Statistics, or Math Central. These sites will give you resources to use and allow you to converse with other teachers via email.

Math

Mathematicians of the Seventeenth and Eighteenth Centuries
URL: http://www.maths.tcd.ie/pub/HistMath/People/RBallHist.html

Almost 100 mathematicians and scientists who made their contributions in the 17th and 18th centuries are featured here, including René Descartes, Isaac Barrow, Isaac Newton, and Henry Cavendish.

Related Areas: *Science; Social Studies*

Mathematics and Problem-Solving Task Centers
URL: http://www.srl.rmit.edu.au/mav/PSTC/index.html

K-6 educators can find a number of word problems to try on their class at this site. Updated monthly, visitors are encouraged to scroll through the extensive archives and submit their own problems. An email list, GOTTAPROB-L, has been set up to assist teachers, students, and other educators to communicate and talk about problem solving.

Mathematics Curriculum
URL: http://www.dpi.state.nc.us/Curriculum/Mathematics/grade1.htm

A series of math strategies at this Web site covers the competency goals students are expected to reach at each grade level. Included are concepts such as counting, making sets, identifying ordinal position, and comparing numbers. Each plan features activities and ideas for increasing learning by tying concepts together.

Related Areas: *Teacher Resources*

Mathematics K–7
URL: http://www.est.gov.bc.ca/.curriculum/www/irps/mathk7/mathtoc.htm

Grouped by grade level, at this site you will find a collection of hands-on lessons, extension ideas, and resource lists. Topics include number concepts, measurement, and data analysis. Many of these lessons can also be integrated into other subjects.

Related Areas: *Teacher Resources; Math; Science; Technology/Internet; Language Arts/Languages; Social Studies*

Math

The Mathematics of Cartography
URL: http://cml.rice.edu:80/~lanius/pres/map/

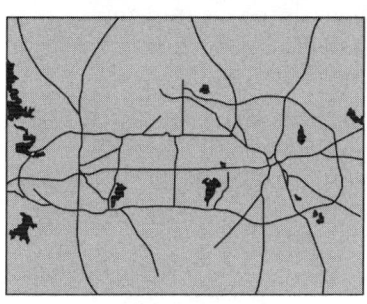

What exactly is a map? What is the history of mapmaking? What mathematics do you use when making a map? This site attempts to answer these questions as well as provide some fun word problems to try out while online.

Related Areas: *Social Studies; Science*

Math Forum
URL: http://forum.swarthmore.edu/

Formerly known as the Geometry Forum, this updated and expanded Web site has something of value for everyone involved in mathematics, be they students, teachers, parents, professors, or those who just like math. The Student Center offers aid for the confused, while the Teacher's Place is chock full of classroom plans and activities. There are sections on every topic of math, project ideas, search tools, links, and updates on key issues currently facing the mathematics community.

Math Homework Help
URL: http://www.erols.com/bram/

Are your students having trouble with homework? Then have them take advantage of this service, a collection of links to helpful math sites and individuals. You can also email the site's author to get geometry, algebra, and even calculus advice.

Related Areas: *Science*

 Integration Idea

When will I ever use this in real life? Answer that question and find out who are the people behind some of math's greatest theories. Use the mathematicians site and math of cartography as research tools for your students to find those answers.

115

Math

The Math League
URL: http://www.mathleague.com/

The Math League is dedicated to bringing challenging mathematics materials to students. You can find out about math contests for elementary students, educational software, books designed to stimulate interest in math, and a reference guide to math topics for grades 4-8, complete with examples, definitions, and explanations.

Related Areas: *Science*

MathMagic
URL: http://forum.swarthmore.edu/mathmagic/

MathMagic is a K-12 telecommunications project that provides strong motivation for students to use computer technology while increasing their problem-solving and communications skills. MathMagic posts challenges in four categories, divided according to grade level. Registered teams of students work together to solve them.

Related Areas: *Science*

The Mathman
URL: http://www.shout.net/~mathman/

The materials at this Web site will teach your students to discover patterns, visualize mathematics, and "learn to learn." A section entitled "Get Ready for Calculus" aims to introduce young children to some basic calculus concepts.

Related Areas: *Science*

MathMania
URL: http://csr.uvic.ca/~mmania/

Knots, graphs, sorting problems, and finite machines are all discussed at this site, an attempt to have students experience math the way professional mathematicians experience it. Tutorials, stories, puzzles, activities, exercises, and a glossary are included in each section.

Related Areas: *Science*

Math

Mathman's Home Page
URL: http://www.macatawa.org/~mathman/

Celebrate math time with Mike "the Mathman" Harmon as he offers helpful math and study hints, answers your math questions, suggests games, and just acts goofy.

Related Areas: *Science*

Math Online Helpline
URL: http://www.kqed.org/Cell/math/mathmenu.html

Sponsored by the KQED Center for Education and Lifelong Learning (CELL), this K-12 mathematics site is divided into four distinct sections. The lesson section offers perplexing problems to solve, like "How do you approximate a broken heart?" The Math News and Events section is a nicely organized collection of the latest goings-on in the world of mathematics, while the Math Resource Center provides other quality links for teachers and students to visit.

MathsNet
URL: http://www.anglia.co.uk/education/mathsnet/

MathsNet combines the study of math, computers, and the Internet into one whopping package. Besides pages on logos, spreadsheets, and graphs, you will also find ones dedicated to specific educational software such as Excel, puzzles and problems to solve, and an ongoing math debate.

Related Areas: *Science; Teacher Resources; Technology/Internet*

 Integration Idea

Each of these sites — the Math League, Math Magic, MathMania, and MathsNet — offer a math challenge to meet the level of your students working individually or with a partner. Set up the beginning of your class to be "brain exercise time" by completing one of these online challenges. This will help get your students in the spirit of thinking critically for the rest of the day!

Math

Mayan Math
URL: http://hanksville.phast.umass.edu/yucatan/mayamath.html

 4-6

Can you count in Mayan? This site will teach you how. Incorporate Language Arts into your lesson by having your students research the lost Mayan culture and then give a presentation.

Related Areas: *Art & Music; Language Arts/Languages; Social Studies; Teacher Resources*

The Maze Man
URL: http://members.aol.com/TheMazeMan/index.html

 4-6

Don't let this puzzle master's alias fool you. There's more than just mazes offered at this Web site. Improve students' vocabulary, math skills, and general creativity with these educational and recreational puzzles. Word searches, number games, movie trivia, it's all here. Have your students try to solve one and then see if they can create their own!

Related Areas: *Science; Teacher Resources; Language Arts/Languages; Art & Music*

MegaMath
URL: http://www.c3.lanl.gov/mega-math/index.html

 K-6

The MegaMath project brings some of the most unusual and important mathematical ideas to elementary school classrooms so young people and their teachers can think about them together. Each of the seven activities listed has an Activities and Evaluation page and covers subjects such as infinity, graphs, and algorithms. Easily one of the best math sites on the Web.

Related Areas: *Science*

The Mid-Atlantic Eisenhower Consortium
URL: http://www.rbs.org/eisenhower/index.html

 K-6

This site is primarily intended to support math and science educators and reform efforts in the Mid-Atlantic region. There's enough content here, however, to help those living outside the area as well.

Related Areas: *Science; Teacher Resources*

Math

Monster Math

URL: http://www.lifelong.com/AcademicWorld/MonsterMath/

Your students are invited to a Monster Math Surprise Party! Each page asks them to solve a math problem. If they do it correctly, then they move on; incorrectly, they get help. Problems are addition, subtraction, multiplication, and division. The better they do, the harder the questions get.

The National Council of Teachers of Mathematics

URL: http://www.nctm.org/

At this official page of the NCTM, you will find updates on all of the latest math happenings across the United States, as well as online journals, job information, scholarships, and more.

Related Areas: *Science; Teacher Resources*

Newtonia

URL: http://wwwcn1.cern.ch/~mcnab/n/index.html

Anything having to do with the who, what, and where of Isaac Newton can be found here. For example, get the lowdown on whether or not he really got hit by that apple!

Related Areas: *Science; Social Studies*

Integration Idea

Take the fear out of doing math by integrating it with other subjects for example, Mayan Math can also cover social studies and language arts. Students can be split into groups that research each aspect of the Mayan culture and make a presentation of that information to another class. Maze Man and Monster Math take ordinary computation skills and turn them into exciting but challenging activities for groups or individuals. Once students are comfortable with the puzzles they can make their own.

Math

North American Steam Locomotive
URL: www.arc.umn.edu/~wes/steam.html

First visit the train museums and then discuss their different speeds and different places they've traveled. Start discussions on how long it would take to get from one place to another. Split the students into groups, have them choose a train, and use the information listed to figure out the time of arrival. This site can also be adapted to help students figure out distance.

Related Areas: *Teacher Resources; Social Studies*

Onboard Fabrics Catalog—Kid's Fabrics
URL: http://www.onboardfabrics.com/onboard_catalog.cgi

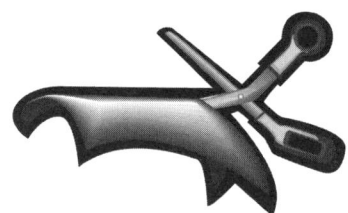

This site lets you use sewing to explain measurement using fabric samples and their prices per yard. Students can try half- and quarter-yard measurements as a challenge. They can then use the information here to write word problems.

Related Areas: *Arts & Music; Teacher Resources*

Online Calculator
URL: http://www.math.scarolina.edu/cgi-bin/sumcgi/calculator.pl

This Web site functions as a basic calculator, just in case you or your students don't have one handy!

Related Areas: *Technology/Internet; Teacher Resources*

Online Mathematics Dictionary
URL: http://www.mathpro.com/math/glossary/glossary.html

Do you know what a bijection is? How about a lattice point? Have your students check out this online dictionary to see how many mathematical definitions they already know.

Math

Paint Estimator
URL: http://www.btw.com/applets/paint_calc.html

Teach estimation and measurement at the same time. Have your students guess the perimeter of the room and the height of the walls. Enter the information onto this site and estimate how many gallons of paint it will take. Hit calculate and see if you are correct.

Related Areas: *Technology/Internet; Teacher Resources*

Paper Folding
URL: http://www.lwcd.com/paper-folding/

Paper folding is a simple, novel, hands-on approach to mathematics. This site shows some sample uses of paper folding in the classroom. A useful way to teach fractions and tessellations to elementary school students.

Related Areas: *Art & Music*

PBS Mathline
URL: http://www.pbs.org/mathline/

In an effort to strengthen students' math knowledge using the latest technology, the Public Broadcasting System has created this popular project, aimed at middle and elementary school students. Teacher-participants enroll through their local public television stations, and once online, they become members of a learning community of 25-30 fellow participants, coordinated by a facilitator. Videos and online materials to help students learn about probability and statistics. Through a national bulletin board, participants can interact with fellow teachers across the nation and with experts on mathematics.

Integration Idea

> Introduce estimation as an everyday occurrence. Students can estimate distance and the speed a train travels after reading information about it at the North American Steam Locomotive site. The fabrics catalog and Paint Estimator site allows you to view fabric prices by the yard and estimate what their cost would be for less than a yard. Or, you can figure out how much paint a room needs?

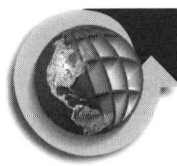

Math

Population Estimates by Age, Sex, and Race 1990–1994 `K-6`
URL: http://govinfo.kerr.orst.edu/pe-stateis.html

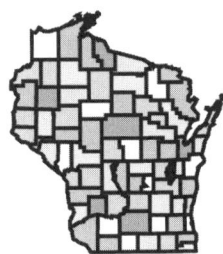

Integrate geography, problem-solving, and math using this site. Click on a state's abbreviation (have students name it), pick a county, read the chart, discuss why there are changes in population year to year, split into groups to make a graph of the information.

Related Areas: *Teacher Resources; Social Studies*

Probability `K-6`
URL: http://www.iit.edu/~smile/ma8919.html

Using colored golf balls students can practice the skills of probability. This site, complete with lesson plans, will help even your primary students get involved with probability.

Related Areas: *Teacher Resources*

Rodriguez Communications: Hispanic Market Consultancy `4-6`
URL: http://www.rodcom.com/uspop.htm

Integrate social studies with math using this site, a market survey of the Hispanic community in the United States. Have students read the text, interpret what the table explains, and then demonstrate how the percentages were compiled.

Related Areas: *Social Studies; Teacher Resources*

Smile Program Mathematics Index
URL: http://www.iit.edu/~smile/mathinde.html

These activities will have your students smiling for math. There are plenty of mathematics lessons available at this site for all grade levels. Each lesson has been written by teachers for teachers, and includes working with manipulatives.

Related Areas: *Teacher Resources*

Some Card Probabilities—Table Version
URL: http://www.math.unb.ca/~knight/3083/Cards2.html

Playing cards are used here to teach probability. Students starting in third grade will be able to use this site (with teacher assistance) to visualize probability. Split students into groups with a deck of cards and have them complete the chart on their own.
Related Areas: *Teacher Resources; Science*

Stanley Park Chase
URL: http://familyware.com/chase/Default.htm

Help Dexter find the missing gold in Stanley Park by answering math questions correctly. Each correct answer gets you to the next page. One wrong answer and you'll have to start over again.

Systemic Math & Science
URL: http://www.ncrel.org/ncrel/mands/mathsci.htm

Sponsored by the North Central Regional Educational Laboratory (NCREL), this site provides in-depth information and hands-on strategies designed to aide educators and community members in bringing about systemic improvements in mathematics and science education in local schools.

Related Areas: *Science*

 Integration Idea

Looking to do hands-on activities but are short on supplies? Make use of everyday objects to teach probability such as a deck of cards or golf balls. The probability sites on these pages will also give you lessons to use in the classroom. When students are ready to add to the concept ask them to bring in items that they can use to teach the class a probability lesson such as gum balls. What is the probability that you will get a yellow gum ball from a jar?

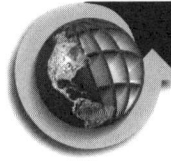

Math

Tangram
URL: http://www.aie.nl/~geert/java/public/Tangram.html

 4-6

This site allows your students to manipulate tangram pieces to create their own online design which can then be published here.

Related Areas: *Technology/Internet; Teacher Resources*

Tile Installation Information
URL: http://www.bedrosians.com/flrpatt1.htm

 4-6

Looking for a practical use of math on the Web? Have your students plan the floor tile layout for a room with established dimensions using a pencil, graph paper and this site. Explain that the tiles need to be evenly cut in their diagram and that they'll need to explain what they've done.

The Total Yellowstone Page Map
URL: http://www.Yellowstone-Natl-Park.Com/map.htm

 K-6

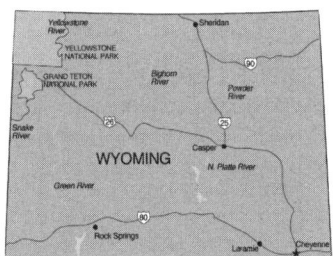

Take a vacation to Yellowstone. Use the mileage chart at this site to have your students determine the number of miles on a trip to three or more places. Click on hotel accommodations and they can figure out room prices, including the 7% tax.

Related Areas: *Social Studies; Teacher Resources; Science*

USNO Master Clock Time
URL: http://tycho.usno.navy.mil/what.html

 K-3

What time is it in your town? Primary students can practice telling time using different time zones. You can strengthen their critical thinking skills by having them reason the number of hours ahead or behind of a certain state.

Related Areas: *Science*

Math

Welcome to the Virtual Science and Mathematics Fair '95

URL: http://www.vpds.wsu.edu/fair_95/

K-6

A math and science fair held by your elementary school students? This site shows a fair held by college students with lesson ideas you can use in your elementary classroom. Challenge your students to produce their own science or math fair projects.

Related Areas: *Teacher Resources; Science; Art & Music; Language Arts/Languages*

Word Problems for Kids

URL: http://juliet.stfx.ca/people/fac/pwang/mathpage/math1.html

4-6

This Web site contains word problems for students and teachers in grades 5-12. See how good your students' problem-solving skills are. Complete solutions are available upon request to teachers with email addresses.

World Wide Web Virtual Library: Mathematics

URL: http://euclid.math.fsu.edu/Science/math.html

K-6

The math index located here will make a great home page for math wizards and neophytes alike. The site links to online resources for math teachers and students and is organized by categories such as mathematical software, electronic journals, math education, and so on.

Related Areas: *Teacher Resources*

 Integration Idea

The Tangram site allows you to work on the logical thinking process without needing a set for every student. Make skills practical for students by having them find the perimeter and area of the classroom. Use the tile site to have them compute the number of tiles they would need in various sizes. Compute miles traveled in Yellowstone or the cost plus tax of a hotel room. What time is it in Spain right now? Students can integrate these skills into social studies and language arts through a project.

YELLOW PAGES
SCIENCE

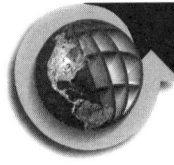

Science

About Temperature
4-6

URL: http://www.unidata.ucar.edu/staff/blynds/tmp.html

About Temperature is an excellent, information-packed Web resource for any class studying the physical concepts of temperature. You'll find data on thermometers, temperature scales, kinetic theory, thermal radiation, and much more.

Related Areas: *Math; Teacher Resources*

Accu-Weather
4-6

URL: http://www.accuweather.com/web/welcome.htm

Get the latest weather information for your area via Accu-Weather's Web site. Learn where new storms are brewing and see the latest hurricane graphics. Satellite images, Doppler radar, and weather maps are all available here.

All About Meteorology
K-6

URL: http://www.weather.com/weather_whys/teachers_resources/all_about/meteo/all_about_meteo.html

Do any of your students want to become a meteorologist? If so, here's the site to find out how to get started. It tells you what you need to do to become a meteorologist, a "spotter," or just a "backyard observer." Included is information on how to predict the weather by merely walking outside.

Science

Amazing Space: Education Online from the Hubble Space Telescope
URL: http://www.stsci.edu/pubinfo/amazing-space.html

Amazing Space is a set of Web-based lessons designed by teachers in collaboration with scientists at the Space Telescope Science Institute. The lessons in Amazing Space are interactive and use Hubble Space Telescope images to teach science and math concepts and skills. Take the student astronaut challenge, or make some solar system trading cards!

Related Areas: *Math; Teacher Resources*

American Museum of Natural History
URL: http://www.amnh.org

A number of online scientific explorations are available at this museum's home page. "Amber: Window to the Past" for example, contains information on how animals and insects get caught in this sticky stuff and become preserved for centuries on.

Related Areas: *Math; Social Studies*

Animal Tracks Online
URL: http://www.nwf.org/nwf/atracks/

Animal Tracks Online, developed by the National Wildlife Federation, contains a collection of environmental education lessons and activities read for classroom use. Subjects are divided into five major topic areas: Air; Habitat; People and the Environment; Wildlife and Endangered Species; and Water. Each section includes an introduction, general background, information, fun facts, things you can do to help the environment, and a glossary of terms and classroom activities.

 Integration Idea

Weather is a theme that elementary teachers often encounter in their science curricula. These sites will help you relate this scientific study to the Internet. Accu-Weather will give your class up-to-date weather information, and About Temperature will explain the system of degrees we use to measure warmth and coolness. At the same time, the All About Meteorology site will encourage the future "weather-watchers" in your group to pursue careers in meteorology.

Science

The Appalachian Trail
URL: http://www.fred.net/kathy/at.html

Take a long walk through the Appalachian trails and calculate your distance using this site. View some of the tourist information and complete a tour guide for hikers. Great introduction into one of the longest nature trails in the U.S.

Related Areas: *Language Arts/Languages; Social Studies; Teacher Resources; Math*

Apollo 11 Mission to the Moon
URL: http://www.gsfc.nasa.gov/hqpao/apollo_11.html

Sponsored by NASA, the Apollo 11 site is a valuable resource for those studying this historic space mission. Relive the historic flight as you read recollections of the astronauts, key White House documents, a retrospective analysis, and a bibliography. You can also view short video clips of the most exciting moments of the mission.

Related Areas: *Social Studies*

Archaeology and the Big Dig
URL: http://www.mos.org/ed/bigdigarch/bigdigstart.html

The Big Dig takes you to Spectacle Island in Boston Harbor. Excavations of the island reveal important information about Native Americans and their use of the harbor's resources. You can view what the site looks like, the tools and food remains that were found there, and information about what has happened to Spectacle Island over the last 10,000 years.

Related Areas: *Social Studies*

B-Eye:
The World through the Eyes of a Bee
URL: http://cvs.anu.edu.au/andy/beye/beyehome.html

Have you ever wondered how other creatures see the world? Here you can find out. This Web page shows you how the world looks through the eyes of a bee. Then you can choose an item to be viewed in the gallery and see how a bee would look at it.

Science

Bad Science
URL: http://www.ems.psu.edu/~fraser/BadScience.html

What is bad science? According to the site's author it's "well-understood phenomena which are persistently presented incorrectly by teachers and writers." This page seeks to remedy misconceptions in meteorology, chemistry, astronomy, and physics.

Birds: Our Environmental Indicators
URL: http://www.nceet.snre.umich.edu/Curriculum/toc.html

By the end of this extensive, comprehensive 12-day project, middle school students will understand the role of birds as environmental "indicators," and the reasons some birds are endangered. This site goes through a day-by-day overview of the project, experiments and activities for students, and extra curricular ideas to try after the project is finished.

Related Areas: *Teacher Resourcess*

BugWatch
URL: http://www.bugwatch.com/index.html

 From ants to wasps, you'll find just about every major insect species here, along with close-up photographs and well-written essays.

 Integration Idea

> Supplement a study of insects with a trip to BugWatch. This unique site offers pictures of all types of bugs with descriptions and even some recommendations for bug watching. Be sure to look at their bee section, and follow it up with a visit to B-Eye: The World through the Eyes of a Bee. Here your students will have the opportunity to view objects through the eyes of a bee. After that, have a bug hunt, and see how many of the different types of bugs from BugWatch you can find!

Science

Cascades Volcano Observatory
URL: http://vulcan.wr.usgs.gov/home.html

With real-time data, photo archives, and more than enough information on the active volcano range in the North American west coast, this site is a great stopping point for students and teachers looking for data on what makes volcanoes go boom.

Related Areas: *Social Studies*

Cells Alive
URL: http://www.cellsalive.com/

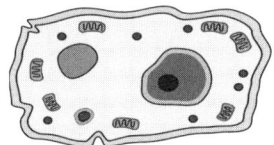

View wonderful videos of cell processes at this site: a view afforded nowhere else in the world! Learn about what lurks in your water supply, and how white blood cells fight germs. Gross fun.

ChickScope
URL: http://vizlab.beckman.uiuc.edu/chickscope/

ChickScope began as an online project for primary and secondary schools in the Illinois area. Using this site, students were able to learn about chicken embryology by examining several eggs through a high-powered microscope over the Internet. Although the experiment is over and the chickens have hatched, your students can still use the extensive amount of information located at this site to learn about biology. There are photos, video clips, notes and observations from other students, and some really bad chicken jokes.

Comet Observation Home Page
URL: http://www.encke.jpl.nasa.gov/

Looking for quality photos of Hale-Bopp for your class? Then be sure to include this site in your astronomy curriculum. Aspiring star-gazers will enjoy reading the in-depth story detailing how Hale-Bopp was discovered and viewing this complex images and animations of its path.

Science

Coral Forest
URL: http://www.blacktop.com/coralforest/

The content team behind this site has developed an interdisciplinary, hands-on Teacher's Guide for grades K-6. The objective of this guide is to present material that will encourage students to think about the complexity of coral reefs and their surrounding environment, as well as the threats that the reefs are currently facing.

Related Areas: *Teacher Resources; Social Studies*

Cornell's Solid Waste Activities
URL: gopher://eelink.umich.edu:777/11/activities/cornell

This gopher site provides background information, lesson plans, and activities to help grades K-6 learn about solid waste. There is also a glossary of terms for your students to learn.

Related Areas: *Language Arts/Languages; Teacher Resources*

Coastal, Energy, and Environmental Information and Resources Clearinghouse
URL: http://www.leeric.lsu.edu/

Teachers looking for quality lesson plans and activities centering on the environment will find exactly what they need at this site, sponsored by the Louisiana Energy and Environmental Resource Information Center. A number of educational resources are included at this site, as are links to other online resources and hands-on science programs.

 Integration Idea

> Your class will be amazed by the development of chicks from the site called ChickScope. Find the "Previous Editions" for pictures and diagrams that explain the chicks' growing process. Then back up a bit and visit Cells Alive. This site will introduce your class to the basic unit of life and will illustrate the actual size and shape of such cells. Your class will improve their understanding of cells with an experiment using a microscope. Have them scrape the inside of their cheeks and examine these skin cells up-close.

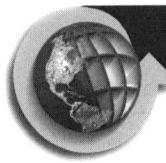

Science

The Cub Den
URL: http://www.nature-net.com/bears/cubden.html

With a literally roaring welcome, this site introduces young visitors to the world of bears. Included here are ten basic facts about bears, other "amazing facts about bears," and bear-related books for young readers. Older students can head over to the Bear Den for even more grizzly data.

Current U.S. Weather
URL: http://www.mit.edu:8001/usa.html

A graphical weather map of the United States, complete with the latest radar image from an orbiting weather satellite. Students can click on any location and receive an up-to-the-minute weather forecast!

Related Areas: *Teacher Resources*

Current Weather Maps and Movies
URL: http://www.rs560.cl.msu.edu/weather/

View the latest weather satellite images from more than a dozen satellites circling the globe.

Dan's Wild Wild Weather Page
URL: http://www.whnt19.com/kidwx/

This site is designed for children from 6 to 16 who want to learn about weather. Topics include clouds, temperature, pressure, humidity, climate, lightning, and hurricanes. There's even a teachers' section with weather units, a "make a weather station activity," links, and more.

Dinosaur Exhibit
URL: http://www.hcc.hawaii.edu/dinos/

Online dinosaur lovers can visit a free, permanent exhibit of dinosaur fossils for public viewing on the Web. Fossils from some of the largest creatures that ever existed are here, as is an audio tour.

Science

Discovery Channel School
URL: http://www.school.discovery.com

While this site was designed to go hand-in-hand with teachers using the Discovery Channel and the Learning Channel in the classroom, this site has enough materials and information to keep students busy for hours TV or no TV.

Related Areas: *Social Studies; Math; Teacher Resources*

Discovery Online
URL: http://www.discovery.com/

The Discovery Channel, known for its award-winning educational programming, also offers a Web site boasting original interactive content with film, music, photography, and illustration. Like the Discovery Channel School, you don't have to subscribe to cable to make use of the online resources.

Related Areas: *Social Studies; Math*

Dr. Bob's Interesting Science Stuff
URL: http://ny.frontiercomm.net/~bjenkin/science.htm

 Devoted to the wonders of science and technology, this site has unusual and thought-provoking science information for grades 4 and up! Get in touch with Dr. Bob himself via an interactive, online Web form. This site continues to grow on a regular basis, and Bob responds quickly and regularly to any correspondence.

 Integration Idea

Most children are naturally curious about severe weather occurrences such as thunder storms, lightning, and hurricanes. Your students will find lots of information about these events at Dan's Wild Wild Weather Page, while you will discover a "flurry" of ideas for lesson plans about weather patterns. Have your class check the climatic conditions in your area daily with help from Current U. S. Weather and Current Weather Maps and Movies. Do they agree with your local weather forecast? Why or why not?

Science

Earth and Sky
URL: http://www.earthsky.com

More than 950 public and commercial radio stations carry the popular Earth and Sky radio series. Now, your students can use the Web and RealAudio software to listen to the show's hosts discuss popular science and astronomy subjects.

Earth Day Resources
URL: http://www.cam.org/~cdsl_ps/Earth_Day/earthday.htm

This Earth Day site gives you plenty of ideas of how to involve your class in projects to help save the environment. There are things to do, ideas, resources, and student projects. In the What Can I Do section, students can learn about pollution, the ozone layer, acid rain, eco-wise shopping, and conserving energy.

Related Areas: *Social Studies*

The Electronic Zoo
URL: http://netvet.wustl.edu/e-zoo.htm

Eagles, earwigs, worms, wolves, snails, snakes, bullfrogs, and bison—they're all waiting for you at this Web site! The Zoo incorporates the best animal resources on the Internet, including telnet sites, gopher databases, anonymous ftp sites, and other Web pages. It's full of excellent graphics, photos, and information on biology, veterinary medicine, environmental science, and ecology. Students can click on images in the opening graphic to learn about different animals.

Energy Education from the California Energy Commission
URL: http://www.energy.ca.gov/education/index2.html

If your class is studying energy, this is the place to be. Follow the road map and stop at all different kinds of energy to learn about each. There are science projects, saving energy, alternative fuel vehicles, and wind energy sites to name a few. Also included are super scientists and puzzles by someone named Percy.

Related Areas: *Teacher Resources*

Science

Entomology for Beginners
URL: http://www.bos.nl/homes/bijlmakers/ento/begin.html

Entomology, for those unfamiliar with the term, is the study of insects. In the first section of this site, you can click on an insect's body part and go to that area to read about it. Then read and learn about the metamorphosis of insects (both simple and complete metamorphosis).

EPA Stratospheric Ozone Protection Page
URL: http://www.epa.gov/docs/ozone/index.html

This Web site contains information about the science of ozone depletion, United States regulations designed to protect the ozone layer, information on methyl bromide, flyers about the UV index, and other topical environmental information aimed at the general public.

Eureka!
URL: http://cybershopping.com/eureka/

Did you know that comets die? Or how many miles are there in a light year? Visitors to this Web site will find lesson plans, science fair projects, trivia questions, and online catalogs—all relating to the various fields of science.

Related Areas: *Math; Teacher Resources*

> ⚠ **Integration Idea**
>
> The best time to teach conservation is while children are young and their habits are still forming. Help your students understand the importance of conserving energy with a visit to Energy Education from the California Energy Commission. Your class will encounter many different ways that energy is created and how it may be saved. Another source for conservation material is Earth Day Resources. This site has abundant suggestions for how your students can conserve energy in their daily lives.

Science

The Exploration of the Earth's Magnetosphere **4-6**
URL: http://www-spof.gsfc.nasa.gov/Education/Intro.html

This site contains a student-centered tour of the Earth's magnetic field and is a great cross-curricular source for earth or space science. Students will discover earth's magnetosphere with interactive exercises and topics ranging from Aurora light to electrons and ions.

The Exploratorium **K-6**
URL: http://www.exploratorium.edu

Located in the Palace of Fine Arts in San Francisco, the Exploratorium is a museum of science, art, and human perception. It features more than 650 interactive exhibits. Its ExploraNet Web site makes many of these exciting exhibits, such as vocal vowels, color vision, and a mysterious fading dot, available to young Internauts.

Related Areas: *Art & Music*

Eye of the Storm **4-6**
URL: http://www.orlandosentinel.com/hurricane/

Using this Web site, students can track hurricanes and tropical storms along the eastern seaboard, gaining insight about these destructive forces of nature. Read about the different hurricane categories and terms. The site includes sound advice on what to do before, during, and after a hurricane.

Finding Your Way with Map and Compass **4-6**
URL: http://info.er.usgs.gov/fact-sheets/finding-your-way/finding-your-way.html

Using this site, your students will learn about how to properly use maps and compasses to get from point A to point B. Issues such as topography, distance, scale, and determining direction are covered. Compass use is also introduced with a sample exercise for students to try.

Related Areas: *Social Studies*

Science

Fish FAQ K-6
URL: http://www.wh.whoi.edu/homepage/faq.html

This site is a "bouillabaisse of fascinating facts about fish." There is so much information about fish, your students will be thoroughly stuffed when they get finished with the answers. "How do porcupine fish inflate themselves?" "How many eggs do salmon have?" and "What do oysters and clams eat?" are just a few questions here.

The Florida Aquarium K-6
URL: http://www.sptimes.com/aquarium/default.html

You don't have to worry about tapping on the glass at this aquarium! This official Web site of the Florida Aquarium in Tampa Bay offers plenty of materials and data on various water creatures, including hands-on activities and photographs.

Forensic Files 4-6
URL: http://forensicfiles.bc.sympatico.ca/

Turn your students into sleuths! Have them solve a mystery by gathering scientific information, analyzing and reviewing their findings to come to a conclusion. They will work with Newton Beagle to solve an international heist of an endangered species.

Related Areas: *Language Arts/Languages*

 Integration Idea

> Hurricanes are an awesome display of the force of nature that most children find confusing and frightening. Your students will gain understanding of these storms through a trip to Eye of the Storm. They will have access to the latest satellite images and current tracking maps. Review map reading skills at Finding Your Way with Map and Compass, and then have the class use the blank tracking map from the first site to record the progress of a real or hypothetical hurricane.

Science

The Franklin Institute Science Museum
URL: http://sln.fi.edu/

A great spot on the Web for teachers and future scientists, the Franklin Institute Science Museum in Philadelphia offers numerous interactive exhibits such as "The Heart: A Virtual Exploration," an extensive guide to Net science and teaching resources, and a monthly online magazine for anyone interested in inquiry-based science education using telecomputing.

Related Areas: *Math; Language Arts/Languages; Social Studies*

The Froggy Page
URL: http://frog.simplenet.com/froggy

Billed as the "link to froggy things from various places on the Net" the Froggy Page is a fun, educational Web site that students of all ages and grade levels will enjoy. It has a clickable database of pictures and sounds of frogs from around the world, plus froggy tales from Aesop, Aristophanes, and Grimm. Ribbit!

Related Areas: *Art & Music; Social Studies; Language Arts/Languages*

Goddard Space Flight Homepage
URL: http://www.gsfc.nasa.gov/

The official Web site for Goddard Space Flight, this site includes sections on Current Events (like comet Hale-Bopp), Space Sciences, Earth Sciences, Goddard Organizations, Public Services and Information, and Educational Programs.

Gulf of Mexico Environmental Program
URL: http://pelican.gmpo.gov/

The goal of this program is to "protect, restore, and maintain the health and productivity of the Gulf of Mexico ecosystem." Of special interest for all grade levels are the curriculum and activity guides, lesson plans, and online tutorials. Anyone studying or teaching earth sciences should go to this site.

Science

Hadrosaurus
URL: http://www.levins.com/dinosaur.html

The world's first dinosaur skeleton was found in 1858. Now it has its own Web site! Go back in time and climb down into the 30-foot ravine in Haddonfield, New Jersey, where the skeleton was found.

Related Areas: *Social Studies*

Hands-On Children's Museum
URL: http://www.wln.com/~deltapac/hocm.html

This Web museum is a colorful, fun place for young students to learn about science. Exhibits change every few months. Their current exhibit theme focuses on the forest and the animals that live there. Included in this unit is a wildlife matching game, tree and forest jokes, and links to related sites.

Related Areas: *Social Studies; Art & Music*

Helping Your Child Learn Science
URL: http://www.ed.gov/pubs/parents/Science/index.html

This site is provided by the U.S. Department of Education to help your students learn science. Although designed for parents, there is plenty of information for teachers to help their students learn to love science. Tons of activities to try at home, in the classroom, and in the community.

 Integration Idea

> Kids love animals, and you can use the resources of the Internet to supply the ideas and information for an extensive study of all living creatures! The Franklin Institute of Science Museum has just what you need to get started in its online exhibit "The Circle of Life." If slimy green critters are what your students like, take them to The Froggy Page. The Hands-On Children's Museum, meanwhile, has its own display related to living things that you can't miss. Plants and animals take precedence in this online thematic experience!

141

Science

History of Science, Technology, and Medicine K-6
URL: http://www.asap.unimelb.edu.au/hstm/hstm_ove.htm

This online index has links to biographies, subject histories, and links to museums and other science history sites.

Related Areas: *Social Studies*

inQuiry Almanack 4-6
URL: http://www.fi.edu/qa96/qanda3.html

This online magazine (e-zine) is created by science staffers at Philadelphia's Franklin Institute. It contains hands-on classroom lesson plans and activities with a science theme. There are always links to online resources, which give you one more great reason to integrate the Internet into your curriculum! Back issues are also available.

Related Areas: *Teacher Resources*

Insects K-3
URL: http://www.ed.uiuc.edu/YLP94-95/Mini-units/Griffin.Insects/

This unit provides a fun, cross-curricular method for teaching your K-4 students about insects! They will learn about insects in four main curriculum areas—language arts (read stories with insects as main characters), science (brainstorm animals they think might be insects, then later examine actual specimens), art (use their imagination to paint pictures of insects), and music (learn how to clap to rhythms using insect names).

Related Areas: *Art & Music; Language Arts/Languages*

Intellicast Weather K-6
URL: http://www.intellicast.com

Sponsored by MSNBC, this site has up-to-the-minute weather maps and forecasts for locations around the world.

Related Areas: *Social Studies*

Science

International Wildlife Coalition
URL: http://www.webcom.com/~iwcwww/welcome.html

The IWC is a wildlife protection organization fighting to save endangered species and protect wild animals. Their Web site is chock full of newsletters, links to similar organizations, and a teacher's kit on whales. Discover whale facts such as how they sleep and how some whales sing. Find out about body parts on both baleen and toothed whales.

The International Wolf Center
URL: http://www.wolf.org/

Hundreds of Minnesota teachers and students use this site to enhance their study of wolves. The project organizes links to resources on the Internet and archives valuable wolf-related information. For example, a Fish and Wildlife Office provides regular telemetry data from collared wolves in the Superior National Forest. Students use a map to monitor the animals' movements. The site features pictures of wolves, the sounds of wolf howls, and more.

Invention Dimension
URL: http://web.mit.edu/invent/

Do your students have a hankering to figure out who invented the automobile? Well, this site should sate their curiosity for awhile, as it has information on a number of inventions and inventors, some famous, some obscure.

Related Areas: *Social Studies; Math*

 Integration Idea

> Introduce your students to the fun of collecting with these two Web sites. Your class will enjoy the mini-unit activities from Insects, and they will get the whole "buggy" story when they visit inQuiry Almanack since their "Spotlight" section focuses on insects. Have the group collect some bugs and determine which ones are insects and find their type. If they enjoy bug collecting, your class might also welcome the opportunity to search for and collect leaves.

Science

Jim Lovell and the Flight of Apollo 13
URL: http://www.mcn.org/Apollo13/Home.html

Your students can learn about the life of Apollo 13 hero, Jim Lovell, from his childhood and college days through to his later Naval Astronautical career, and discover not only his biographical information but scientific facts as well. Find out the facts behind the famous motion picture.

Related Areas: *Language Arts/Languages*

Kid's Page
URL: http://www.epa.gov/OGWDW/kids/

The Office of Ground Water and Drinking Water has put together a series of drinking water activities for teachers and students. There is a project to build your own water cycle, a bloopers section containing common mistakes about keeping our water supply safe, word games, and lessons on the water treatment process.

Related Areas: *Teacher Resources*

Kids Did This!
URL: http://sln.fi.edu/tfi/hotlists/kids.html

This Web site includes many different links to a variety of school projects created by and for kids. Included here are links to school newspapers and miscellaneous subjects, such as national parks. Find out what other kids and classrooms are doing online.

Related Areas: *Art & Music; Language Arts/Languages; Math; Social Studies; Teacher Resources*

Kid's Web News
URL: http://www.wylandkids.com/

Wylands Kid's News gives students a variety of ways to explore marine life. For example, there is an excellent coloring book with a large number of fish, whales, and dolphin pictures to be printed. Each picture comes with several fascinating marine facts as well.

Related Areas: *Art & Music*

Science

KidSource Online Education
URL: http://www.kidsource.com/kidsource/pages/education.homework.html

So your students need help with a homework assignment? An idea for a school project? KidsSource has the answers in the form of a generous, up-to-date listing of homework helper sites on the Net. Recent offerings include Moon Facts, A World Wide Web Digital Library for Schoolkids, and more.

KIE Internet Education Project
URL: http://www.kie.berkeley.edu/KIE.html

The Knowledge Integration Environment (KIE) is pioneering the use of the Internet in K-12 science classrooms. KIE works to encourage appropriate science materials on the Web and the effective use of Internet tools as educational technology. It also offers science projects to use in your classroom, collections of evidence culled from schools across the globe, science software, and the chance to talk with other educators and scientists.

Related Areas: *Math; Teacher Resources*

Lessons on the Senses of Touch, Taste, and Smell
URL: http://www.classroom.net/SensesExer.html

Elementary students will enjoy participating in any of these 12 experiments having to do with one or more of the senses. To show that pain receptors are not located in the epidermis, for instance, you can perform this demonstration on yourself. "Sterilize a small sewing needle and the skin of a finger by wiping with an alcohol swab. Carefully slide the needle through the skin of the finger by sliding it just under the epidermis. Students can see that the needle is actually under the epidermis, but that there is no pain involved. (Students love this appearance of torture to their teacher!)

 Integration Idea

> Welcome your class to the world of water with curriculum ideas from the Kid's Page. This site has great resources for you in teaching the importance of water conservation and water facts. Encourage your students to summarize the importance of water to people. Then have them use a new perspective; instruct them to visualize the importance of water to other animals using Kids Web News. What ways can your students conserve water? Formulate a plan to implement that will reduce the amount of water your class uses at school and at home.

Science

Liftoff to Space Exploration
URL: http://astro-2.msfc.nasa.gov/

Your students can find out about the latest NASA missions via this neat Web site. Get the skinny on shuttle liftoffs, mission operations, top space headlines, and what it takes to be an astronaut! Be sure to check out the Kid's Space section, which has a lot of fun space quizzes, puzzles, and articles for younger students.

Related Areas: *Teacher Resources*

Live from Mars
URL: http://quest.arc.nasa.gov/mars/

This site provides an enormous amount of information and activities relating to the red planet. There is a What's New section providing the latest Martian news. Mars Today gives you a picture of current conditions on Mars and its relationship to Earth. There are also live video clips, a photo gallery, and a teacher's lounge with a number of lesson plans from other teachers. The Kid's Corner contains poems, artwork, and writings by kids—as well as a section of student stumpers.

Related Areas: *Teacher Resources*

The Mad Scientist Network
URL: http://128.252.223.239/~ysp/MSN/

Billing itself as the "laboratory that never sleeps," The Mad Scientist Network (MSN) is a collection of scientists, high school teachers, and university faculty from around the globe who field questions about science. Have a science question that you can't find a satisfactory answer to? Send it to this site, and you'll get a concise answer within a reasonably short period of time. If you don't have a specific question in mind, you can head over to the Random Knowledge Generator, which searches the MSN library to select several questions at random.

Making a Pinhole Camera
URL: gopher://ericir.syr.edu:70/00/Lesson/NewLesson/Science/Camera

Using a three-pound coffee can, construction paper, a shoe box, masking tap, aluminum, cardboard, and a few tools, students can create their own cameras, take pictures, and develop them. This creative lesson plan introduces students to photography and how light works in exposing film. Enterprising students can later post their favorite pictures on the Internet as an extracurricular project.

Related Areas: *Art & Music*

Science

Map Machine Atlas

URL: http://www.nationalgeographic.com/resources/ngo/maps/

The Map Machine Atlas, provided by *National Geographic*, lets your students quickly pinpoint the country they need information about. Each country's page contains maps, flags, facts, and profiles.

Related Areas: *Social Studies*

The Martian Sun-Times

URL: http://www.ucls.uchicago.edu/MartianSunTimes/

 Students can learn meteorology from this creative role-playing experience in which they play investigative reporters for a Martian newspaper. They will compare Martian weather to Earth weather. Activities and lesson plans are included in the site for teachers.

Related Areas: *Language Arts*

MathMol Hypermedia Textbook for Elementary Schools

URL: http://www.nyu.edu/pages/mathmol/textbook/elem_home1.html

MathMol brings your students a science textbook via the Net. The grade 3 chapter covers the differences between water, solid, liquid, and gas. In grade 4, your students will study what matter is, states of matter, energy, and how to measure it. And finally, the grade 5 section covers atoms, elements, compounds, and mixtures.

Related Areas: *Math*

 Integration Idea

> Space exploration is a favorite scientific study for elementary children, and these sites will put your students in touch with current space missions and Mars explorations. Begin with a venture to Liftoff to Space Exploration, and be sure to allow your students to try some activities from "Kid's Space." Visit Live from Mars to get the story on exploration to the "Red Planet." After your students have familiarized themselves with Mars, have them create a "Martian's Guide" to the Earth or your country, state, or city. You will find curriculum resources and much information to help you at The Martian Sun-Times.

Science

Miami Museum of Science
URL: http://bird.miamisci.org/hurricane/

This Web site, provided by the Miami Museum of Science, gives visitors answers to many questions about hurricanes by actually taking you inside a hurricane. There is also information on hurricane survivors and a section on how to have your students build their own weather instruments.

Microworlds—Exploring the Structure of Materials
URL: http://www.lbl.gov/MicroWorlds/

The words "material world" mean something different to the scientists at the Lawrence Berkeley Laboratory. Students can use this Web site to explore a variety of science topics. The site includes plenty of scientific photographs, graphics, quizzes, and interactive follow-up activities for curious young scientists. Be sure to read the section about the Advanced Light Source, a humongous instrument for probing atoms and molecules.

Missouri Botanical Garden
URL: http://www.mobot.org/welcome.html

Your students can take a virtual tour of this world-famous botanical garden and view the extensive pictures of plants at the image gallery, as well as follow the great links to other botany sites on the Internet.

Monarchs and Migration
URL: http://www.sci.mus.mn.us/sln/monarchs/

Discover what other classes around the country and Mexico are doing to learn about butterflies. There is a list of ideas for your class such as raising butterflies, creating butterfly artwork, learning about metamorphosis, and seeking out local butterfly locations for field trips.

Related Areas: *Art & Music*

Science

Mrs. Chagnon's Chicken Page
URL: http://www.geocities.com/EnchantedForest/7672/chickens.html

Whoever thought chickens could be so interesting? This site describes the day-to-day development of eggs. See how fast the chick is formed in the egg and also check the changes in the weight of the egg through your computer screen.

MTU Volcanoes Page
URL: http://www.geo.mtu.edu/volcanoes/

When your students visit this Web site, they will have access to a worldwide volcanic reference map, the latest volcanic activity, remote sensing of volcanoes, pointers to other volcano sites, an online glossary of terms, and some great volcano jokes!

Muscle Page for Kids
URL: http://danke.com/Orthodoc/kidmuscle1.shtml

This site gives your students wonderful graphics of all of the muscle groups. See the shoulder, chest, belly, and thigh muscles and find out how they work together to help you move. Learn how your body works with gravity, what the muscle with the longest name is, and how to maintain good posture.

Related Areas: *Health/PE*

Integration Idea

The most delicate and beautiful creatures of the insect world are the butterflies. Send your class on a butterfly excursion with Monarchs and Migration. Find out how children across the country are learning about monarch butterflies, and you may want to participate, too. Your students can examine butterfly gardens and plants in general at the Missouri Botanical Garden. Perhaps your class will want to plant a butterfly garden and make a journal of their observations or catch monarch caterpillars and raise them to maturity.

Science

NASA Shuttle Web
URL: http://shuttle.nasa.gov/

Information about the history of the space shuttle program in general, as well as more detailed data about recent and upcoming missions, can all be found at this NASA site. Pictures, video, and sound clips are included.

National Audubon Society
URL: http://www.Audubon.org/

Young students studying the effects of fish depletion should pay a visit to the online headquarters of the National Audubon Society. Students can take a tour of a swamp sanctuary, view 500-year-old cypress trees, and learn about Florida 'gators. Find out what birds live in your state and what their migrating patterns are.

National Science Teachers Association
URL: http://www.nsta.org/

The The NSTA Web site is home to K-12 science-related projects and curriculum information. It also offers online forums devoted to astronomy, medicine, psychology, and more. A great resource for use in the classroom.

Related Areas: *Teacher Resources*

National Wildlife Federation
URL: http://www.nwf.org/nwf/

National Wildlife Federation has been helping teachers for over 60 years, and the legacy is continued in their official Web site, which houses environmental lesson plans, activities, workshops, and lots of fun online games and riddles for students to try! Be sure to stop and say hello to Ranger Rick!

Related Areas: *Social Studies; Teacher Resources*

Science

Natural Disaster Reference Database 4-6
URL: http://ltpwww.gsfc.nasa.gov/ndrd/cgi/ndrd.cgi

Those benevolent people at the NASA Goddard Space Flight Center have been good enough to provide hungry earth science educators with this Web site, a bibliographic database covering every type of natural disaster, from fires to tsunamis. The articles cover everything from prevention, research, and relief to the causes of the disasters. In addition, there are links to disaster images and other disaster databases.

Neuroscience for Kids K-6
URL: http://weber.u.washington.edu/~chudler/neurok.html

This Web page has been created for elementary and secondary school students and teachers who would like to learn more about the nervous system. Let your students enjoy the activities and experiments on their way to learning more about the brain and spinal cord.

Related Areas: *Health/PE*

Newton's Apple K-6
URL: http://ericir.syr.edu/Projects/Newton/index.html

Now that this popular PBS science show has gone online, you can easily access lesson plans and experiments from this series. You'll find activities indexed by subject matter or episode. Topics cover everything from acid rain, bicycles, the human eye, and karate to recycling, spelunking, and yeast (for bread).

Related Areas: *Health/PE*

Integration Idea

While studying about wildlife and/or habitats integrate the Internet into your lesson by visiting the Audubon Society and National Wildlife Federation Web pages. Read about the various species of birds and other animals that live in North America and view their habitats. Take your students on a nature walk and make a list of what animals live in your area and note their habitat.

Science

The Nine Planets
URL: http://seds.lpl.arizona.edu/billa/tnp/

 Enjoy space travel but don't have the time? Take a multimedia tour of the solar system through text, pictures, sounds, and an occasional movie. Each planet and major moon is briefly described and illustrated with pictures from NASA spacecraft.

An Online Guide to Meteorology
URL: http://covis.atmos.uiuc.edu/guide/guide.html

 This comprehensive site offers students an in-depth look at the various forces of nature that affect our world. Thunderstorms, tornadoes, air pressure, clouds, snowstorms, and the ins-and-outs of weather forecasting are all covered here. For the younger grades, there is an Especially Elementary section, which contains hands-on lesson plans and activities, integrating other curriculum areas besides earth science.

Related Areas: *Teachers Resources*

Paleontology Server
URL: http://ucmp1.berkeley.edu/

The University of California's online Museum of Paleontology is an interactive natural history museum kids will love. Inside, students can learn more about "The Tree of Life," browse photos of Great White sharks, and explore fossil records.

Related Areas: *Social Studies*

Photosynthesis Directory
URL: http://esg-www.mit.edu:8001/esgbio/ps/psdir.html

This site is a complete hypertextbook chapter on photosynthesis. Your students can follow the interface of the chapter and learn the process and applications of light reactions, dark reactions, and other ways plants photosynthesize.

Science

Pittsburgh Zoo
URL: http://zoo.pgh.pa.us/index.html

Visit the Pittsburgh Zoo at this site and learn about many of its inhabitants. There are sections on wildlife, research and conservation, education—even a "Kid's Kingdom"!

Prem's Fossil Gallery— Beneath the Calamities Tree
URL: http://dev.uol.com/~prem/fossil.html

If your students hunger for trilobites, graphtolites, and fossil plants, then this site should give them plenty to chew on! There are lots of fossil-hunting facts and pictures to download, including links to other paleontological Web pages.

PSC Meterology Program Cloud Boutique
URL: http://vortex.plymouth.edu/clouds.html

The PSC Meterology Program has developed this site to provide explanations of and access to detailed pictures of some basic cloud forms such as cirrus and lenticular. The cloud images are relatively large in order to show detailed structure and features. The purpose of this "boutique" is to provide a general cloud reference and is not intended to be an all-inclusive list.

 Integration Idea

> Use the meteorology sites listed on these two pages to assist your collection of resources in creating a unit on weather. Each site has facts and figures you can use to better explain different weather patterns to your students. The Guide to Meteorology site should soon have movies available, so be sure to keep an eye out!

Science

Purdue Weather Processor
URL: http://wxp.atms.purdue.edu/

WXP is a software package that was developed at Purdue University in the Department of Earth and Atmospheric Sciences. It is intended to be a general purpose weather visualization tool for current and archived meteorological data. The products available at this server are derived from the data obtained from the National Weather Service, the University of Wisconsin, and WSI Corporation.

The Python Page
URL: http://member.aol.com/cybrstorm/

Discover the exciting world of pythons at this site. Your students may choose which type of python to study—Burmese or Balinese. There is also a link to medical information for those who may keep snakes as pets (but not for those who may occasionally encounter them).

Redwoods: California's Redwood Canyons
URL: http://redwoods.com/~ebarnett/redwood.canyons.html

Use your computer to take your class on a photo tour of the Redwood canyons via the Internet. See and learn about the world's tallest trees and find out about the different ecological areas that exist in these canyons. Plenty of wonderful pictures.

Running the Nile
URL: http://www.adventureonline.com/nile/index.html

Let your students join a team of kayakers attempting to descend the Victoria Nile River in Uganda, Africa. Read their daily journals, meet the team, and find out what happens. Along the way, use the Nile Classroom section to gather classroom activities and lessons.

Related Areas: *Language Arts/Languages; Social Studies*

 Science

The Salmon Page
URL: http://www.riverdale.k12.or.us/salmon.htm

K-6

Think you know all about salmon? Why not head over to this site and find out! Here, your students will discover the life cycle of salmon, with pictures showing the development from eggs into adults. In addition, there is information on how to catch and cook salmon, school salmon projects, and the latest salmon news.

Science Daily
URL: http://www.sciencedaily.com

4-6

Get the gist on the latest science news and headlines via this Web site, which provides access to such periodicals as *Discover, Scientific American, Popular Science,* and other, more obscure journals.

Related Areas: *Social Studies; Language Arts/Languages*

The Seasons
URL: http://www.wentworth.com/seasons.html

4-6

This comprehensive, hands-on lesson plan challenges students to explore why and how the seasons change. During a group discussion, students explain why the seasons vary, why weather changes from season to season, and why it's light or dark outside when they go to bed at certain times of the year. Then, they create a model of the sun and earth from styrofoam balls to show the position and angle of the bodies at various times of the year.

Related Areas: *Teacher Resources*

 Integration Idea

Teach the about the habitats and weather patterns of different countries and states in the U.S. without ever leaving the classroom. Go to California via the Redwoods site, or head over to Africa through the Running the Nile site. Look at a python up close or explore the theory behind why the seasons change. These sites will allow your students to experience sights they may not otherwise encounter due to their location.

Science

Sea Turtles
URL: http://kingfish.ssp.nmfs.gov/tmcintyr/turtles/turtle.html

 Your students can learn plenty about sea turtles at this information-filled site. After learning some basic facts about these salt-water reptiles, they will read about the Endangered Species Act of 1973. Includes pictures and information about those sea turtles that are endangered.

Sea World Animal Information Database
URL: http://www.bev.net/education/SeaWorld/

This Sea World site gives you enough facts about animals to start your own safari. Included are: common name, class, order, family, size, weight, life span, gestation, diet, and fun facts. Students can send questions to the whale Shamu, take an animal quiz, or find out about the different types of zoology careers available.

Shangri La
URL: http://aleph0.clarku.edu/~rajs/Shangri_La.html

Bearing no relation to the fictional utopia created by novelist James Hilton, this Web site attempts to present the natural and geographical aspects of the Himalayas, the highest mountain range on Earth. Take a tour of the mountains, view its natural wildlife, learn about how they were created, and about the brave men and women that tried to scale it. The collection of photos here are stupendous and make for an excellent first-time view into this enormous and unique ecosystem.

Related Areas: *Art & Music; Language Arts/Languages; Social Studies*

Smithsonian Gem and Mineral Collection
URL: http://galaxy.einet.net/images/gems/gems-icons.html

 Those among your class who enjoy collecting rocks will get a kick out of this Web site, as it features some of the prettiest gems and minerals on earth. Descriptions of each mineral are included, along with several photos.

 **Science**

Solar System Live
URL: http://www.fourmilab.ch/solar/solar.html

K-6

At this site, your students can view the solar system and see the actual position of all the planets around the sun in real time. The controls allow you to set time and date, viewpoint, observing location, and other orbital elements so your class could, for example, track a comet.

Space Calendar
URL: http://NewProducts.jpl.nasa.gov/calendar/

4-6

This Space Calendar allows your students to see what the latest space-related happenings and events are occurring each day. Every listing links to further information about the subject.

Space Educators' Handbook
URL: http://tommy.jsc.nasa.gov/~woodfill/SPACEED/SEHHTML/

4-6

Head over to this site to find space exploration movies, comics about the history of aviation, and an excellent section that teaches about space and science technology by using science fiction pulp novels and comic book covers to dispel current myths.

Related Areas: *Language Arts/Languages*

 Integration Idea

Integrate the Internet into your oceans unit by having your students read about the life of the salmon using the site on p. 155. Purchase salmon for students to taste or go fishing for salmon. Learn what the term endangered means and have your students use the Sea Turtles site as a research tool. Purchase a turtle to keep in the class and observe its habits. Use it as a prompt for writing stories and have students keep a journal of what they observe the turtle doing. Conclude your unit with a trip to Sea World via the Internet.

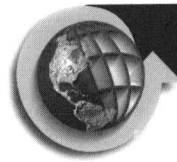

Science

Space Telescope Electronic Information Service
URL: http://www.stsci.edu/

This site provides visitors with a guide to the inner workings of the Hubble Space Telescope, as well as a number of photos taken via Hubble. Educational activities and resources are also available.

Spiders Home Page
URL: http://diogenes.sedl.org/scimath/pasopartners/spiders/spiderhome.html

The Spiders Home Page starts you on a seven-lesson study of arachnids and aims at debunking some old myths about our eight-legged friends. Lessons include: "Spiders! Scary or Nice?" "Spiders Catch Prey," "Spiders Life Cycle," "Natural Enemies," and "Spiders Live Everywhere."

Related Areas: *Language Arts/Languages; Teacher Resources*

StarChild
URL: http://starchild.gsfc.nasa.gov/

StarChild Project is a wonderful interactive site for younger students, with big, clickable graphics, large text for easy reading, and simple hyperlinks that help students learn new terms. Youngsters will learn about galaxies, planets, stars, suns, and moons. The pages are well-organized—clicking on any item on the home page will give you a single page of basic definitions and links to related terms and colorful images or photos.

Sugar Glider Page
URL: http://www.rtis.com/nat/user/regrove/

This odd-named animal is fast becoming a popular pet in the United States. This site will give your students plenty of information on these adorable marsupials, which are similar in size and appearance to the American flying squirrel. Sounds, scent, diet, and health are just a few of the topics covered here.

Science

Super Science HomePage
URL: http://www.superscience.com/home.html

This site is designed to encourage students, teachers, and parents to do scientific experiments. It includes ideas for experiments, advice on performing and presenting experiments, an online contest, information on exciting books and multimedia titles, and how to apply for science grants.

The Telegarden
URL: http://www.usc.edu/dept/garden/

This telerobotic installation allows Web users to view and interact with a remote garden filled with living plants. Members can plant, water, and monitor the progress of seedlings via the tender movements of an industrial robot arm.

Related Areas: *Technology/Internet*

Theater of Electricity
URL: http://www.mos.org/sln/toe/toe.html

This Museum of Science hosts this online tour through the world of electricity. Section topics include: history, sparks, touching lightning, Franklin's kite, safety quiz, and teacher resources with lessons and experiments.

Related Areas: *Teacher Resources*

Integration Idea

Encourage your students to become active participants of science. Have them think of something they would like to invent. Build up this idea by discussing the idea that scientists create inventions to make life easier, and conduct experiments to see if their inventions work. Use the Theater of Electricity, Super Science, and Thinking Fountain (page 164) sites to build interest and download experiments to try out during class.

Science

Thinking Fountain
URL: http://www.sci.mus.mn.us/sln/tf/

 Presented by the Science Museum of Minnesota, Thinking Fountain is a collection of online "card files," all aimed at encouraging students to investigate and learn about the scientific world. Clicking on the fanciful collage, allows visitors to travel through the various card topics. The Card Clusters section groups cards that have a common theme or resource, while Mind Maps illustrate how to use the cards in the classroom. Students can create their own cards to be added on to the site if they wish.

Tiger Information Center
URL: http://www.5tigers.org/

The Tiger Information Center site explores all types of tigers, from those in the jungle to those in captivity. Special attention is paid to tiger ecology and how to keep these beasts from becoming extinct. There is a wonderful section called Cubs'n'Kids, which has fun facts and tiger quizzes your students can try out. Don't miss the Online Tiger Adventure, where you get to track an escaped tiger.

The Tornado Project Online
URL: http://www.tornadoproject.com/

 More than just your ordinary tornado Web site, this site is loaded with tornado myths, oddities, personal experiences, tornado chasers, and information on how to stay safe during a tornado attack.

The Tree of Life
URL: http://phylogeny.arizona.edu/tree/phylogeny.html

An online project linking various biology Web pages, showing the infinite diversity of life on our planet and the relationships they share from the smallest ameoba to the largest whale.

Science

Turtle Trax
URL: http://www.turtles.org/

At this site, your students can learn about actual sea turtles and find out why some of them are endangered. They can listen to turtle sounds, read turtle essays and poetry written by sixth graders, see student turtle-inspired art, print out coloring pages, and much more.

Related Areas: *Art & Music: Languauge Arts*

USA Today Weather
URL: http://www.usatoday.com/weather/wfront.htm

See the *USA Today* forecast of temperatures on a map and find out where it will be raining. Go to the topic index and get connected to files on weather subjects from acid rain to Zulu time. There is an "Ask Jack" question-and-answer section, a weather almanac, Celsius-Fahrenheit conversions, and forecasts for areas outside of the United States.

Related Areas: *Social Studies*

Views of the Solar System
URL: http://bang.lanl.gov/solarsys/homepage.htm

The largest, most complete educational tour of our solar system, this site includes information on the sun, the planets, asteroids, meteors, and comets, as well as images and animations of every celestial phenomenon.

⚠ Integration Idea

While studying habitats and life science visit Turtle Trax and The Tree of Life sites. These sites will help you integrate language arts, music, and art into your science lesson. For example, you can have students read the turtle essay and then attempt to write their own. The class can choose their favorite essay and then submit it to the site. These are two very student-friendly sites.

Science

Virtual Cave
URL: http://www.goodearth.com/virtcave.html

This virtual cave is an amalgation of all the best caves in the world. Your students can surf this cave without the trademark claustrophobia spelunking often induces. There is no other grotto in the world (or cyberspace) quite like this one!

Virtual Cell
URL: http://ampere.scale.uiuc.edu/~m-lexa/cell/cell.html

Explore a virtual plant cell at this site. Your students can zoom, turn, and cut into the image in their browser window. The easy-to-understand online instructions will enable your students to have a successful journey though the inner workings of the cell.

Related Areas: *Technology/Internet*

Virtual Frog Dissection Kit
URL: http://george.lbl.gov/ITG.hm.pg.docs/dissect/info.html

Designed for high school biology classes, this Web site, created by the Lawrence Berkeley Laboratory, allows students to explore the anatomy of a frog without dissecting a real animal. They can turn the frog over, remove skin, and highlight various organs and systems. Researchers used data from high-resolution imaging to create this one-of-a-kind site.

Related Areas: *Technology/Internet*

The Virtual Sun
URL: http://www.astro.uva.nl/michielb/sun/kaft.htm

Take a virtual tour through the single most important celestial body for our survival, our sun. This tour shows the excitement not always obvious to us here on earth. Your students will love the images and movies.

Science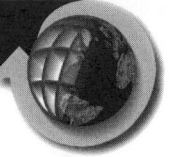

The Visible Human Projects
URL: http://www.nlm.nih.gov/research/visible/visible_human.html

The Visible Human Project creates complete, anatomically detailed, three-dimensional representations of the male and female human body. The current phase of the project involves collecting CAT, MRI, and "cryosection" images of a male and female cadaver at one millimeter intervals. An interesting site for all students and teachers of anatomy.

Related Areas: *Health/PE*

Volcano World
URL: http://volcano.und.nodak.edu

Perfect for students studying volcanoes, NASA's Volcano World contains timely updates about volcanic activity worldwide, historical eruption reports, information on how volcanoes work, and guidance on becoming a volcanologist. Also of interest is an online Web form you can use to sign up your class for the popular, year-round Ask a Volcanologist Project.

Related Areas: *Teacher Resources*

Water Resources and Information
URL: http://h2o.usgs.gov/public/watuse/index.html

 Your students can answer questions on the topics that interest them such as water use in the United States, water data and measurements, and water use in your home. Detailed answers are provided for each question. Color maps help tell you how much water your state uses.

 **Integration Idea**

Incorporate the Internet into your biology lessons. The Virtual Cell Web site allows your students to dissect a cell online and then define the different parts. Along the same lines, the Virtual Frog Dissection site allows your students to dissect a frog and define the internal organs without having to clean up any mess. You can follow this up with having students view their own cheek cells under a microscope.

Science

The Weather Channel Site Guide
URL: http://www.weather.com/index.html

This site provides you with graphs, daily weather information, weather history, and a page of the how-and-whys of weather to use in class. The site also has a glossary and a TV schedule for taping educational weather programs to use in the classroom.

Related Areas: *Language Arts/Languages*

Weather Glossary for Storm Spotters
URL: http://www.nssl.noaa.gov/~nws/branick2.html

This glossary contains weather-related terms that may be either heard or used by severe local storm spotters or spotter groups. In an attempt to standardize communication in this field, these professionals have created a great online weather resource that is detailed and current.

Weather Online
URL: http://www.weatheronline.com

Find out the latest on tropical storms and other big weather events. Complete forecasts and graphics for your local area with the Local Weather section can be found here. The Weather Tools section is the largest compilation of links to weather sites on the Net. Be sure to check out the adventures of Weatherboy!

Weather System Visualization
URL: http://www.ugems.psu.edu/~owens/WWW_Virtual_Library/

Head over to this online index to locate some of the best weather-related sites on the World Wide Web. Headings include maps, forecasts, satellite images, movies, and climate.

Science

The Weather Unit
URL: http://faldo.atmos.uiuc.edu/WEATHER/weather.html

This online unit helps your class learn all about weather, from climate to precipitation. In the science section, there are lesson plans for the seasons, condensation, and light and heat. There are also cross-curricular lesson plans for math, reading and writing, art, social studies, and even drama.

Related Areas: *Art & Music; Language Arts/Languages; Math; Social Studies; Teacher Resources*

Welcome to Earth RISE
URL: http://earthrise.sdsc.edu/

Earth RISE is a graphical, easy, and fun to use database of photos of the earth from space. These photos were taken by astronauts out the windows of the space shuttle. Earth RISE contains photos from the past 15 years and is a great resource for all students, educators, and the general public interested in our planet.

Welcome to the WhaleTimes SeaBed!
URL: http://www.whaletimes.org/whahMPG.htm

Integrate science, language arts, and math using this site. Your students can view the sea mammals, read about them, estimate how much classroom space they would take up, and then actually figure it out. Check the kids page and help write the Whale Tale with students from all around the world. There's lots to do!

Related Areas: *Art & Music; Language Arts/Languages; Social Studies; Teacher Resources; Technology/Internet; Math*

⚠ **Integration Idea**

Need resources for gathering information on weather? All the sites on these two pages have weather-related data instantly available for students to use. Some even have lesson plans and areas designed specifically for kids! Use the Weather Channel site to chart weather changes in different areas. Then have students create a graph of the temperature changes in a certain region.

Science

Wendell's Yucky Bug World
URL: http://www.nj.com/yucky/roaches/

Future entomologists should get a kick out of this site, also known as the "Yuckiest site on the Internet!" Bug World contains more than any student would ever want to know about these resilient, but often very annoying creatures. There are quizzes, multimedia shows, and plenty of fun facts. Those with the big bug questions can ask resident experts, or follow a day in the life of the site's mascot, Ralph Roach. Best of all, visitors can share their favorite bug stories with other visitors in the Tall Tales section. A Web site definitely not for the faint of heart!

Related Areas: *Language Arts/Languages*

Whales: A Thematic Web Unit
URL: http://curry.edschool.Virginia.EDU/go/Whales/

This site provides your class with an entire unit about whales using language arts, math, science, and social studies subject areas. There are book reviews, homework suggestions, and lesson plans provided for you. Check out the glossary of whale terms for your students to learn.

Related Areas: *Language Arts/Languages; Math; Social Studies; Teacher Resources; Technology/Internet*

The Why Files
URL: http://whyfiles.news.wisc.edu

The Why Files, a project of the National Institute for Science Education, is an electronic exploration of the science behind the news. Twice a month you'll find new features on the science (as well as math, engineering, and technology) of everyday life. The site's boundaries are broad—from outer space to cellular biology, from dinosaurs and dragon lizards to the statistics of political polling.

Related Areas: *Social Studies; Math*

The Wild Ones
URL: http://www.columbia.edu/cu/cerc/WildOnes

The Wild Ones is an international club that provides students aged 7-13 a place to share information about endangered species, different habitats and environments, and each other. It's also an ever-growing, online educational network providing teachers and their students opportunities to design and work on collaborative scientific investigations.

Related Areas: *Social Studies; Language Arts/Languages; Teacher Resources; Technology/Internet*

Science

Windows to the Universe
URL: http://www.windows.umich.edu

K-6

And what a large window it is! This user-friendly site attempts to include as much basic information as possible on earth and space science. Whether it's the planets themselves, the people who discovered them, planets in the arts, or how they were pictured in classical mythology, you'll find it all here. Updates on the latest scientific discoveries are included, plus information on the basic physical laws.

Related Areas: *Language Arts/Languages; Social Studies; Math; Art & Music*

The Wonderful Skunk and Opossum Page
URL: http://elvis.neep.wisc.edu/~firmiss/mephitis-didelphis.html

K-6

Your students will enjoy this site, which describes itself as "a celebration of two underdogs in the animal kingdom." Lots of information on tracks of each animal, chemical composition and cleaning information on skunks and their scent, along with stories and pictures. There is even help on what to do with injured animals and troublesome ones.

Related Areas: *Language Arts/Languages*

The World of Benjamin Franklin
URL: http://sln.fi.edu/franklin/rotten.html

4-6

Benjamin Franklin is famous for being many things—a scientist, an inventor, a statesman, a printer, a philosopher, a musician, and an economist. This wonderful Web site gives you information on each of his remarkable accomplishments. To help your students learn even more about Ben Franklin and his world, try taking a look at some of the recommended resource materials, enrichment activities, and glossary.

Related Areas: *Art & Music; Social Studies*

⚠ Integration Idea

Have an information seek and find. List the Wendell's Yucky Bug World, the whale unit, the Wild Ones, the Wonderful Skunk and Opossum Page, and Ben Franklin's site addresses on the board along with questions to be answered. Have students use these sites to find their answers and form an eight-minute presentation informing the class on one or two facts they discovered that were interesting. These sites are very student-friendly and some have movie and sound clips.

Science

Worm World
URL: http://www.nj.com/yucky/worm

From the people who brought you the popular Bug World comes this intriguing examination into the underground world of earthworms, planarians, and other simple-celled, slithering organisms. Follow host Wendell Worm as he takes visitors on a tour of worm biology and interviews some of his more obscure worm cousins. Students can find out why worms are one of nature's best recyclers, download video clips of a worm being born, or contribute their own worm-related artwork.

Yes Magazine
URL: http://www.islandnet.com/~yesmag/

Yes is Canada's Science Magazine for Kids. Inside its pages you'll find Science and Technology news, and hands-on projects such as paper airplane designs, a newspaper dome, and a giant tower using only spaghetti and marshmallows. Be sure to try the brain bumper science questions

You Can with Beakman and Jax
URL: http://www.youcan.com

The theme of this Web site, based on the popular television show Beakman's World, is "A good question is a powerful thing!" The site is full of science questions and educational links that get students thinking about science in their everyday lives. Gross, fun, and educational!

The Zooary
URL: http://catt.poly.edu/~duane1/zoo.html

Which animal is known as the "chicken of the trees?" Don't know? Then maybe you need to stop at The Zooary, a collection of resources and materials for all those who are interested in biology, physical science, and ecology.

Science

Zoo Net—All about Zoos!
URL: http://www.mindspring.com/~zoonet/

ZooNet has a comprehensive list of links to zoos in the United States and over the world plus an extensive set of images. There is a special children's section as well. If you are looking for any information on zoology, check here first.

Integration Idea

Looking to take a visit to the zoo? These online zoo sites are excellent, especially for primary teachers who are introducing animals to their students. In addition to the animal info, the Zooary site has career information. Have your students create a classroom zoo mural highlighting the animals they learned about. Ask the students to write either a list of facts or a short story about each of their favorite animals.

YELLOW PAGES
SOCIAL STUDIES

Social Studies

1492: An Ongoing Voyage

URL: http://sunsite.unc.edu/expo/1492.exhibit/Intro.html

Set the time machine for 1492, and set sail with Christopher Columbus and his crew. This in-depth study from the Library of Congress examines life in America before the European's arrival. A fine example of how students can visit museums without leaving their desks.

1996 Notable Children's Trade Books in the Field of Social Studies

URL: http://www.ncss.org/online/resources/notable/home.html

This excellent site features a bibliography of social studies trade books along with short summaries of the plot. Prices and reading levels are also included. Have students figure out the price of buying books for a math lesson.

Related Areas: *Language Arts/Languages; Math; Teacher Resources*

4-H . . . More Than You Ever Imagined

URL: http://www.fourhcouncil.edu/index.htm

You can get your students involved in helping the environment by looking up the various events and activities listed at this site. The 4-H club's mission is to involve youth in critical issues that affect their everyday lives. Information for adults who want to get involved with youth development is here as well.

Related Areas: *Language Arts/Languages*

A-Bomb WWW Museum

URL: http://www.csi.ad.jp/ABOMB/index.html

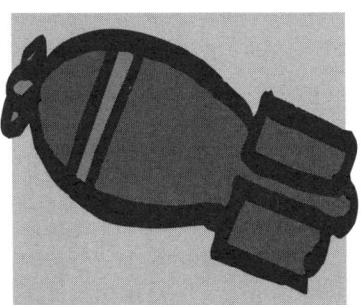

The dropping of "Fat Man and Little Boy" helped to end WWII. But was it necessary? This site examines the impact that the event had and its repercussions for those living in Japan. Included are interviews with a child who survived the Hiroshima bombing and children that live in that city today.

 **Social Studies**

Abraham Lincoln Assassination
URL: http://members.aol.com/RVSNorton/Lincoln.html

 Learn about the 1865 conspiracy trial, the final hours of John Wilkes Booth, and Mary Surratt, the first woman ever to be executed by the U.S. government. You'll also find information on Lincoln's life and accomplishments, and links to Lincoln books you can order online!

Academy of Achievement
URL: http://www.achievement.org

Far from being just another museum, the Academy of Achievement brings you face-to-face with extraordinary individuals who have shaped the twentieth century with their accomplishments. Influential role models such as Wynton Marsalis, George Bush, Colin Powell, and Rosa Parks are all profiled and interviewed here. Designed to give students inspiration, encouragement, and the will to achieve, the academy profiles the essential elements of achievement shared by all academy members, such as passion and perseverance.

Related Areas: *Language Arts/Languages*

AFROamerica
URL: http://www.afroam.org/

This site allows you to study the African-American culture from contemporary as well as historical perspectives. Pages focus on news, history, art, and other topics. You'll even find a kid's page full of activities focusing on history, geography, and vocabulary.

Related Areas: *Art & Music; Language Arts/Languages; Social Studies; Math*

 Integration Idea

> Your students will become experts in the field of social studies when they explore famous figures of African-American history. AFROamerica includes historical accounts from the very beginning of slavery, and Abraham Lincoln Assassination addresses Lincoln's role in ending the slave trade. Many leaders of African-American culture are also members of the Academy of Achievement. Have your students use the resources located there to choose an outstanding individual in history who has had some impact on African-American culture and develop a resume for him or her. The resumes will be written for an imaginary organization for consideration in an achievement award.

Social Studies

The Age of Imperialism 4-6
URL: http://www.smplanet.com/imperialism/toc.html

During the late nineteenth and early twentieth centuries, the United States pursued an aggressive policy of expansionism, extending its political and economic influence around the globe. That pivotal era is the subject of this online history resource, which includes lesson plans and information of use to both educators and students.

Related Areas: *Teacher Resources*

Alaska K-6
URL: http://tqd.advanced.org/3140/k-beach.html

Can't get to Alaska anytime soon? Visit the Alaska Web site and see what life is like on the Kenai Peninsula! This site is complete with color photographs and descriptions of Alaskan wildlife, climate, food, and lifestyle and was created by a 13-year-old student!

Related Areas: *Language Arts/Languages;*

The American Immigration Home Page 4-6
URL: http://www.bergen.gov/AAST/Projects/Immigration/index.html

What types of people have emigrated to America? Where did they come from and what were their reasons for immigration? This site, created by a tenth grade history class, attempts to answer these questions and more. The project aims to give information not only on how immigrants were treated, but also why they decided to come to America. Other topics covered include how much assimilation has taken place among various immigrant groups and what immigrants find distinctive about America.

American Memory from the Library of Congress K-6
URL: http://rs6.loc.gov/amhome.html

This site consists of primary source and archival materials relating to American culture and history. These historical collections are the key contribution of the Library of Congress to the National Digital Library. A must for anyone learning about U.S. history.

Related Areas: *Teacher Resources*

Social Studies

The American Presidency
URL: http://www.grolier.com/presidents/ea/ea_toc.html

View the biographies of all the presidents, their wives, and their vice-presidents. Find out their elections results, presidential programs, and even the scandals that graced their office terms. This site also has photos and articles on the branches of the government broken down into small subtopics. There's even a section on how to use the site as a study guide.

Related Areas: *Language Arts/Languages; Teacher Resources*

America's West
URL: http://www.AmericanWest.com/

Let your students explore the west, from the frontier and pioneer days to the present. Westward expansion, cowboys, Indians, trappers, and scouts are all discussed and described. Familiar names include Doc Holliday, Daniel Boone, and Billy the Kid.

Ancient World Web
URL: http://atlantic.evsc.virginia.edu/julia/AncientWorld.html

Designed to search by subject or region, this extensive online index will help you and your students find any information you need that has to do with ancient history and cultures.

 Integration Idea

Children love to pretend, and a favorite imagination exercise is pretending to be a cowboy! Introduce your class to the characters of the old west with an online hike to America's West. There are links to just about every type of cowboy your kids can round up. Your students will see what these buckaroos actually looked like through a pictorial tour of western images at the American site. Have your students write tall tales about a figure from the west and draw portraits to share with their stories.

 **Social Studies**

Anne Frank Online
URL: http://www.annefrank.com/

Over one million children under the age of 16 died in the Holocaust. Anne Frank was one of them. This Web site, created by the U.S. Anne Frank Center, attempts to educate Internet users about her life and times, the holocaust, and her justly famous diary. A well-designed photo scrapbook of Anne and her family can be found here, as well as selections from her diary and information on its publishing history.

Related Areas: *Language Arts/Languages*

Antarctica Live
URL: http://www.antdiv.gov.au/aad/exop/sfo/mawson/video.html

Your students will love connecting to this site to see live video captures, updated hourly, from the Mawson Antarctic Station, an Australian scientific outpost at the bottom of the world. Visitors can also click on a link to see Mawson's location on a world map. You and your students can learn more about living in Antarctica by visiting a similar site.

Related Areas: *Science*

Appalachian Log Homes
URL: http://alhloghomes.com/main.phtml

When discussing with your students the different types of homes people live in, head over to this site to view some actual log cabins. What are the benefits of living in such a home?

Archiving Early America
URL: http://earlyamerica.com/

Looking for some 18th century U.S. documents? If so, this site is the place to be, as it warehouses tons of historical documents and maps. Of special note is George Washington's journal of a trip he took to the Ohio Valley and a copy of the first copyright law.

Related Areas: *Language Arts/Languages*

Social Studies

Ask the Amish
URL: http://www.800padutch.com/askamish.html

Lancaster County, Pennsylvania is home to thousands of Amish residents who live separately from modern society and have no modern conveniences, including cars and electricity. The Pennsylvania Dutch Visitors Center offers this Ask An Amish Expert service to allow students from around the world to ask questions concerning this unique American culture.

At Home in the Heartland Online
URL: http://www.museum.state.il.us/exhibits/athome/welcome.htm

This is an interactive museum focusing on Illinois life from 1700 to the present. Students will need to use critical thinking skills to answer the questions provided about the exhibits. Learning goals and objectives are provided for teachers, as are several fun activities.

Related Areas: *Language Arts/Languages; Teacher Resources*

Atlapedia
URL: http://www.atlapedia.com/

The Atlapedia contains key information concerning every country of the world. Each country profile provides facts and data on geography, climate, people, religion, language, history, and economy, making it an ideal site for use by students of all ages.

Related Areas: *Science*

 Integration Idea

> What would it be like to live without the modern conveniences of a regular household? Ask the Amish answers questions about a group of people who live this way today. Compare their lives to the lives of people in the 1800s in Illinois by going back in time with At Home in the Heartland Online. In early America, people built homes made of logs. Even now some people choose log homes, and you can see how these buildings have changed by visiting Appalachian Log Homes. Is it surprising that people still have log homes? Would your students ever choose to give up some of the conveniences that they have?

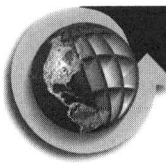

Social Studies

Atlas of the United States
URL: http://fermi.jhuapl.edu/states/states.html

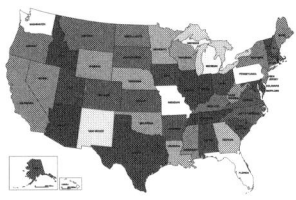

One-stop research is found at this Web site. Students can research all 50 states from this one Web site. Each state listing comes with a topographic map, a county map, and links to Yahoo and other geography-related sites.

Related Areas: *Art & Music; Math; Science*

Atlas of the World
URL: http://cliffie.nosc.mil/~NATLAS/atlas/index.html

A simple site containing maps of every region of the earth. Appropriate for use by both young and old students of geography alike.

Related Areas: *Science*

The Betsy Ross Home Page
URL: http://www.libertynet.org/iha/betsy/index.html

Was there ever really a Betsy Ross who sewed the first U.S. flag? According to the creator of this site, there was! You and your students can find a history of Ross' life, as well as some flag trivia, etiquette, and a picture gallery of different U.S. flags in history.

Big Bus
URL: http://www.pcola.gulf.net/~ptlg/new/BIGBUS.html

What is a world view? Do your students have a world view? If not, this site, which is an online global magazine and forum for kids, should help them look beyond their own backyards. Peruse the articles from students on subjects ranging from Thailand to Coca-Cola, cathedrals to the English language. Listen to different types of music from other countries. Contributions and comments are encouraged.

Related Areas: *Language Arts/Languages; Science; Art & Music*

Social Studies

Biography.com
URL: http://www.biography.com/

This is the official site for the popular A&E show *Biography*. The best things about it are the biography quizzes and anagram games that your students can play online. There's also a database of brief biographies on everyone from Nero to Emile Zola.

The Britannica Guide to Black History
URL: http://www.EB.com:180/blackhistory

 From this site, students can examine nearly 400 years of African-American history through five distinct time periods – from the struggles of slavery through the successes of the Civil Rights Movement.

Cairo: Culture and History
URL: http://pharos.bu.edu/Egypt/Cairo/index2.html

A plush, colorful Web site containing a well-organized collection of information about Cairo, Egypt. Includes an in-depth history of the city and the country, a colorful picture gallery, maps, and much more. Links to related sites are also provided.

 Integration Idea

Encourage your students to look beyond their surroundings by helping them develop a "world view." Big Bus is a great place to start! Your students will read about peacemakers and their countries. One key to the creation of a "world view" is experience. Provide the experiences your students need by touring countries via the Web. Show them the location of each country on the globe by finding it on the Atlas of the World. (Be sure to make Cairo: Culture and History a spot on your tour!) When your class has visited a variety of countries and uncovered the stories of their people and customs, they will be prepared to see with a "world view."

Social Studies

Canadian Museum of Civilization
URL: http://www.cmcc.muse.digital.ca/cmc/cmceng/welcmeng.html

Students will love "The Great Adventure" tour at this Web museum, which "whisks visitors to far-flung corners of the world" to experience cultural diversity. Displays include a Japanese home, Amsterdam architecture, and an Egyptian pyramid.

Castles of the World
URL: http://www.castles.org

What are some of the homes other people have lived in? You can view color photos of castles from all over the world. Each one has an explanation on its construction. Questions about these famous castles can also be sent via email.

Related Areas: *Art & Music; Language Arts/Languages;*

Census Bureau
URL: http://www.census.gov/

Future geographers and cartographers will find plenty to interest them here. Try out the mapping service to generate high-quality, detailed maps, or select a country to get detailed census information on population, housing, education, labor force, income, poverty levels, and much more.

Related Areas: *Science; Math*

City.net
URL: http://www.city.net/

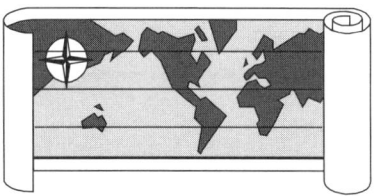

Use this handy site to browse Web sites located around the world, or learn about the various countries on the globe. Just click on any location on the world map at this site and a list of Web servers in that region of the world (or country) is displayed. A unique way to gather data about some of the most popular countries, cities, regions, and continents on planet Earth.

Related Areas: *Language Arts/Languages; Teacher Resources*

Social Studies

The City of Hiroshima
URL: http://www.city.hiroshima.jp

This site gives a brief history of the city of Hiroshima, presents extraordinary photographs of the damage done due to the atomic blast, and discusses the city's commitment to peace.

The Civil War in Miniature
URL: http://serve.aeneas.net/ais/civwamin/

Created by a Civil War buff, this Web site provides a cursory version of the War, complete with historical photos, maps, facts, tidbits, short stories, and graphics.

Civil War Lesson Plan
URL: http://www.smplanet.com/civilwar/civilwar.html

A fully developed lesson plan for a unit on the Civil War. Contains links to other Internet sites, a list of recommended books with plot summaries, ideas for cross-curricular links, and critical thinking activities. Perfect for upper-elementary students.

Related Areas: *Teacher Resources*

Integration Idea

> A common theme in early childhood education is homes. Your students will enjoy learning about the homes of people in other countries with this study. Take them to "The International Village" of the Canadian Museum of Civilization for a tour of homes. Then find Castles of the World to see some unusually large homes. What would it be like to live in one of these homes? Have your students draw comparisons between their own homes and the ones they see on the Web. Talk about the different types of housing that are available, and point out that where you live may determine whether you have a house, apartment, or other home.

Social Studies

Civil War Photograph Collection
URL: http://rs6.loc.gov/cwphome.html

4-6

A must visit for all students studying America's Civil War, the Library of Congress-sponsored Civil War Photographs Collection contains more than 1,000 online images, most of which include scenes of military personnel, preparations for battle, and battles' after-effects. The collection also includes portraits of both Confederate and Union officers, and a selection of enlisted men.

CNN Interactive
URL: http://www.cnn.com/

K-6

This online news site provides up-to-date information on current events. There are news summaries and links for full texts on subjects ranging from politics to travel to entertainment. If you have QuickTime, you can download movies of the latest major news events. How does the information presented on this Web site differ from that presented on television?

CRAYON (Create Your Own Newspaper)
URL: http://www.eg.bucknell.edu/~boulter/crayon

K-6

Students keeping up to date on national, world, and online news will find a wonderful tool at this site. Crayon is the Internet's first free custom newspaper creator. Just click on the name and the contents of your paper, then click on "create." A few seconds later, the newspaper pops up in your Web browser, allowing you to read current headlines from any one of dozens of national newspapers, *Time* magazine, or any other Internet-connected news outlet.

Related Areas: *Language Arts/Languages*

C-SPAN
URL: http://www.c-span.org

4-6

The popular cable TV channel now has an online site featuring live RealAudio coverage of Senate and House floor action. There are also lesson plans for educators and a special feature on Alexis de Tocqueville.

Social Studies

Custer Battlefield Historical and Museum Association
URL: http://intuitive.com/custer

 4-6

A nonprofit educational group, the association focuses on the study and dissemination of information about General Custer, the battle of Little Big Horn, and the Plains Indian Wars. Biographies of Custer, Sitting Bull, and maps of the battlefield can be found here.

Daily Almanac
URL: http://erebus.phys.cwru.edu/~copi/events.html

 4-6

Have your students connect to this site on any day to find out what historical events occurred on this day in history. Also includes sunrise, sunset, special events, days until Christmas, birth and deaths of famous figures, phases of the moon, and more.

Related Areas: *Science; Language Arts/Languages*

Dazhdbog's Grandchildren
URL: http://sunsite.oit.unc.edu/sergei/Grandsons.html

 K-6

Great site revealing the daily life, law, literature, humor, etc., of Russian life. In the mythology section, find out how the Russians got their name!

Related Areas: *Language Arts/Languages; Art & Music*

 Integration Idea

> Welcome your students to the world of current events with the help of online resources. Unlike newspapers that can be outdated by the time they are delivered, these Internet resources are as dynamic as the news they report. CNN Interactive and C-SPAN will inform your class of the day's national and global events. For a look at the date in history, read the Daily Almanac. Compare the recorded historical events of the day with the current happenings. Your students could even use the news reports to create a short "broadcast" that could be given at the beginning of each day.

Social Studies

The Diary of Virginia Park
URL: http://home.sprynet.com/sprynet/robincam/ameliavp.htm

Virginia "Ginger" Park Shook was a close friend of Amelia Earhart for many years. This Web site contains entries from Shook's diary as she and her friend traveled across the country by train in 1912. Images and sounds of Amelia Earhart are also available here.

Related Areas: *Language Arts/Languages*

The Dr. King Timeline Page
URL: http://buckman.pps.k12.or.us/room100/time line/kingframe.html

View and read the descriptions done by a first grade class on Dr. King in the form of a time line. You can also view many other pictures, stories, and activities done by these students.

Related Areas: *Art & Music; Language Arts/Languages*

Earth Day Groceries Project
URL: http://www.halcyon.com/arborhts/earthday.html

Teach your students respect for the earth by participating in this nationwide art activity sponsored by your local grocery store. Joined together on the Internet, thousands of school children have decorated 78,973 paper grocery bags to celebrate Earth Day and increase environmental awareness at their schools and communities. At this site you can read all the reports from past years and find out how to participate for the next one.

Related Areas: *Art & Music; Language Arts/Languages;*

Edison National Historic Site
URL: http://www.nps.gov/edis/ed000000.htm

This site is a wonderful place for your students to learn about one of America's great inventors. The Kid's Corner, for example, has a biography of Edison, descriptions of his inventions, and a time line of his life.

Social Studies

Elections and Electoral Systems Around the World
URL: http://www.keele.ac.uk/depts/po/election.htm

`4-6`

A large database of links organized alphabetically according to country. While you're here, be sure to stop by the other political resources offered at this Web site, like the online list of constitutions and treaties.

Electronic Ellis Island
URL: http://wwwald.bham.wednet.edu/museum/museum.htm

`K-3`

Alderwood Elementary School in Bellingham, Washington would like to invite you to their Virtual Museum! Their mission statement is to chronicle and celebrate the diversity of the many cultures around our world through the eyes of children. An excellent example of getting kids involved with educational technology at an early age.

Related Areas: *Technology/Internet*

Encyclopedia of Women's History
URL: http://www.teleport.com/~megaines/women.html

`K-6`

What began as a way for students to participate in Women's History Month has evolved into a Web site featuring descriptions of women throughout history, with charming spins that only children could give. There are also hyperlinks to other women's history sites and the U.S. Census' statistics on women in America.

Integration Idea

Best friends are very important, and even famous people in history have had these special people in their lives. The Diary of Virginia Park tells the story of young girls on an exciting trip. As you read the diary, you will discover that one of these young women was Amelia Earhart! Earhart is also listed at the Encyclopedia of Women's History. Read the description of her there, and compare the historical representation with the young girl described by Virginia Park. Remind your class that all great heroes have grown up and often experienced many of the same things that they deal with every day, including having good friends.

Social Studies

Ethnologue Database

URL: http://www.sil.org/ethnologue/

A completely statistical guide to possibly every language spoken around the world. For some eye-opening statistics about Native American languages, check out the U.S.A. section.

Everton's Genealogical Helper

URL: http://www.everton.com/

Designed for the beginner researcher as well as the more experienced genealogist, this site can help you and your students research their family trees. If you're doing a unit on genealogy, you'll find the site a must with its online resources, libraries, search engines, and biweekly magazine.

Exploring Ancient World Cultures

URL: http://eawc.evansville.edu/index.htm

This Web site focuses its magnifying glass on eight ancient world cultures: Egypt, China, Greece, the Roman Empire, the Islamic World, India, and Medieval Europe. An overview of each culture, its significance, and essays on the importance of studying ancient cultures are all included here.

Extend a Hand to Help

URL: http://www.intac.com/PubService/rwanda/fund

After discussing community help and foreign aid, your students can pick a nonprofit organization from this large online index to send a donation. Descriptions are provided about each humanitarian aid group.

Social Studies

FedWorld
URL: http://www.fedworld.gov/

The National Technical Information Service (NTIS) introduced FedWorld in November 1992 to help with the challenge of accessing U.S. government information online. In an electronic age when more and more government agencies are racing to get online, FedWorld can help you keep up with the flood of information worldwide by providing a comprehensive central access point for locating and acquiring government information. More than 130 government bulletin boards and databases can be accessed here.

FleetHouse: Canada
URL: http://www.fleethouse.com/fhcanada/fhc_expl.htm#panel

FleetHouse: Canada, a Vancouver, British Columbia based electronic publication, is your comprehensive guide to Canadian travel. Use this site to create a bulletin board explaining about life in Canada. Draw a flag for each province, calculate the refund on the seven percent tax you will be owed, and write about the country's history.

Related Areas: *Art & Music; Language Arts/Languages; Math; Science; Social Studies;*

Flints and Stones
URL: http://www.ncl.ac.uk/~nantiq/menu.html

Welcome to the Stone Age! This exhibition takes your students you into the lives of the inhabitants of Britain and northwest Europe, where you must hunt and gather for survival. Try the food quiz at this site to see if you could survive as a hunter/gatherer today.

> **Integration Idea**
>
> Here you will find two sites to complement a study of world cultures. Exploring Ancient World Cultures introduces your students to several ancient cultures with all of the information you need to explain their development. Flints and Stones addresses the lifestyle of the Stone Age hunter/gatherers. Compare the behaviors and societal patterns of these groups. Your students may work in groups, each assigned to an ancient people, and create projects of their choosing that reflect an understanding of how the people lived.

Social Studies

From Revolution to Reconstruction
URL: http://odur.let.rug.nl/~welling/usa/revolution.html

This site is an American history textbook complete with graphics and historical essays. Each summary gives a complete account of American history from the colonial period to modern times.

Related Areas: *Language Arts/Languages; Teacher Resources*

From the Ground Up
URL: http://www.GateWest.net/~green/

From the Ground Up began as a teachers' lesson guide on food, agriculture, and sustainable development. This online version is divided into five lessons: the history of agriculture and a description of sustainable development; soil; agriculture and chemicals; the real cost of food; and how these elements are connected. This site is adaptable to meet the needs of intermediate-level students.

Related Areas: *Science; Math; Language Arts/Languages; Teacher Resources*

Frontline Online
URL: http://www.pbs.org/wgbh/pages/frontline/

In the past few years, PBS's show *Frontline* has delivered some of the best news stories on television. Now, many of their best episodes are online, along with teacher guides, transcripts, maps, RealAudio excerpts, charts, graphics, expanded interviews, readings, discussion boards, and more. Perfect for upper-elementary students and beyond!

Related Areas: *Teacher Resources; Language Arts/Languages*

GeoGame Project
URL: http://www.gsn.org/gsn/proj/geog/

Sponsored by the Global SchoolNet, the GeoGame Project is a popular, email-based activity that helps students learn geographic terms, learn how to read and interpret maps, and increase awareness of geographical and cultural diversity.

Social Studies

Geography Quiz
URL: http://hammer.ne.highway1.com/trivia/geogfram/geogfram.html

Created by a fourth grade teacher in Massachusetts, this Web page offers a new geography quiz question for elementary-aged students each week during the regular school year. Links to related interactive maps and resources are also provided.

GeoNet Game
URL: http://www.hmco.com/hmco/school/geo/indexlo.html

Students can play a game that tests their knowledge of geography. There are a series of six games, all focusing on knowledge of the different areas of the United States, including the south, northeast, Midwest, and west.

Related Areas: *Language Arts/Languages*

Global Online Adventure Learning
URL: http://www.goals.com

Explorers of all ages will get a kick out of this site, which follows the real-life adventures of scientific investigators from around the world. Follow the young Laffitte brothers as they travel across the Pacific Ocean, or Karen Thorndike as she attempts to be the first woman to single-handedly sail around the world. In the process, students learn about global navigation, geography, and strengthen their map skills!

Related Areas: *Science*

 Integration Idea

Have you been wondering how it might be possible to spice up your geography lessons? Then these sites are for you! Global Online Adventure Learning exposes your students to geographical concepts masked in adventurous expeditions. In addition, the GeoGame Project and GeoNet Game are enjoyable activities that incorporate map usage and geographical knowledge. The Geography Quiz is a page with a new question every week for your explorers to tackle. Use these sites as enrichment activities to liven the ho-hum daily lessons of geography.

Social Studies

The Great Chicago Fire and the Web of Memory
URL: http://www.chicagohs.org/fire/index.html

The legend says that Mrs. O'Leary's cow was responsible for the fire that destroyed Chicago. But what really happened? This site combines known facts, legends, and multimedia with various eyewitness accounts for a fascinating examination of the most memorable blaze in U.S. history.

Related Areas: *Language Arts/Languages*

Great Kiva Online
URL: http://www.sscf.ucsb.edu/anth/projects/great.kiva/

Students of Native American architecture, music, and artifacts will find lots to love about this site! It contains a three-dimensional reconstruction of a Great Kiva, an architectural feature found in many prehistoric Anasazi communities in the Southwestern U.S. This particular model was created using archaeological records from the excavated Chetro Ketl Great Kiva, which is located in Chaco Canyon in northwestern New Mexico.

The Hall of Multiculturalism
URL: http://www.tenet.edu/academia/multi.html

This rich site is a must-visit for educators looking for links to the latest online multicultural resources. You'll find links to the Multicultural Pavilion, the Africa Home Page, Japan Window, Diversity Links, Hispanic Heritage, and more.

Hawaii's Cultural and Educational Page
URL: http://www.search-hawaii.com/hawaii/vacation/culture.shtml

Students can be tour guides for Hawaii after visiting this site. Incorporate all the subjects by holding a Hawaiian culture fair. Students can use math skills to purchase shirts, caps, and hotel rooms. After learning how canoes are made, try to make one out of foil and see if it will float holding one paper clip at a time. The activities are endless.

Related Areas: *Art & Music; Language Arts/Languages; Math; Social Studies; Science*

Social Studies

Henry Ford Museum and Greenfield Village K-6
URL: http://hfm.umd.umich.edu/index.html

Celebrate the spirit of innovations in America at this site. The Henry Ford Museum is filled with objects created by innovative men and women in the fields of transportation, communication, agriculture, industry, domestic life, and the decorative arts. Check out the featured exhibits which examine the world of Motown and American clock makers, for example.

History Index K-6
URL: http://galaxy.tradewave.com/galaxy/Social-Sciences/History.html

Head over to this extensive index, created by the World Wide Web Library, when you're having trouble finding Net information on a particular historical subject or time period.

Related Areas: *Teacher Resources*

The History/Genocide Project 4-6
URL: http://www.iearn.org/iearn/hgp/

This international, nonprofit, telecommunications project focuses on the Holocaust in an effort to promote education and awareness about one of the most brutal and harrowing periods of history. Features include lesson plans and information on study trips.

Related Areas: *Teacher Resources*

 Integration Idea

> How can your students tour an archaeological site as it was when its creators built it? The Internet provides virtual tours for just this purpose. One such tour is Great Kiva Online, an excellent journey through a model of a building of the Anasazi, ancestors of the Pueblo. Take the tour of the Great Kiva, and then visit The Hall of Multiculturalism for their list of Native American resources. What Native American archaeological sites are currently being excavated? Create some Native American art based on the samples at the Kiva and the other resources.

Social Studies

The History Buff's Page
URL: http://www.historybuff.com

With a extensive, searchable, library, students interested in conduction research on the history of America or journalism should find something of interest here. Did you know Edgar Allen Poe created a newspaper hoax about a balloon?

The History Channel Time Machine
URL: http://www.historychannel.com/

Speeches, problem-solving games, exhibits with audio clips, teacher's guides, resource lists, a calendar of events you can contribute to, and lots more are all available at this comprehensive site, an online extension of the popular cable TV channel. Primary students can team up with intermediate students by drawing a picture of a time machine and listening to them read the information or by playing games together.

Related Areas: *Language Arts/Languages; Art & Music*

History in the USA
URL: http://www.historyplace.com/tourism/usa.htm

Travel to see all of the historic sites in the United States via the Web. All sites have beautiful pictures and explanations. Some sites have audio!

Related Areas: *Art & Music; Language Arts/Languages; Teacher Resources*

The History Net
URL: http://www.thehistorynet.com/

Sponsored by the National Historical Society and the History Group of Cowles Enthusiast Media, this may be the most extensive and content-rich site devoted to history on the Internet. With hundreds of articles and images taken from issues of various history-related magazines, the site offers something to all students of history—whether they're studying American history, world history, famous wars, the wild West, or women's history. There are eyewitness accounts of world-turning events, personality profiles of people who made history, interviews with noted historians and heroes, and daily history quizzes to keep you on your toes.

Related Areas: Language Arts/Languages

Social Studies

History of Piracy
URL: http://www.filmzone.com/cutthroat/highseas/highseas.html

Arrrr me hearties! Head over to this site to shiver your timbers and rattle your bones! Learn about some real pirate rogues and hear of the horrible games they would play and what would happen to the losers. Find out how pirates meted out justice, what they ate, and meet the source of virtually all the pirate legends we know today.

The History Place
URL: http://www.historyplace.com

This visually elegant Web site offers graphic time lines of World War Two and the life of Abraham Lincoln. Also included is a photo journal of JFK, a featured speech of the week, and a hot list of historically related tourist sites.

Holidays on the Net
URL: http://www.holidays.net/

The Holidays Web site contains information not only on Thanksgiving, Martin Luther King, Jr. Day, Christmas, and Valentine's Day, but also on Passover, Ramadan, and other less known holidays. The sites contain facts and information about each holiday, along with links to other sites that may contain games, recipes, and much more.

 Integration Idea

> Kids are always interested in pirates, and the History of Piracy Web site is just the place for them to get all of the details about the guys they love to hate. Your students can then discover that there is more to the story of William Kidd, the famous captain and well-known pirate, when they search for him at The History Net. Like the outlaws of the old west, the infamy of pirates has led to a form of idolization among young people. Your students will get the whole story from these sites that will likely change their views of piracy.

Social Studies

Horus
URL: http://www.ucr.edu/h-gig/horuslinks.html

K-6

If you're searching for quality historical information on the Net, you can do no better than Horus, a comprehensive, well-organized index of history sites on the Web. The site is grouped into four different categories: histories of specific countries and places; areas of history; online services about history; and Web tools.

Related Areas: *Technology/Internet; Teacher Resources*

How a Bill Becomes a Law
URL: http://www.vote-smart.org/reference/primer/billlaw.html

4-6

Students will learn through this online document step by step how a bill becomes a law and what the responsibility is for each branch. They will also be introduced to legal terms defined in the article on which they can be assessed.

Related Areas: *Teacher Resources; Language Arts/Languages*

How Far Is It?
URL: http://www.indo.com/distance/

4-6

Using this site, students can find the distance between cities, their populations, latitude and longitude, elevation, and telephone area code. Visitors type in the names of the cities, like New York and London for example, in the appropriate areas and click on the "Look it up" button. Within a matter of seconds the shortest distance between the cities is displayed. You can also link to an online map if you want to view the cities.

Related Areas: *Math; Science*

Human Rights Web
URL: http://www.hrweb.org

4-6

Includes an introduction to human rights, a short history of the human rights movement, biographies of prisoners of conscience, human rights legal and political documents, and human rights issues, debates, and discussions. Appropriate for use by gifted elementary students.

Social Studies

Ice Ages

4-6

URL: http://www.museum.state.il.us/exhibits/ice_ages/

This interactive museum takes you and your students on a step-by-step trip through the Ice Ages. Students are given three questions to answer before they begin to ensure comprehension. A great way to begin learning about the prehistoric world.

Related Areas: *Language Arts/Languages; Science*

India Online

4-6

URL: http://IndiaOnline.com/

Learn all about India via this Web site designed to be a "one-stop kiosk for information on the Indian Subcontinent." Students visiting here will discover new things about Indian society, culture, and food.

 Integration Idea

How many times have your students told you that you were not being fair? Fairness is extremely important to elementary students. This is why they will be so surprised to read about the oppressive conditions people endure in other countries. Human Rights Web will explain these problems to your students. Have them research countries with unresolved human rights issues at the Index of Resources for Historians. They can share their findings with their classmates.

Social Studies

Israeli Keypals
URL: http://ietn.snunit.k12.il/keypals.OLD.htm

Are you planning a lesson or activity that could be made more dynamic by connecting your students to individuals or a class in Israel? You'll find links to lists of classes seeking Israeli keypals, and Israeli classes seeking keypals in other parts of the world.

Related Areas: *Teacher Resources*

Kelsey Museum of Archaeology
URL: http://www.umich.edu/~kelseydb/

The Kelsey Museum displays artifacts found during digs made by the University of Michigan from 1926 to 1935. Head to the Greek and Roman Gallery at this Web site to view the head of a satyr or visit the Egyptian and Near East gallery to find a gold mask from an Egyptian mummy.

Related Areas: *Science*

Kids Connected
URL: http://www.ncss.org/online/kids/home.html

Sponsored by the National Council for Social Studies, Kids Connected takes you to places where you can look at live pictures from around the world, listen to TV stars talk about school, and find fun sites to surf. As the site says, "You'll find cool stuff from around the world here and if you're not careful, you might learn something about social studies, too."

Related Areas: *Teacher Resources*

Kids Do Care
URL: http://www1.sympatico.ca/Contents/DNA/kidsdocare/

Kids Do Care is a new Web project aimed at getting kids involved with activism and the federal government. It's specifically aimed at Canadian kids, but there's no reason that students from other countries can't take advantage of the resources here too! "Political Friends" section allows visitors to send questions to the Prime Minister of Canada, while "What do you think" provides a chance for kids to talk about their concerns. There are also several surveys and tips on how to help out in your community and government.

Social Studies

Kids Voting USA
URL: http://www.kidsvotingusa.org

Did you know that kids can vote? Thanks to Kids Voting USA, a nonprofit, nonpartisan, grassroots program, students in 40 states will be able to go to official polls, with parents and guardians in tow, and cast their own ballots in their own polling booths on the same issues and candidates as adults do. The group's central aim is to teach the importance of being informed and of voting.

Kid's Window
URL: http://jw.stanford.edu:80/KIDS/kids_home.html

Ever wonder what a leaky faucet sounds like in Japan? How about a turkey? If so, head over to the Kid's Window site, a fun and interactive look at the land of the rising sun designed especially for kids. There are recipes to try, language and origami classes, popular Japanese folk tales in both Japanese and English, a reference picture dictionary, and sound bites galore!

Related Areas: *Language Arts/Languages*

LatinoLink
URL: http://www.latinolink.com/

This site is perfect for integration into your social studies curriculum and for use by Latino students. The site contains engaging stories and articles, columns, and photography dealing with important political and social issues in the Latino world.

Related Areas: *Language Arts/Languages; Art & Music*

 Integration Idea

> Elections are very exciting for people who follow them and know the candidates and issues. Your students will become a part of the election frenzy when they visit Kids Voting USA. Voting, however, is not the only part of being a good citizen. Kids will find a list of books related to democracy and citizenship from Kids Connected. Encourage your class to describe a good citizen, and email a world leader with their opinions. You may reach the Prime Minister of Canada through Kids Do Care. An early start is one way to promote awareness of current events and politics among young people!

Social Studies

Learning about the Senate
URL: http://www.senate.gov/about/index.html

This site informs you about the senate and allows for visitors to email comments to senators. Take your students on a tour through the history of Congress and its members. Included is a glossary of terms and a virtual tour through the United States Capitol with descriptions of each room.

Related Areas: *Language Arts/Languages*

The Library in the Sky
URL: http://www.nwrel.org/sky/Classroom/Social_Studies/Multicultural/Multicultural.html

This is an excellent site to gather information for social studies reports on cultures, languages, and countries. Each site is broken down into subsites for greater detail and includes a lesson plan. Beware: some sites tend to take awhile to download.

Related Areas: *Art & Music; Language Arts/Languages; Teacher Resources*

Magellan Global Adventure
URL: http://www.schurmann.com.br/ingles/index.htm

Make history or at least watch it as it happens! Learn about Magellan and his historical adventure while watching it come alive day by day through the Schurmann sailing crew. Lesson activities will be provided along with photographs and an email address so your students can have their questions answered.

Related Areas: *Math; Science; Teacher Resources; Technology/Internet*

Map Stats
URL: http://www.census.gov/datamap/www/index.html

Students can work on learning the 50 states by viewing this online map. State abbreviations are provided, and students can guess the state name before clicking on it and viewing its name and flag.

Social Studies

Mapmaker, Mapmaker, Make Me a Map
URL: http://loki.ur.utk.edu/ut2Kids/maps/map.html

Meet Will Fontenez, a cartographer at University of Tennessee. Fontenez has created a Web site for young students that describes the many different kinds of maps available such as political, physical, road, and weather. Be sure to have your class try the mapmaker crossword puzzle.

Related Areas: *Science*

Maps in the News
URL: http://www-map.lib.umn.edu/news.html

Contains detailed maps of cities and countries currently in the news. Current offerings include Bosnia, the Middle East, and Taiwan.

Related Areas: *Science*

Mariners' Museum
URL: http://www.mariner.org/

Located in Newport News, Va., the Mariner's Museum is one of the most prestigious Maritime museums in the world, documenting over 3000 years of seafaring. This online tour includes the Museum's permanent and temporary collections, and an extensive trip through the history of man's relationship with the sea. There are photos galore, "Marifacts" of the month, information on educational opportunities, upcoming events and exhibitions, and, of course, the museum shop.

Related Areas: *Art & Music*

 Integration Idea

Develop map skill in your students by using these map sites. Map Stats will help students in recalling capitals while Mapmaker gives examples of types of maps and a glossary of mapping terms. Mapmaker also has a downloadable crossword puzzle that can be used for assessment. Use Maps in the News to incorporate current events in your geography lessons.

Social Studies

Martin Luther King, Jr.
URL: http://www.seattletimes.com/mlk/index.html

 Martin Luther King, Jr., the man, the movement, and his legacy are all discussed at this site, sponsored by the *Seattle Times*. Your students can follow past dialogues between students from Alabama and Washington or take an interactive quiz. The study guide for teachers helps make the site effective in the classroom.

Related Areas: *Teacher Resources*

Maya Quest '97
URL: http://www.mecc.com/maya97/

This exciting site changes weekly. It is an on going search for the lost Mayan cities. Researchers communicate with schools via email as they are on their trip. You can have students calculate miles or rolls of film, write newspaper columns, or draw pictures of what they think Mayan cities would have looked like.

Related Areas: *Art & Music; Math; Language Arts/Languages; Science; Social Studies; Teacher Resources*

Monticello
URL: http://www.monticello.org/

 Visit the Virginia home of Thomas Jefferson, Monticello online. A Day in the Life takes your class through the entire day with Jefferson. A Matter of Fact gives your class many details on Jefferson's accomplishments, and younger children can click on the kid's section to find letters written to Jefferson by modern-day students.

Related Areas: *Language Arts/Languages*

Mount Vernon Educational Resources
URL: http://www.mountvernon.org/education/

George Washington is waiting to have you over for a visit at his home on the Web. You and your students can tour his plantation, learn about his life, see some famous pictures of home, and then take an online quiz to see what you learned.

Related Areas: *Teacher Resources; Language Arts/Languages*

Social Studies

Multicultural Book Reviews for K–12
URL: http://www.isomedia.com/homes/jmele/joe.html

Reviews, written by educators, of African-American, Jewish, Asian, and Latino children's literature. Included are reading grade levels and easy-to-understand ratings. Contributions are encouraged so feel free to submit!

Related Areas: *Art & Music; Language Arts/Languages; Teacher Resources;*

Multicultural Calendar
URL: http://www.kidlink.org:80/KIDPROJ/MCC/

Find out how people celebrate common holidays, such as Christmas and New Year's in America and Europe, as well as more unusual holidays like the Hindu celebration of Deepavali in Malaysia. The calendar is always growing and your students are welcome to add their own entries. Also included are ideas for teachers to incorporate the calendar into their lesson plans.

Related Areas: *Teacher Resources*

Multicultural Mask
URL: http://arlo.wilsonhs.pps.k12.or.us/masks.html

This is an excellent way to incorporate cooperative learning, art, social studies, and literature into one fun project. This project could be adapted to primary if paper plates were used and done as a teacher lead project.

Related Areas: *Art & Music; Language Arts/Languages*

 Integration Idea

Incorporate visits to the homes of past and present presidents using the Monticello and the Mount Vernon sites. These sites will show your students pictures of the estates and give them background on the president who lived there. Conclude your lesson by going to the White House. See pg. 220 for the address.

Social Studies

Multicultural Thematic Curriculum Planner on Native Americans

URL: http://www.lennox.k12.ca.us/lessonplan/NatAm/ThemPlanNA.html

With this extensive third grade cross curricular unit, your students will learn about Native American art, geography, literature, and lifestyle. An assessment and resource list are included.

Related Areas: *Art & Music; Health/PE; Language Arts/Languages; Math; Science; Teacher Resources*

Multicultural Trivia Challenge

URL: http://dune.srhs.k12.nj.us/WWW/trivia/welcome.htm

"I ordered my courtiers to kiss my dead wife's hands as she sat enthroned next to me. She was rotting already, but I didn't care. Who am I?" Think your students might know the answer? How about yourself? This fun, regularly updated social studies contest is open to students and teachers of all grade levels, although each challenge can only have one student winner and one teacher winner. Winners will be determined by the earliest submitted correct answer along with an honor roll of the next ten runners-up. The questions are tough, but don't worry. If you don't know the answer you can always contribute your own fun multicultural fact to the Web site.

Related Areas: *Technology/Internet; Language Arts/Languages*

Mungo Park

URL: http://www.mungopark.msn.com

Social studies teachers will find lots to love about Microsoft's Network's Mungo Park online adventure magazine! The site provides exciting, provocative, and timely stories, as well as incredible sound, video clips, and file photos of great expeditions and adventures. Mungo Park has four main sections: Interactive Expeditions, which retraces the steps of famous explorers; At the Park, which is a place to participate in live chats with explorers; World Lit, which features contributions from best-selling authors, who are invited to take an adventure travel trip and then pen an essay exclusively for Mungo Park; and Drum, which includes regular columns written by other journalists and writers worldwide.

Related Areas: *Science; Language Arts/Languages*

Social Studies

My Hero
URL: http://www.myhero.com/

My Hero! is an interactive, online project for students at all levels. At the heart of the project is the belief that there are and always have been positive role models for children. My Hero! draws much needed attention to the unsung heroes in every community and walk of life.

Related Areas: *Teacher Resources; Technology/Internet; Science; Math; Health/PE; Art & Music; Language Arts/Languages*

National Geographic Online
URL: http://www.nationalgeographic.com/

This incredible free online service gives you and your students access to exclusive *National Geographic* content that's updated every day. Simply apply for your online "passport" at the home page, then click on the icons to link directly to content-rich articles, maps, geography quizzes, and more. Chat with Society photographers, writers, and artists, and exchange ideas with the leading scientific minds of our time.

Related Areas: *Science*

National Performance Review Home Page
URL: http://www.npr.gov/

Students can access this interactive World Wide Web home page and help reinvent the U.S. government. Students can examine U.S. National Performance Review documents, access Vice President Al Gore's Electronic Open Meeting, and search a database of reinvention success stories. After visiting, they can offer their suggestions for improvements.

Second to fourth grade teachers will find the Native American unit very helpful for increasing their repertoire of thematic lessons. This site will give you ideas for such subjects as art, literature, and math. This site also includes various book titles. In addition, the Multicultural trivia site lends itself to a computer center by sponsoring a daily trivia question. Have students work in pairs to research the answers and submit their findings. Integrate other cultures into your thematic unit by sending students to the National Geographic site.

Social Studies

National Public Radio
URL: http://www.npr.org/

Students interested in current events can tune into this Web site to keep up with the latest news developments every hour. In addition, there are special features on national elections, music, and other cultural programs. You need the RealAudio plug-in to be able to listen to the broadcasts however.

Related Areas: *Language Arts/Languages; Art & Music*

A Nation Divided—
The U.S. Civil War 1861–1865
URL: http://www.historyplace.com/civilwar/index.html

You can use this site to help with research or build interest in the Civil War. The photos and their captions are a great source of information.

Related Areas: *Language Arts/Languages; Teacher Resources*

Native American Pow Wow Singers
URL: http://niikaan.fdl.cc.mn.us/fdltcc/guest/spirit/home.html

Created by a group of pow wow singers in the Western U.S., this Web site contains background information, photographs, sound clips, and links to other sites related to one of the oldest traditions in the Native American culture. A fascinating site about a still largely misunderstood culture.

Related Areas: *Art & Music*

Native Net
URL: http://www.fdl.cc.mn.us/natnet/

NativeNet is designed to promote dialogue and understanding regarding indigenous peoples of all parts of the world, as well as current threats to their cultures and habitats (such as the rainforest).

Social Studies

North American Steam Locomotive
URL: http://www.arc.umn.edu/~wes/steam.html

Enhance your lessons on transportation by visiting these train museums via the Web. This site has spectacular color photos of famous locomotives in history with descriptions. Some pages will take awhile to download however.

Related Areas: *Art & Music; Teacher Resources*

Notable Citizens of Planet Earth
URL: http://www.tiac.net/users/parallax/

This online biographical dictionary contains incredible information about more than 18,000 people — from ancient times to the present day. Information includes birth and death years, professions, positions held, and other achievements. The dictionary is completely searchable as well.

Online Map Creation
URL: http://www.aquarius.geomar.de/omc/omc_intro.html

Here's a great, interactive way to teach students about mapmaking and geography. Visitors fill out an online form, submit their entries, and a Web page featuring their simple map creation will be returned to their browser. This map can later be saved onto your computer for printing. You can include political boundaries, bodies of water, or the topography. If you are unfamiliar with certain terms, fear not. There's several helpful how-to pages to aid first-time visitors with their map creations.

Related Areas: *Math; Science*

 Integration Idea

> Integrate current events and research into your study of Native Americans by using the Pow Wow Singers site, Notable Citizens, and Native Net. These sites keep a collection of articles dealing with current issues concerning Native Americans as well as historical facts. Have students download the music samples from the Pow Wow singers and discuss what sound they are hearing and why is the drum so important. Incorporate how the Civil War affected native American life through the information on the Nation Divided site.

Social Studies

Online NewsHour
URL: http://www1.pbs.org/newshour/

The NewsHour with Jim Leher recently began offering the latest breaking news on the Web, which is professionally presented by a Net-savvy team of online journalists. The site offers direct, online links to the journalists who write each day's offerings, and forums where debates take place on a variety of topics. One of the best news sites on the Web.

Operation Desert Storm
URL: http://www.geocities.com/Athens/6506/

Your students will find plenty of information on all of the aspects of this war, including weapons, soldiers, POWs, and military presence. The soldiers section includes interviews and profiles. There's even information on how your class can send care packages and letters to soldiers still in the Gulf and Bosnia.

The Original Titanic Home Page
URL: http://gil.ipswichcity.qld.gov.au/~dalgarry/

Created by a 13-year-old Webmaster and Titanic aficionado, visitors can get a tour of the ship from its builder, meet the passengers and crew, and otherwise read about "the ship that God couldn't sink."

Oyez Oyez Oyez
URL: http://oyez.at.nwu.edu/oyez.html

This U.S. Supreme Court Web resource offers online audio files of complete oral arguments of many of the landmark cases argued before the court. Your students can access dozens of these files, including *Roe vs. Wade* and *United States vs. Nixon*. Background information and the voting record are provided for each case.

Related Areas: *Language Arts/Languages*

Social Studies

Parliamentary Elections Around the World   4-6
URL: http://www.universal.nl/users/derksen/election/home.htm

 Wondering when Albania holds their national elections? If so, head over to this site, which not only lists election dates for most countries, but the various political parties and their leanings as well.

PBS Democracy Project   4-6
URL: http://www.pbs.org/democracy

This project is specifically focusing on engaging youths in civic education and the democratic process. The "Correspond with correspondents" section, for example, enables students to interview reporters. Eligible voters can also find out how and where to register.

The Peters Projection Project   4-6
URL: http://www.webcom.com/~bright/petermap.html

Maps help create our world view. They tell us who we are in relation to the others on the earth. The Peters Projection was created in 1974 to address some of the problems of existing maps, including distortions and biases. The importance of the Peters map goes beyond its superior portrayal of sizes and proportions. It leads visitors to a new view of the world. One square inch anywhere on this map is equal to the same number of square miles.

Related Areas: *Science*

 Integration Idea

Make the study of civics a hands-on project for students. Students can compare how other countries conduct parliamentary election to our election system by visiting the Parliamentary Elections Web site. Explain that our country depends on volunteers, challenge your students to volunteer in their neighborhoods, and send them to the PBS Democracy Project to learn more on civics. This site also offers lesson ideas for teachers.

Social Studies

Photo Tour of the Civil Rights Movement
URL: http://www.seattletimes.com/mlk/movement/PT/phototour.html

This is an excellent introductory site to begin discussion on the Civil Rights Movement. The photos begin with Rosa Parks in 1956 and continue up to the election of the first female black governor in 1989. The extensive list of photos encourage discussion and come along with well-written descriptions.

Related Areas: *Language Arts/Languages; Teacher Resources*

Powerful Symbols
URL: http://www.powersource.com/gallery/objects/default.html

This site works well in conjunction with a lesson on Native Americans as it discusses the way different tribes viewed animals and nature according to their beliefs. Each animal is described briefly and some have a folk tale to follow. Created by a wired Cherokee tribe.

Related Areas: *Art & Music; Language Arts/Languages*

Presidents of the United States
URL: http://www.ipl.org/ref/POTUS/

Your students will learn many interesting facts about each United States president including background information, election results, cabinet members, presidency highlights, and some other odd facts. There are also links to biographies, historical documents, and audio/visual files.

Project Cape Town: Education and Integration in South Africa
URL: http://curry.edschool.Virginia.EDU/go/capetown/home.html

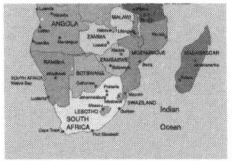

Anyone studying culture or race relations, whether in America or around the world, should make this site a priority. It draws its material from three schools in the South African capital that were among the first to become racially integrated, immediately prior to the election of Nelson Mandela. Text, still images, sound, and video depict four actual scenarios where teachers were challenged with educating children whose cultures were different from their own. Visitors are asked to compare the different classes and provide their own comments on the situation.

Related Areas: *Language Arts/Languages*

Project Central America
URL: http://www.adventureonline.com/pca/

K-6

You and your students will enjoy Project Central America, an adventure-driven, distance learning project that focuses on the myriad number of countries beneath the United States. Educators and cyclists traveled 1900 miles throughout Central America visiting classrooms and various points of interest. Stop in and learn all about it.

Rabbit in the Moon
URL: http://www.halfmoon.org/

While a lot of the information here is aimed at Mayan experts, students should cruise by as well. The most notable part is the virtual tour of a Mayan Governor's house that can be downloaded. The site also contains a language chart, sound files and hieroglyphics, information on Mayan books, instructional materials, and workshops. You can even send a Mayan greeting card to a friend!

Related Areas: *Art & Music; Math; Teacher Resources*

Radio Free Europe
URL: http://www.rferl.org/

Radio Free Europe/Radio Liberty broadcasts news and current affairs programs daily in two dozen languages to 25 million listeners across Central Europe and the former Soviet Union. This site is a treasure trove of information for students looking for the "other side of the story" as told by local journalists reporting live from these important countries—both in English and their native languages.

Related Areas: *Language Arts/Languages*

 Integration Idea

Increase students' knowledge of other cultures by visiting the Cape Town and Central America sites. At Cape Town, students will be able read how a once segregated country is now dealing with integration in their schools. Then take your students to Central America and let them explore the area online. Assign each student a country to research and complete a poster which lists general information, economic statistics, government information, and a picture of their flag.

Social Studies

Regia Anglorum—Anglo-Saxon, Viking, Norman, and British Living History
URL: http://www.ftech.net/~regia/regblurb.htm

Explore the life and crafts of the late Viking Age Britain. This "living history" Web site is centered around a reconstructed village of the time. Related articles with wonderful pictures show the weapons, warfare, and crafts of the day, such as leather working, glass and amber working, and braid weaving.

Related Areas: *Art & Music; Language Arts/Languages*

RETANet
URL: http://ladb.unm.edu/retanet/

RETANet (Resources for Teaching about the Americas) makes accessible resources and curriculum materials about Latin America, the Spanish Caribbean, and the U.S. Southwest. Visitors can find more that 65 lesson plans dealing with culture studies, a searchable annotated database of resource materials, and an archive of photographs of Latin America and the Caribbean. Teachers can also collaborate with their Spanish-speaking counterparts in a bilingual chat area.

Related Areas: *Language Arts/Languages; Teacher Resources*

The Royal British Columbia Museum
URL: http://rbcm1.rbcm.gov.bc.ca/

This Web version of one of the largest museums in the world includes exhibits such as Natural History, Modern History, Open Oceans, and First Peoples. The fascinating displays range from the soft-bodied Vampire Squid to totem poles.

Related Areas: *Science*

Running the Nile 1996
URL: http://www.adventureonline.com/nile/index.html

Class activities, maps, and pictures are included at this site. Students can view different maps of Uganda, figure out the temperature change mathematically, study the history of Uganda, read a message from their king, learn the language, or listen to the national anthem. This site has it all. You will need to click on Uganda background to access some of this information.

Related Areas: *Art & Music; Language Arts/Languages; Math; Science; Teacher Resources*

 **Social Studies**

Russia on the Net
URL: http://www.ru

 A large database of Russian and Russia-related Web resources. Organized in a friendly, colorful subject tree, you'll find links to the Russian media and news outlets, arts and culture, business, government and legislation, science and education, and personal Web pages created by Russians about their homeland.

Seeds of Change
URL: http://horizon.nmsu.edu/garden/

Sponsored by the Smithsonian Institution, this educational Web site teaches about diversity and history by looking at the evolution of agriculture and cuisine throughout the world. For each season of the year, you'll find some great activities to explore, and plenty of advice on how to create your own school garden. In addition, your students can learn about why what we eat and grow helps to determine our culture, and how the search for food has changed the course of history — most notably in 1492.

Related Areas: *Science*

The Seri Cultural Center
URL: http://www.folkart.com/~latitude/sonora/culture.htm

Explore the world of the Seri Indians, who live in the desert by the sea. Their environment has shaped their lives, and this is reflected in their art. See sculptures made out of ironwood, which is so heavy it sinks—or learn about baskets woven so tightly they hold water.

Related Areas: *Art & Music*

 Integration Idea

> Send your students on a cultural information seek and find. Explain that they will be given 20 minutes to find the answers to questions from the Regina Anglorum, RETNA, Running the 1996, Russia on the Net, or the Seri Center site. Have students work in pairs on only one site. Once they are done have them present the information to the class. As a side note, the RETANet site has links to various Latin American embassies and their snail mail addresses that your students can contact.

Social Studies

Sitka, Alaska
URL: http://www.sitka.com/

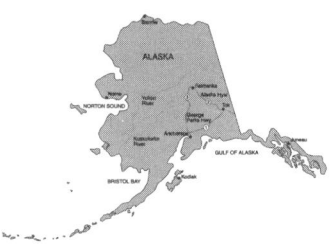

Visit Alaska and see the sites. You can teach across the curriculum with this site. Students can figure the cost of a room, recreation and food while studying the history and lifestyles of Sitka, Alaska. Students can also view the Web pages of other Alaskan students and send them email.

Related Areas: *Art & Music; Teacher Resources; Language Arts/Languages; Math; Science*

Smoky Says
URL: http://www.smokeybear.com/index.html

Only you can prevent forest fires, and at this site Smoky gives you his rules for fire safety. There are several games students can play to test their fire safety knowledge: in "How do I prevent a forest fire?" there is a multiple choice test; in "Can you make a campfire right?" there is a word scramble; and in "Who puts out forest fires" there is a crossword puzzle.

Related Areas: *Science*

Social Studies Bookmarks
URL: http://www.mcps.k12.md.us/curriculum/socialstd/ss.bookmarks.html

A perfect online starting point for K-12 social studies teachers. Created by a school staffer in Maryland, this single site contains links to more than 1,000 online sites which contain information about African-American history, Asian resources, election links, European history, and more.

Social Studies Innovations
URL: http://www.grundy-center.k12.ia.us/ssi/index.html

Contains a small collection of curriculum and social studies units with goals, objectives, media, classroom activities, assessments, and student and teacher guides for teaching units.

Related Areas: *Teacher Resources*

Social Studies

South Africa Tour
URL: http://osprey.unisa.ac.za/south-africa/home.html

 Get online to take a colorful tour of the southern-most country on the African continent. Learn about the various cities in South Africa, the country's inhabitants, and the animals that live there too.

Soviet Archives
URL: http://sunsite.unc.edu/expo/soviet.exhibit/entrance.html

This exhibit is the first public display of the highly secret internal record of Soviet Communist rule. Material long used for one-sided political combat has now become fodder for shared historical investigation into the post Cold War era. Included are internal workings of Soviet politics, and how Soviet-American relations were conducted in the past.

Stamp on Black History
URL: http://tqd.advanced.org/2667/

This Web site takes students on a tour through American black history by focusing on those black artists and leaders that have had the good fortune to have their likenesses captured on postage stamps.

Related Areas: *Science; Math; Art & Music; Language Arts/Languages*

 Integration Idea

> The history of government gives students an appreciation for their constitutional freedoms and fosters an understanding of other cultures. Assist your students in developing this knowledge by having them compare the history of the South African government with the Soviet government. Lastly, have them compare their findings with their government. Have them discuss why they would change or keep it the same.

Social Studies

TerraQuest
URL: http://www.terraquest.com

About twice a year, the creators of TerraQuest send a collection of swarthy souls out into the wilderness to gather information on ancient cultures and distant lands — all for the benefit of your K-12 students! The nice thing about this site is that there is so much scientific, historical, and geographical information available here that students won't feel left out if a particular project is already over and done. Past expeditions include trips to Antarctica and the Galapagos Islands. The latest project, HighSights '96, followed blind mountain climber Erik Weihenmayer as he ascended the 3,000 foot sheer face of El Capitán, in Yosemite National Park.

Third Grade Technology Integration Project: Our City
URL: http://www.microstore.com/ardis/ypsiinfo/ypsiindex.html

Third graders at Ardis Elementary School in Ypsilanti, Michigan recently studied their school and their community. The results of this research can be found on the World Wide Web! This is an excellent example of one method of how to integrate social studies, language arts, and technology in a primary-level classroom.

Related Areas: *Language Arts/Languages; Technology/Internet*

Thomas: Legislative Information on the Internet
URL: http://thomas.loc.gov/

The U.S. Congress' Thomas Web site has access to: the full text of all 1993-96 and recent 1997 House and Senate bills, including summaries and chronologies of pending legislation; the *Congressional Record*, updated daily; and email directories for House and Senate members and committees. The site is a must visit for educators and students studying the U.S. government and the legislative process.

Social Studies

The Total Yellowstone Page
URL: http://www.Yellowstone-Natl-Park.Com/index.html

Use this Web site to take your class on a tour of Yellowstone Park. Pictures, maps, and sounds will make you feel as though you are there in person. Students can also send email queries to park officials. Be sure to check out the great bear stories and humor pages.

Related Areas: *Art & Music; Math; Science; Teacher Resources*

Tour of the United Nations
URL: http://www.pbs.org/tal/un/index.html

Tour the UN through descriptions and pictures. This site is equipped with lessons ready to be printed. Click on links and then skim down to ride the CyberSchoolBus and win prizes for your class.

Related Areas: *Teacher Resources*

Treasures of the Czars
URL: http://www.times.st-pete.fl.us/Treasures/Default.html

Rather than fly to Florida, your class can see the breathtaking treasures left over from the reign of the Romanov czars on the Web for free! This exhibit is said to be one of the largest collection of items ever sent out of the country by the Moscow Kremin, so don't miss it!

Related Areas: *Art & Music*

Integration Idea

Take your students where they have never been before without leaving the classroom. Go mountain climbing with TerraQuest, see the sites at Yellowstone, or tour the United Nations. Some of the sites have lesson plans you can download or an email address that your students can send their questions to.

Social Studies

A Tribute to the *R.M.S. Titanic*   4-6
URL: http://www.fireflyproductions.com/titanic/

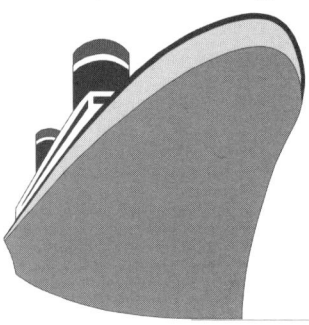

Learn the history behind the largest catastrophe on the water. Discuss the construction, measurements, and amount of utilities needed to accommodate everyone. Incorporate fractions; for example: ask what would be a third of the 40,000 towels taken. Use foil to build a ship and see how long it will float after adding one paper clip at a time.

Related Areas: *Language Arts/Languages; Math; Science; Teacher Resources; Art & Music*

U.S. Gazetteer   K-6
URL: http://www.census.gov/cgi-bin/gazetteer

Want to know how many people live in your town? With the U.S. Gazeteer it's a piece of cake. Just enter the name of the town you want to search for, or a five-digit zip code, and within seconds you will get statistics on population and links to an online map.

Related Areas: *Science*

UNITE (Unite Now In Tolerance & Equality)   K-6
URL: http://www.sssas.pvt.k12.va.us/MS/UNITE/Home.html

A student-led, grassroots, online organization that has created models for tolerant communities and ways of putting them in practice in schools across the United States. Perfect for inclusion in racial, ethnic, and religious tolerance lessons and activities.

The United Nations CyberSchoolBus   K-6
URL: http://www.un.org/Pubs/CyberSchoolBus/

Head over to the Curriculum Corner to involve your class in several exciting and in-depth units that cover topics such as urbanization and global health. Looking for some interactive projects? Events Orbit has plenty of short-term social studies projects and activities for your classroom. There's also an abundance of resource materials on global trends and various countries, quizzes and games from Dr. Data and Prof. PhotoQuiz, and a model U.N. discussion area.

Related Areas: *Language Arts/Languages; Art & Music; Science*

Social Studies

Universal Survey of Languages
URL: http://www.teleport.com/~napoleon/

4-6

A guide to languages around the world, both real and invented, with examples and not-too-complex text on linguistic theory and the like.

Related Areas: *Teacher Resources*

USA CityLink
URL: http://usacitylink.com/

K-6

This site is billed as "a city's interface to the world...the Internet's most comprehensive listing of World Wide Web pages featuring U.S. states and cities." From Alabama to Wyoming, students will find a bounty of information about hundreds of cities, such as geography (lots of maps and graphics!), weather, culture, and much more.

Related Areas: *Math; Science*

USA Counties 1996
URL: http://govinfo.kerr.orst.edu/usaco-stateis.html

K-6

Social studies teachers will find lots to love about this information-rich site. Here you and your students can quickly and easily unearth geographic and raw census data about every single U.S. state and county in the United States. Click on the map of the U.S. and zoom in as close as a county or as far away as a state.

Related Areas: *Science*

Integration Idea

Integrate geography into your math lesson by using the population statistics from the US Gazetteer, USA Counties, or the Citylink site. Have your students graph the population changes. If you're looking for project ideas, the UN CyberSchoolBus site is an excellent source of information for students and teachers with ongoing projects.

Social Studies

Voices of Youth
URL: http://www.unicef.org/voy/

 4-6

What do your students think about war? World hunger? This Web site, created by UNICEF as part of its 50th anniversary celebration, gives students a chance to share their opinions with peers from around the world. The Meeting Place asks students to give their opinions and share drawings about global problems, while The Learning Place offers educators a chance to engage their students with a collection of online activities.

Related Areas: *Language Arts/Languages*

Vote Smart
URL: http://www.vote-smart.org/

 4-6

Having trouble telling the candidates apart? Confused about some of the issues? Then head over to this site which lists candidates' voting records and biographies in a simple, easy-to-read format. Lots of good information for students studying the inner workings of the U.S. Government.

Web 66
International WWW School Registry
URL: http://web66.coled.umn.edu/schools.html

 4-6

After learning about different countries take your students on a field trip to wherever they want to go using email. Visit the school Web pages of other countries through this site, and make some keypals!

Related Areas: *Language Arts/Languages; Teacher Resources*

Web Museums
URL: http://www.lam.mus.ca.us/webmuseums/

 K-6

Planning a trip to a museum downtown or across the country? Look no further than this online Guide to Museums and Cultural Resources. It provides a comprehensive index of information about museums, aquaria, historical parks and other cultural institutions, and thousands of links to the institution's Web sites. Best of all, this site features a powerful search engine to help you find the museum you're looking for quickly and easily.

Related Areas: *Science*

Social Studies

Welcome to GlobaLearn
URL: http://www.globalearn.org/

 GlobaLearn, Inc., a not-for-profit corporation, was incorporated in August of 1993 with a mission "to prepare children for global citizenship and develop in them the skills, awareness, and determination to become responsible stewards of the earth." They have since hosted a number of excellent Internet projects and expeditions designed to teach students about the world around them.

Welcome to North Georgia
URL: http://www.ngeorgia.com/

This site has it all: Native American history, Georgia history, pictures of heritage trails, and sound clips. You can creates a cross-curriculm unit using this site alone as it lends itself to many cooperative activities.

Related Areas: *Art & Music; Language Arts/Languages; Math; Science; Teacher Resources*

What Do Maps Show?
URL: http://info.er.usgs.gov/education/teacher/what-do-maps-show/index.html

This activity involves using eight lesson plans to help students understand and use maps. Created by the U.S. Geological Survey, this free package includes a large teaching poster, eight lessons, three reproducible maps from which you can create a map packet for each student, reproducible activity sheets, and a detailed teaching methodology.

Related Areas: *Math; Science*

 Integration Idea

Allow your students to dialogue with other students from around the world on topics about war, hunger, or anything else that affects their world. The Voices of Youth and GlobaLearn site prompts students for these discussions and debates. Teachers can locate schools to share in this exchange by going to the Web 66 site.

Social Studies

White House

URL: http://www.whitehouse.gov

This Web site is your "Interactive Citizens Handbook" to the White House. Students can take an interactive tour, listen to recorded messages from the President and Vice President, read a detailed account of family life at the White House, and leave a message in a virtual Guest Book.

The White House for Kids

URL: http://www.whitehouse.gov/WH/kids/html/home.html

Think of the White House for Kids Web site as a child-friendly version of the official. Follow Socks the cat as he takes your students on a tour of the White House and its history. A special section on White House kids and pets is also included.

Related Areas: *Teacher Resources; Language Arts/Languages*

The World of the Vikings

URL: http://www.pastforward.co.uk/vikings/index.html

Here's an excellent site for information on ancient runes, Icelandic sagas, how to make mead, links to other Viking-related research projects, educational resources, museums, and online mailing lists. This is the definitive guide to Viking resources on the Net.

World Population Clock

URL: http://sunsite.unc.edu/lunarbin/worldpop

This site contains a population counter which is reloaded and updated in your Web browser every 30 seconds. How much does the clock change in those 30 short seconds?: A net increase of 111 human beings.

Related Areas: *Science; Math*

Social Studies

World Surfari
URL: http://www.supersurf.com

K-6

Each month this Web site takes visitors on a tour of a particular country, such as Jamaica. Tons of interesting facts about each area is available here, including geography, government, people, history, and more. There's also tips on speaking the language, and how to make the local cuisine.

WorldTime: Interactive World Atlas
URL: http://www.worldtime.com

4-6

WorldTime is a free online service that features a unique interactive world atlas, information on local time, and sunrise and sunset times in several hundred cities, and a database of public holidays worldwide. Your students will find the clickable globe easy to operate to find the information they need. An amazing example of how Web site developers can make full use of the Internet's multimedia capabilities.

Related Areas: *Science*

World War II in Europe Timeline
URL: http://www.historyplace.com/worldwar2/time line/ww2time.htm

4-6

Enhance your language arts and social studies lessons with this site. The photos come with well-written descriptions and discuss topics that go in conjunction with *The Diary of Anne Frank*.

Related Areas: *Language Arts/Languages*

> ### ⚠ Integration Idea
>
> Where does the president live and what are his pets' names? Your students can learn the answers to these questions and more by visiting the White House sites. These sites are extremely friendly to the lower elementary grades. You can also set up a scavenger hunt for students using these Web pages. Challenge them to find certain designated facts from both sites and see how long it takes them to obtain the answers.

Social Studies

World War One—Trenches on the Web
URL: http://www.worldwar1.com/

Trenches on the Web is your one-stop source of information about The Great War—World War One. This site contains information about the people, places, and events that comprised one of the worst calamities of modern history. Entire kingdoms vanished in the clash, and the map makers of the day were busy indeed. The "trenches" (main areas of the site) are set up in such a way as to allow you to explore the war at your own pace, in your own manner, and includes a time line of the war, reenactments, recent television programs devoted to the war, Virtual Reality objects from the war, and World War One literature.

Related Areas: *Language Arts/Languages*

Yahoo Maps
URL: http://www.proximus.com/yahoo/

Encourage your students to learn their address so they can participate in this map making site. It creates a map of your exact location no matter where in the U.S. you are located. Create real road maps using addresses input by your students. This site allows for an excellent math lesson and possible art activity for making brochures on places to visit.

Related Areas: *Art & Music; Math*

YELLOW PAGES
TEACHER RESOURCES

Teacher Resources

1996 Digest of U.S. Education Statistics
URL: http://www.ed.gov/NCES/pubs/D96/

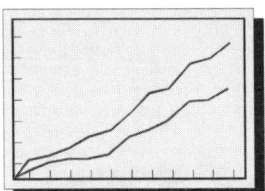

The U.S. Department of Education National Center for Education Statistics (NCES) has recently made the full text of the 1996 *Digest of Education Statistics* available via the Internet. Includes information about thousands of education topics, from elementary to postsecondary education and everything in between.

Academic Employment Network
URL: http://www.academploy.com/

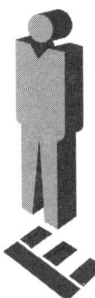

This is the place to head to if you are an educator looking for a new position, or an administrator looking to fill a position. Search by state for the best faculty, staff or administrative jobs, or post your own ads here via email or an interactive Internet form. There's also a collection of employment resources for educators to help with things like relocation and certification requirements.

Related Areas: *Technology/Internet*

The Academy Curriculum Exchange
URL: http://ofcn.org/cyber.serv/academy/ace/

This site is a collection of lessons for grades K-12 on all subjects. Each subject is broken down by grade level. Note that the lesson plans were written in paragraph form, which makes them challenging to read.

Related Areas: *Language Arts/Languages; Social Studies; Math; Science; Technology/Internet*

The Amazing Picture Machine
URL: http://www.ncrel.org/ncrtec/picture.htm

The Amazing Picture Machine is a Web page created by NCRTEC (North Central Regional Technology in Education Consortium) to help educators easily find graphic resources on the Web. Hundreds of different types of pictures and photos are indexed here, from aircraft to World War II. Teachers and students working on school Web sites will find lots to love about this site!

Related Areas: *Technology/Internet*

Teacher Resources

American Association of School Administrators
URL: http://www.aasa.org/

Sure, the Internet provides great resources for classroom teachers, but what about those higher up in the bureaucracy? Where are all the good Web sites for school administrators? Well, look no further! The American Association of School Administrators (AASA) has posted a Web site aimed at serving the 16,500+ K-12 administrators in North America, particularly those working at the central-office level. Those looking for work can cruise by the Job Bulletin, which displays the latest jobs available. Others can read about the latest congressional actions regarding education, skim school-related news releases, and read about upcoming conferences and programs.

American Federation of Teachers
URL: http://www.aft.org//index.htm

The AFT provides quality information not only for K-12 educators, but also for health professionals, public employees, higher education professionals, and school-related personnel. Sections like Lessons for Life deal with educational reform efforts, while other areas discuss grassroots initiatives and educational standards. If you're wondering what issues affect you and your coworkers, this is one of the best places to find out.

Armadillo
URL: http://riceinfo.rice.edu/armadillo

Armadillo's full of resources and instructional materials relating to Texas, the Lone Star State. The content supports an interdisciplinary course of study with a Texas theme and includes hyperlinks to dozens of other Web and gopher education sites.

Integration Idea

You will find everything you need to introduce your students to the State of Texas by surfing three sites with a Texan flavor. Armadillo is full of lesson information and curriculum ideas relating to this state. Offer your class a visual experience as well by visiting The Amazing Picture Machine. A search of "Texas" will reveal images of wildflowers and tornadoes. The Academy Curriculum Exchange has an excellent elementary social studies section which will provide lesson suggestions related to states in general, community, and geography. Some of the materials here will ideally fit into your tour of Texas. Yahoo!

Teacher Resources

Ask An Expert Services
URL: http://www.askanexpert.com

Astronauts, zookeepers, and authors from around the world will answer questions about their careers posed by your students. In all, more than 250 experts are listed on this single Web page. They're ready and willing to add their unique knowledge to your lesson plans, activities, and projects via the Internet! When emailing an expert, type *Ask an Expert Question* as your subject line; include your return email address in the body of your message so you receive a response; and finally, indicate whether you're using the question(s) in conjunction with a lesson plan or project, and any deadlines you have for a response.

Related Areas: *Language Arts/Languages; Technology/Internet; Art & Music; Health/PE; Science; Math; Social Studies*

Association for Supervision and Curricular Development
URL: http://www.ascd.org/

The Association for Supervision and Curriculum Development is an international, nonprofit, nonpartisan association committed to providing professional development in educational curriculum and supervision, as well as serving as a world-class leader in education information services. Their site contains publications on curriculum development, as well as news and articles on educational issues.

B.J. Pinchbeck's Homework Helper
URL: http://tristate.pgh.net/~pinch13/index.html

This site's motto is: "If you can't find it here, then you just can't find it." Created by a 10-year-old student, this is one of the most comprehensive educational indexes on the Internet. Divided according to subject matter, students as well as teachers should find this site to be an excellent reference tool.

Related Areas: *Art & Music; Health/PE; Language Arts/Languages; Math; Science; Social Studies*

Teacher Resources

Birch Kindergarten Activities
URL: http://leeca8.leeca.ohio.gov/nocs/birch/birch.htm

This incredible site lets the viewer experience animation, audio, and 3D graphics. Created by young students for young students, this "online classroom" caters to kindergarten kids only. Kindergarten email projects are in the works, including Kindergarten Internet Travel via email. A must visit for all kindergarten teachers and students!

Related Areas: *Social Studies; Language Arts/Languages*

Block Scheduling Home Page
URL: http://www.classroom.net/classweb/myhome.html

Your one-stop source of information about block scheduling in the K-12 learning environment. Includes links to dozens of schools who have taken the "block" plunge, and links to anecdotal information about how this new system is working here in the United States.

The Busy Teachers' Web Site
URL: http://www.ceismc.gatech.edu/BusyT/TOC.html

This Web site is designed to provide K-12 educators with a direct source of online teaching materials, lesson plans, and classroom activities. An enjoyable and rewarding experience for the teacher just learning to use the Internet.

Related Areas: *Technology/Internet*

Integration Idea

Welcome to a kindergarten teacher's dream! Birch Kindergarten Activities is a resource for all elementary teachers, but especially those who teach kindergarten. See what is up in this school that caters exclusively to the young child. For still more resources, use The Busy Teacher's Web Site to find a page to complement any teaching theme, and consult B.J. Pinchbeck's Homework Helper for the best sites for kids on the Web. Find the sites that suit the needs of your kindergarten pre-readers!

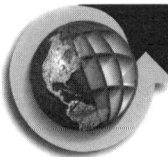

Teacher Resources

Child Safety—A Parent's Guide
URL: http://www.firn.edu/~doe/bin00050/fdle.htm

 Print out a copy of this form for parents to guide them in making decisions about how to keep their children safe wherever they are. You can also use this site to create a safety lesson plan during class for students.

Children Accessing Controversial Information
URL: http://www.zen.org/~brendan/caci.html

The goal for the organizers of this mailing list is to form a community to discuss and develop materials helpful in managing the difficult issue of possible child access to inappropriate material on the Internet.

Children's Television Workshop
URL: http://www.ctw.org/

 All of your students' favorite *Sesame Street* characters are waiting at this site, but that's not all! Here, you'll find lots of quality materials and articles for parents as well as educators. Adults can find out about child development, learning disabilities, and consumer advice, while children can color in pictures of Elmo and take part in a variety of art and music activities. Lots of lesson plans are also available. A great comprehensive site for young children and those that teach them.

Related Areas: *Art & Music; Health/PE; Language Arts/Languages; Math; Science; Social Studies*

Class IV
URL: http://www.edbriefs.com

Rather than combing through tons of print and searching for online information, you can get updated on the latest changes in today's education by heading over to the Class IV Web site. A group of teachers dedicated to keeping educators informed in a rapidly changing world, Class IV publishes *USA Ed.Net Briefs,* a free weekly online newsletter. Each issue is filled with summaries of the week's important education stories, including the source citation for those who need more information. Those wishing to contribute stories are invited to send news about education in their state, town, school district, or school.

Related Areas: *Technology/Internet*

Teacher Resources

Classroom Connect Mailing List Archives
URL: http://www.classroom.net/classroom/maillist.html

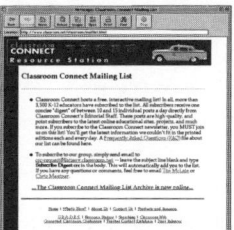

Classroom Connect hosts a free, interactive mailing list with more than 3500 K-12 educators as subscribers (as of Summer 1997). All subscribers receive one concise "digest" of about ten individual posts a day directly from *Classroom Connect's* editorial staff. These posts are high-quality, and point subscribers to the latest online educational sites, projects, and much more. The site also includes an archive of past digests.

Related Areas: *Technology/Internet*

CMargin Notes
URL: http://www.cmargin.com/

CMargin Notes is a free, daily email newsletter that helps K-12 teachers present classroom content and activities within timely, meaningful contexts. Each issue contains brief summaries of news articles selected from dozens of online newspapers and specialty publications. The articles cover topics in ten categories, including: real-world math, real-world science, historical perspectives, economic perspectives, education in the news, kids in the news, fun facts, and real-world data. CMargin Notes gives teachers across all grade levels and disciplines a powerful tool for connecting classroom content to current events and familiar situations.

Related Areas: *Technology/Internet*

Collaborative Lesson Archive
URL: http://faldo.atmos.uiuc.edu/TUA_Home.html

Behind this drab exterior lurks many interesting and well-designed collaborative lessons plans and classroom activities. Until they're better organized, one must sift carefully to find the gems that hide here. There's also a Web bulletin board for comments and an elegant usage chart for the archive.

Related Areas: *Math; Science*

Integration Idea

Have you been seeking a way to communicate with other educators and stay on top of the latest educational information available on the Web? You can do both! Subscribe to a mailing list and peruse their old issues like in the *Classroom Connect* Mailing List Archives, or join a newsletter group such as CMargin Notes. All of the current educational news will come to you when you sign up for Class IV's newsletter. Take advantage of the fast-paced, dynamic nature of the Internet to remain informed and in communication with other educators like you!

Teacher Resources

Community Learning Network (CLN)
URL: http://www.etc.bc.ca/tdebhome/cln.html

The Community Learning Network (CLN) is designed to help K-12 teachers integrate technology into their classrooms. The site contains more than 2,000 links to educational WWW sites on over 100 resource pages — all organized within an intuitive structure. The site provides links to curricular content, instructional materials (lesson plans), background information on technology integration, practical help for teachers looking for keypals/projects, Internet guidebooks, software repositories, mailing lists, school Web pages, a what's-new section, and a link to the site's own online technology courses.

Related Areas: *Technology/Internet*

Computer Skills Lesson Plans 4-6
URL: http://www.dpi.state.nc.us/Curriculum/Computer.skills/lssnplns/Telecomputing/tctoc.html

Looking for a fresh way to get your fifth or sixth grade students to use the Internet? These telecomputing lesson plans will challenge them to use this new technology to find out about the world around them and learn useful research skills.

Related Areas: *Technology/Internet; Social Studies; Language Arts/Languages*

Connections+
URL: http://www.mcrel.org/connect/plus/

This site consists of Internet resources — lesson plans, activities, and curriculum resources — that provide hands-on information to assist educators who use the Internet in the classroom. Some of the best sites on the Net can be found through here. A plus for teachers using cross-curricular units.

Related Areas: *Technology/Internet*

Consortium for School Networking (CoSN) K-6
URL: http://cosn.org

CoSN, one of the oldest professional organizations centering on appropriate use of the Internet in education, offers listings of K-12 resources to educators via their ever-expanding Web site. Includes a new Technology Planning Resources Guide, and live online discussion forums.

Related Areas: *Technology/Internet*

Teacher Resources

Copyright Questions and Answers
URL: http://web.capco.com/capco/QACopyright.html

 Teachers often photocopy documents, articles, and artwork for use in their lesson plans and classrooms. Without understanding the current copyright laws, however, educators can unknowingly put themselves at risk of engaging in illegal photocopying. This online FAQ attempts to guide teachers through current copyright laws and terms such as *fair use*. "What types of works can claim copyright protection?," "What are the penalties for copyright infringement?," and "What if I request permission and don't get a response?" are among the sample questions.

The Council for Exceptional Children (CEC)
URL: http://www.cec.sped.org/home.htm

The CEC is the largest international professional organization dedicated to improving educational outcomes for individuals with exceptionalities, students with disabilities, and/or the gifted. CEC's Web site contains information about current CEC projects and activities, student and high school CEC clubs and organizations, and links to the organization's chapters, federations, and subdivisions.

Council of Chief State School Officers
URL: http://www.ccsso.org/

A nonprofit organization, the CCSSO is composed of public officials who lead the various state departments responsible for elementary and secondary education in the United States. The real gold mine here is the amount of articles and papers on important educational issues. Get the latest scoop on welfare reform, find out how the Telecommunications Act will be implemented, or learn what projects and concerns your state is currently facing, all from this meager little site!

Related Areas: *Technology/Internet*

 Integration Idea

Are you a new educator or just an educator new to the Internet? If so, then these resources are for you! The Consortium for School Networking answers all of your questions related to teaching with the Web, and the Community Learning Network is your source for educational sites that will help you integrate this technology into your daily teaching. Do you still need some real life examples to get you started? Try Connections+ and Computer Skills Lesson Plans for lessons that will get your students using the Internet and acquaint you with the ways of the Web.

Teacher Resources

Creating Lesson Plans
URL: http://www.hcc.hawaii.edu:80/hccinfo/facdev/3.html

Perhaps you construct elaborate, detailed lesson plans. Or perhaps you teach from a few notes. Regardless of your format, you select strategies and methods to help your students move toward your learning goals. This Web site contains an in-depth guide to creating successful lesson plans.

CREDO
URL: http://www.ilt.columbia.edu/projects/copyright/ILTcopy0.html

As more and more schools and classrooms get online, a growing concern of educators is copyright protection. It was for this reason that CREDO, or Copyright Resources for Education Online, came into being. CREDO's aim is to provide a basic guide for educators about protecting your work as well as complying with the existing copyright rules.

Related Areas: *Technology/Internet*

Critical Thinking Primary and Secondary Information
URL: http://www.sonoma.edu/cthink/K12/

Critical thinking skills are the focus of this site. Lessons to help your students learn to be more efficient thinkers, discussion groups for teachers via email, in-service information, articles to help you better understand the levels of critical thinking, and more are all available here.

Related Areas: *Technology/Internet*

CyberBee
URL: http://www.cyberbee.com/

Looking for some quality Web sites for your classroom? Wondering how to best evaluate the Web pages that you find, or what copyright questions you should have in mind when you download material off the Net? Then check out CyberBee, an online magazine devoted to helping educators and students make their way through the Internet hive. Each month focuses on a different educational subject matter, such as science or math, and features tips to not only navigate the Net, but create your own Web materials. Archives are also available to help you locate past articles and activities.

Related Areas: *Technology/Internet; Language Arts/Languages; Math; Science; Social Studies; Health/PE; Art & Music*

Teacher Resources

Daily Report Card News Web Archive
URL: http://www.utopia.com/mailings/reportcard/

 This rich site contains a summary of education-related news as reported by some of America's largest newspapers, magazines, and television news stations. Produced by the U.S. National Education Goals Panel. Very timely and informative for K-12 educators around the world.

Department of Education Grant Guide
URL: http://www.ed.gov/pubs/KnowAbtGrants/

This Web site covers the U.S. Department of Education's discretionary grants process. It addresses the review process, grant funding, administering grants, grant closeout and audit, and includes a glossary of commonly used terms. It also points readers to other federal and nonfederal information sources.

Developing Educational Standards
URL: http://putwest.boces.org/Standards.html

To help K-12 educators keep in touch with the latest educational standards information, Putnam Valley Schools in New York maintains this central Web site with links to this data. A testament to their commitment is this massive list of more than 700 links to related sources.

Related Areas: *Technology/Internet*

 Integration Idea

Give yourself a quick tutorial in lesson plan writing! Visit Creating Lesson Plans for the basic procedures involved in writing effective lessons. Follow this with a primer in enriching your lessons with critical thinking activities and questions at Critical Thinking Primary and Secondary Information. Then apply what you have learned to lessons involving the Internet with help from the CyberBee page "Curriculum Integration."

Teacher Resources

Digital Portfolio Assessment
URL: http://inet.ed.gov/pubs/OR/ConsumerGuides/classuse.html

In traditional student portfolios, students placed their best work in a folder, along with their evaluation of the strengths and weaknesses of the material. These days, computer-created "digital" portfolios are gaining popularity as an assessment alternative to report cards and standardized testing. Visit this site to find out more about digital portfolios, including how to create them on a personal computer.

Early Childhood Education Online
URL: http://www.ume.maine.edu/~cofed/eceol/welcome.shtml

This Web site is a collaborative effort by various educators to create an easy "starting point" for those teachers, parents, and caregivers that deal with children under eight years old and are looking for helpful information on the Internet. The site collects links to other sites of interest and groups them under such titles as Diversity, Observation and Assessment, Curriculum and Environment, Advocacy for Children, and Professional Development. There's also information about their mailing list and suggestions on how you can help the site grow.

Related Areas: *Technology/Internet*

Early Childhood Educators' and Family Web Corner
URL: http://www.nauticom.net/www/cokids/index.html

This site not only provides an extensive index of the best educational elementary sites around, but also has created plenty of useful material in its own right. For example, the "Together We're Better" calendar has lots of daily questions and activities for students to try. The online index lists plenty of quality sites to visit. Subheadings include: Developmentally Approved Practices, Articles, Educational Debates, and teacher and parent pages.

Teacher Resources

Education Newsletters
URL: http://www.ed.gov/newsletters.html

Let's say you're looking for the latest developments involving government and the K-12 community. Where can you go to find this information? This site, of course — it features five free newsletters dealing with this topic. *Community Updates* focuses on what local communities are learning as they attempt to improve their schools. *OERI Bulletin* describes office priorities and OERI-funded publications. *Improving Schools* helps school, district, and state leaders explore key topics in improving schools. *EdInfo* delivers two to three messages per week from the Department of Education to your email account. *Ed Initiatives* offers a weekly look at progress being made on the Secretary of Education's priorities.

Related Areas: *Technology/Internet*

Education Place
URL: http://www.eduplace.com/hmco/school/index.html

This rich Web site, sponsored by Houghton Mifflin, is loaded with curriculum materials. There is a math section, a reading/language arts center, a social studies area, and a technology center, as well as an activity search and a project center. The activity search allows visitors to specify the subject and grade level of the activity they'd like to look for—a great way to find some intriguing lesson plans.

Related Areas: *Language Arts/Languages; Math; Science; Social Studies*

 Integration Idea

Assessment is a hot educational issue at this time, and these Internet sites address this complicated topic. Early Childhood Education Online, and Early Childhood Educators' and Family Web Corner have many links to get you to whatever area of assessment you want to research. Digital Portfolio Assessment explains the process of creating portfolios and the rationale behind this type of assessment. Use the resources of the Web to evaluate the arguments and proposals and construct your own approach to assessment.

Teacher Resources

The Education Station
URL: http://www.digicity.com

This site contains links to online courses for teachers, educational software, online libraries, Ask an Expert services, and much, much more. It also sponsors a graphical Internet BUS dedicated to K-12 education where you can chat online and get advice from your "wired" peers.

Related Areas: *Technology/Internet*

Education Week
URL: http://www.edweek.org/

American education's newspaper of record is now officially online, with an abundance of K-12 school news and articles for the well-informed educator. The full text of *Education Week* is online, as well as their monthly *Teacher* magazine. In addition, you can find data on 23 key educational issues including school vouchers, charter schools, the Internet, and phonics. Looking for work? Try their job database. For a limited time, you can even peruse the past 15 years of stories from their magazines for free. With such great content, this site will quickly become the first place you go to get the latest information about educational reform, schools, and the policies that guide them.

Related Areas: *Technology/Internet*

Education World
URL: http://www.education-world.com

With over 10,000 online links (and growing daily) in its database, Education World boasts the most comprehensive database for education links on the Internet. Search by keyword, or by topic, or browse the Awards section for extensive reviews of the latest and hottest educational sites of the month.

Related Areas: *Technology/Internet*

Educational Mailing List Archives
URL: gopher://ericir.syr.edu:70/11/Listservs/

Online archives of "back posts" to more than a dozen of the Net's most popular email-based discussion groups devoted to using the Internet in the K-12 classroom. Hosted by ERIC, the Educational Resources and Information Center.

Related Areas: *Technology/Internet*

Educator Bookmarks
URL: http://www.nyise.org/start.htm

Created by the New York Institute for Special Education, this site was designed to serve as a jump page to all areas of your curriculum — online. It more than makes good on this promise, offering over a hundred links via its well-formatted home page. Make this your Internet brower's home page for easy access to a wide range of education links and resources. Disability sites are given special attention!

Related Areas: *Technology/Internet*

EdWeb
URL: http://edweb.cnidr.org:90/

The purpose of this online "hyperbook" is to explore the worlds of educational reform and information technology. With EdWeb, you can hunt down educational resources around the world, learn about trends in educational policy and information infrastructure development, and examine success stories of computers in the classroom.

Related Areas: *Technology/Internet*

Electronic School Online
URL: http://www.electronic-school.com

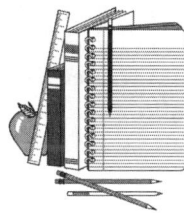

Electronic School is the voice of school leaders who strive to enhance student learning through the judicious and appropriate use of technology. This Web site has all the articles from the print version, additional material not available elsewhere, an archive of past stories, and news and views on the appropriate use of computer technology in schools.

Related Areas: *Technology/Internet*

Integration Idea

What exactly is the "Web?" You will find the definition for this and other technological buzz-words written in terms even the "elementary" can understand at EdWeb. With your new-found knowledge, proceed to Education World or Educator Bookmarks to discover what educational sites the Web has to offer you. Use the Education World Search Engine in order to find the best curriculum resources in the subjects you teach most.

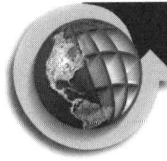

Teacher Resources

eMail Classroom Exchange
URL: http://www.iglou.com/xchange/ece/index.html

Now classroom teachers can find and correspond with pen pals (keypals) from around the world using this site's keypal search engine. Teachers, schools, and students can submit their own pen pals profile to get involved. Perfect for adding powerful Internet components to your cultural, language, history, science, or geography projects and activities.

Related Areas: *Technology/Internet; Social Studies; Science; Language Arts/Languages*

Engines for Education
URL: http://www.ils.nwu.edu/~e_for_e/

Engines is a Web-based "hyperbook" written by education specialists outlining what's wrong with the education system, how to reform it, and how the role of educational technology fits within that reform. A must-read by every "wired" educator.

ERIC & AskERIC
URL: http://ericir.syr.edu

The Educational Resources Information Center (ERIC) is a federally funded national information system that provides, through its 16 subject-specific clearinghouses, online support and resources for K-12 educators. Best known for its collection of thousands of teacher-created lesson plans written for every grade level and curriculum area, and its award-winning AskERIC Q&A service staffed by professional educators to answer questions about all aspects of education. Visitors can also search an in-depth collection of education-related journal articles and research papers in the AskERIC Virtual Library.

Related Areas: *Technology/Internet*

Facility Planning
URL: http://www.cefpi.com/cefpi/

This site is a must for any educators or administrators in the midst of renovating or building new schools in their district. The Council of Educational Facility Planners (CEFPI) has been around since 1965, helping educators create, plan, construct, and renovate facilities to provide the best possible learning environment.

Teacher Resources

The Family Education Network
URL: http://www.families.com/

 This site is aimed a little more towards parents, but it contains such great content that educators ought to find plenty of use for it as well. FEN is dedicated to helping parents and communities play an active role in their children's education and in legislation that affects families. Their Web site offers a combination of news, information exchanges, legislative tracking, exciting projects, health resources, and various other activities related to education. Find out how to improve children's study habits, what to do for children with special needs, and what issues are going on in your community.

Related Areas: *Technology/Internet*

Federal Information Exchange (FEDIX)
URL: http://web.fie.com/

FEDIX contains a wealth of information from federal agencies, including the Federal Aviation Administration, U.S. Department of Agriculture, and NASA. Besides quality educational materials, each federal entity also provides information on its latest K-12 programs, projects, and grants.

The Free Internet Encyclopedia
URL: http://clever.net/cam/encyclopedia.html

This is an encyclopedia composed of information found at various places on the Internet. The MacroReference contains references to large areas of knowledge, FAQs where available, and pointers to relevant resources and specific subjects

Related Areas: *Social Studies; Science; Math; Language Arts/Languages; Art & Music; Technology/Internet*

 Integration Idea

> One language arts experience that all children seem to love is writing to pen pals (aka keypals) via the Internet. Before your class starts to write, however, you need to know how to be sure that the online world is safe for them. Use The Family Education Network to gain the parental perspective on email keypals, and then search ERIC & AskERIC for their guides to using the Internet and creating Net-based lesson plans. When you are ready, Email Classroom Exchange is a perfect source for finding keypals for your students. (Don't forget to include yourself!)

Teacher Resources

From Now On

URL: http://fromnowon.org

Written by veteran school Internet consultant Jamieson McKenzie, From Now On is an online publication whose time has come. Every month McKenzie addresses a hot button issue of interest to the wired K-12 crowd, outlining solutions with a very lucid, hands-on approach. Recent topics include "Protecting our Children from the Internet and the World" (a satire on the CyberPorn controversy); "Creating Policies for Acceptable Use"; "Creating Flexible Tech Plans for Individual Sites"; and "Libraries of the Future."

Related Areas: *Technology/Internet*

Gifted Resources Home Page

URL: http://www.eskimo.com/~user/kids.html

An ideal starting point on the Internet for gifted students, their parents, and educators, this Web page contains links to all known online gifted resources, enrichment programs, talent searches, summer programs, and gifted mailing lists and early acceptance programs. It also contains links to more than five years of TAG-L mailing list archives. It also contains contact information for many local gifted associations and government programs.

Global SchoolNet Foundation

URL: http://www.gsn.org/

Global SchoolNet hosts nearly 100 innovative K-12 Internet projects each year, and continues to find innovative classroom applications for the Net. You and your class can join in right away via this site. Their latest project involves connecting schools worldwide via inexpensive videoconferencing tools such as CU-SeeMe.

Related Areas: *Technology/Internet*

Gopher Jewels

URL: gopher://cwis.usc.edu:70/11/Other_Gophers_and_Information_Resources/
    Gophers_by_Subject/Gopher_Jewels

A jam-packed gopher site full of pointers to thousands of other gopher sites on any subject area. A great place to start your next Internet search for information and find sites to integrate into your curriculum! Updated weekly.

Related Areas: *Technology/Internet*

Teacher Resources

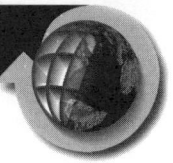

Guidelines for Educational Uses of Online Networks

URL: http://www.ed.uiuc.edu/Guidelines/guidelines.html

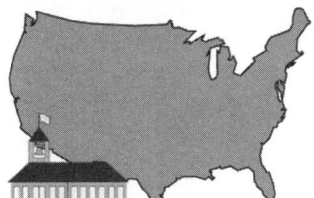

Essays, papers, and columns from some of the world's foremost authorities about proper use of the Internet and other online networks in K-12 schools. Be sure your printer is up and running before you connect here!

Related Areas: *Technology/Internet*

How to Cite Internet Resources in Student Research

URL: http://www.classroom.net/classroom/CitingNetResources.html

From the staff of *Classroom Connect,* this document outlines exactly how to cite online resources in student bibliographies, including email communications, Web resources, and student-created or captured multimedia elements. This is a must read for all students, educators, and library media specialists working in K-12 schools worldwide.

Related Areas: *Technology/Internet*

Integration Idea

Make connections and get involved in Internet projects! The Global SchoolNet Foundation is a premier site for projects and a great way for your class to contact other classes so that you may work together and communicate. If you are interested in connecting with schools in the United States, use the Hot List of K-12 Internet School Sites — USA. Be sure to add your own site to the list, too! If you do use information from other Web sites, you will want to show your students how to appropriately attribute information to its originators, and *Classroom Connect* has your handbook. See our page, How to Cite Internet Resources in Student Research, for all of the answers.

Teacher Resources

InfoList for Teachers
URL: http://www.electriciti.com:80/~rlakin/

Infolist is an online digest of Internet resources for teachers. You can subscribe to Infolist via email or check out the condensed listings posted weekly at this Web site. This is a great place to check for the latest new educational links!

Related Areas: *Technology/Internet*

Instructional Technology Connections
URL: http://www.cudenver.edu/~mryder/itcon.html

Contains links to Theory & Philosophy (Current models, approaches, and ideas), Electronic Journals (Learning, Communications, and Culture), Curriculum Content, Professional Organizations, K-12 Connections (People, Ideas, and Resources), Distance Education (Emerging Technologies and Strategies), and Reflections (A citation index of corollary sources). A must visit for all educators interested in using technology in their curriculum.

Related Areas: *Technology/Internet*

Instructor Magazine
URL: http://place.scholastic.com/Instructor/info/index.htm

Instructor Magazine, one of the oldest and most respected magazines for elementary school educators, is now online. Their site is complete with lesson, integration, assessment, and classroom management ideas. You can also find conference dates and share ideas with other teachers online.

Related Areas: *Art & Music; Health/PE; Language Arts/Languages; Math; Science; Social Studies; Technology/Internet*

Integrating the Internet
URL: http://www.indirect.com/www/dhixson/index.html

This page can help you find primary resources, projects, a weekly newsletter, units of study, and a tutorial to help you plan projects and class home pages. The *Internet Travel Guide* newsletter, for example, provides some perfect starting points, along with tips and tricks for all K-12 educators looking for a way to introduce the Internet into their curriculum.

Related Areas: *Technology/Internet*

Teacher Resources

Intercultural Email Classroom Connections
URL: http://www.stolaf.edu/network/iecc/

This Web site permits educators to search for partner classrooms in other countries. Visitors can use a form to submit their requests for partner classes or to obtain assistance with email projects. It also has links to related mailing lists and other WWW resources. Any teacher looking to connect with other students and cultures over email should head here.

Related Areas: *Technology/Internet*

International Association of School Librarianship (IASL)
URL: http://www.rhi.hi.is/~anne/iasl.html

This site provides information about the association, its publications, and activities. There are selected articles from the *IASL Newsletter* and a collection of documents related to school librarianship. A page of links for school libraries provides a good starting point for Internet exploration.

Internet: A Classroom Resource for All Occasions
URL: http://www.uvm.edu/~jmorris/

"More than any other technology, telecommunications can transform the classroom into an exciting and vibrant learning environment," say the owners of this Web page. This site contains excellent information for newcomers to the Internet who are beginning to integrate it into their K-12 curriculum.

 Integration Idea

> With the rapid change of technology and its effect on education, teachers often find themselves struggling to work the new capabilities into their daily classroom experiences. This is when the integration sites are most important. Internet: A Classroom Resource for All Occasions is a good beginning, and then Integrating the Internet follows with more pointers and suggestions. Ultimately, sites such as *Instructor Magazine* supply the classroom teacher with Web locations that have actual Internet-related lesson plans. Print some lessons or just gather ideas, and you will soon be a "surfing instructor"!

Teacher Resources

Internet Advocate K-6
URL: http://www.monroe.lib.in.us/~lchampel/netadv.html

Internet Advocate is a tremendously useful, hands-on, Internet-based magazine devoted to educators and librarians trying to bring the Internet into their schools, but meeting resistance. In the words of the e-zine: "In addition to helping librarians and educators dispel the notion that the Net is filled with nothing but porn, this resource guide attempts to provide an introduction to the multitude of exciting ways young people are using the Internet in their schools and public libraries."

Related Areas: *Technology/Internet*

Internet Lesson Plans: San Diego City Schools K-6
URL: gopher://ec.sdcs.k12.ca.us:70/11/lessons/UCSD_InternNet_Lessons

Created by a team of teachers in the San Diego City School District, this archive features some of the most innovative lesson plans available online for teachers who are new to the Internet and looking to begin integrating it into their tried and true lessons and activities.

Internet Resource Validation Project 4-6
URL: http://www.stemnet.nf.ca/Curriculum/Validate/validate.html

Here's an excellent site for educators who are concerned about information literacy. Using a simple, no-frills format, students learn the proper questions to ask when examining a Web page in order to make sure the data they retrieve is "accurate, relevant, appropriate, reliable, unbiased, and authoritative." There are also two sample Web pages for students to review and a rating guide to use while online.

Iris Network for Teachers and Educators K-6
URL: http://www.tmn.com/Organizations/Iris/home.html

Iris promotes excellence in education by providing a rich source of student-centered telecommunication projects, professional information, an inviting place to meet colleagues with similar interests, and a forum for developing new and innovative curriculum research.

Teacher Resources

Jenny's Cybrary to the Stars
URL: http://sashimi.wwa.com/~jayhawk/

K-6

Jennifer Levine, a former reference librarian and Internaut, has compiled an impressive list of links to educational and research-related sites on the Web. The central (and most interesting) feature is the Librarian's Site du Jour which highlights sites "with some reference content." Past editions have offered links to Martin Luther King, legal resources, and the Amish. Those fighting city hall to get their school online should visit the "Resources to Help You Persuade Your Board of Trustees" page. There are also links that will keep you up to date with what's going on in cyberspace, how to navigate the Web, library related sites, hot art and business links, and a "Page O' Fun!"

K.I.D.S. (Kids Identifying and Discovering Sites) **K-6**
URL: http://www.scout.cs.wisc.edu/scout/KIDS/index.html

Most online educational publications are created with the teacher in mind. The K.I.D.S. Report, however, is a bimonthly journal of Internet sites selected by and for students. Sites are selected based on their design features, ease of use, content, and credibility. Students choose the art work for the Web site, write the reviews of each resource, and in some cases do the HTML mark-up. The report often revolves around a single theme, which can be easily integrated into the classroom.

Related Areas: Social Studies; Language Arts/Languages; Math; Art & Music; Health/PE; Science

---

K-4 Teacher's Resource Page
URL: http://www.concentric.net/~terrapin/teach.html

K-6

Links to nearly a hundreds online sites of interest to K-4 educators! Contains a classroom page that has age-appropriate links perfect for use by your younger students.

Integration Idea

Evaluation is a high-level critical thinking skill that children should regularly exercise, and the Internet is the perfect outlet for this activity. Introduce your students to the practice of appraising Web material for its child-appropriate content and educational value by studying the Internet Resource Validation Project. Then have them use K.I.D.S. as a prototype for their own list of great sites. What criteria will they use? Jenny's Cybrary to the Stars is an example of how an author's goals and point-of-view mold the end result. If your students chose a "Site du Jour," what characteristics would be required?

Teacher Resources

Kathy Schrock's Guide for Educators
URL: http://www.capecod.net/schrockguide/index.htm

More than just a simple collection of links, educator Kathy Schrock has designed Web evaluation tools, slide shows, and curriculum ideas for students and teachers at the elementary, middle, and high school levels. These are excellent documents that will be helpful to both library media specialists and technology teachers as they work to help students become information literate. Included are online handouts to help students critically evaluate the information they find online.

Related Areas: *Technology/Internet*

Kiddin' Around
URL: http://alexia.lis.uiuc.edu/~watts/kiddin.html

A collection of excellent Internet links for young people, put online by Net veteran John Makulowich. Teachers of young students will find this site to be a useful one-stop source of links for fledgling Internet surfers!

The Learning Kingdom
URL: http://www.learningkingdom.com/

A privately owned company, the mission of the Learning Kingdom is to create the best and most widely used educational software in cyberspace, from whimsical games to comprehensive courses in mathematics, vocabulary, language/arts, science, and critical thinking. Students visiting the site can take the Gaggle Challenge to see how many words they know for groups of animals, or play Blankety-Five Squared, a fun game that will teach them to square two-digit numbers that end in five. Both of these games require a browser that can run Java applets, however.

Related Areas: *Art & Music; Health/PE; Language Arts/Languages; Math; Science; Social Studies*

LION: Librarians Information Online Network
URL: http://www.libertynet.org/~lion/lion.html

A rich resource created and maintained by K-12 media specialists and librarians across the nation! Includes links to information about library automation, library lesson plans, places to buy books online, and a children's literature Web guide. There are also a number of online forums to encourage communication.

LRPnet
URL: http://www.lrp.com/ed/

Searching for access to current federal law statutes and regulations affecting K-12 education? LRPnet, an online resource for education administrators, has made available the full text of the Gun-Free Schools Act, the Individuals with Disabilities Act, and more — free of charge. You'll even find sections of the Elementary and Secondary Education Act.

Make It Happen!
URL: http://www.edc.org/FSC/MIH

This site offers valuable information and useful resources to teachers interested in thematic instruction, interdisciplinary curriculum, inquiry-based learning, technology integration, and inclusion of students with learning disabilities. Appropriate for intermediate and middle-school educators.

Related Areas: *Health/PE*

Making the Connection Online Course
URL: http://www.icondata.com/stores/marketing/main.htm

Making the Connection is an excellent online course ($25) for K-12 educators wanting to know how to integrate the vast resources of the Internet into their curriculum. This immensely popular course takes a project-based approach to learning and using the resources and experiences of teachers on the Net.

Related Areas: *Technology/Internet*

Integration Idea

Making the adjustment to integrating the Internet into daily classroom activities can be an intimidating task without some guidance. Kathy Schrock's Guide for Educators is a terrific resource for any teacher who is facing this transition. Use the many forums of LION: Librarians Information Online Network to find resources related to your areas of interest. When teachers are introduced to the Internet, many question how to use it appropriately for all of their students. Make It Happen! is one example of a teaching method that supports Internet experiences for students of all abilities. Try it!

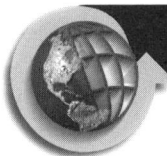

Teacher Resources

Making the Grade
URL: http://www.gse.rutgers.edu/fipse/

If you love teaching but hate grading, or if you are just unsure if your grading practices are as solid as you would like them to be, Jeff Smith and Richard DeLisi of the Graduate School of Education at Rutgers University invite you to link to this site! The pair provide interesting insights into alternative methods of assessing your students' achievement.

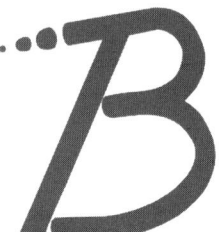

Mining the Internet
URL: http://www.ed.uiuc.edu/Mining/Overview.html

Online columns from educator Judi Harris as they appear in the *Computing Teacher* magazine. Lots of hands-on information from an educator working in the trenches, using the Internet to bring a world of information to her students. Harris is also a well-known educational conference speaker and grassroots advocate for bringing the Internet to K-12 schools across the United States.

Related Areas: *Technology/Internet*

Monsters, Monsters, Monsters!
URL: http://www.coedu.usf.edu/inst_tech/students/gerzoge/index.html

Your classroom can team up with a distant class via email to create strange and colorful monsters via this online unit. The site's authors designed it to introduce young students to the Interenet and to give teachers ideas for how to use the Net in their classroom.

Related Areas: *Language Arts/Languages; Technology/Internet; Social Studies*

National Association of Elementary School Prinicpals
URL: http://www.naesp.org/

Teachers aren't the only ones who can find aid and information on the Net! The NAESP provides plenty of online services for principals, including material on training programs, national conferences, and a host of useful publications and forums. All in all, this is an excellent place for principals to gather together and exchange their thoughts and ideas.

Teacher Resources

National Education Association
URL: http://www.nea.org

Interested in good schools? The National Education Association is, and they've built this Web site to prove it. With more than 2.2 million members, the NEA is one of the largest unions in the country, and their site gives their members the chance to communicate with their peers, learn about important issues, and improve their teaching skills. Find advice on how to use the latest technology in the classroom, visit public schools that are shining examples of positive change, and get tips on how to help your students.

National PTA
URL: http://www.pta.org/

If you think all the PTA does is host bake sales, you should take a look at this Web site. The National PTA is one of the oldest and largest volunteer organizations in the country, and their Web site furthers their mission to get adults involved in their children's education. Not only can you find out who the PTA officers in your area are, you can also take part in online discussions with luminaries such as the Secretary of Education, read guides on how to get families more involved, and learn about educational advocacy programs.

National School Boards Association
URL: http://www.nsba.org/

The National School Boards Association serves as the voice for school boards across the United States and aims "to foster equity and excellence" in public education. From their Web site, you can learn about upcoming conferences, read their latest press releases, training opportunities, and advocacy activities. Publications like *Electronic School, School Board News,* and *The American School Board Journal* keep visitors in touch with the latest educational news.

⚠ Integration Idea

This page brings together three of the most influential and important bodies in education: the National Education Association, the National PTA, and the National School Boards Association. Each group has its own concerns about and plans for the future of the education of American children, but common ground may be found. Keep up with the hot issues of education from all of the perspectives by visiting these sites often. Are your local divisions of these national organizations in sync with national interests?

Teacher Resources

NCSA Education Program
URL: http://www.ncsa.uiuc.edu/Edu/EduHome.html

The National Center for Supercomputing Applications (NCSA) organized this Web site to show students and teachers how they can access educational resources on the Net. Here you'll find links to the Library of Congress database, a database of Internet tutorials, links to K-12 Internet resources, and more. NCSA is responsible for the creation of Mosaic, a graphical Web browser used to access the World Wide Web.

Related Areas: *Technology/Internet*

Non-Profit Prophets **4-6**
URL: http://www.kn.pacbell.com/wired/prophets/index.html

Through this project, students in English, science, social studies, and health select a local or global problem that they want to understand, serve, and solve. Student teams then partner with nonprofit organizations to develop and post a mutually beneficial World Wide Web site. Sponsored by Pacific Bell's Education First Initiative.

Related Areas: *Science; Social Studies; Health/PE*

NOVAE Mailing List Archives **K-6**
URL: http://prism.prs.k12.nj.us/WWW/OII/disc-pub/novae-group/index.html

This URL links you to the archives of this highly informative mailing list for K-12 educators who are networking for the future. You'll find links to informative networking resources, Internet projects, lesson plans, and much more.

Related Areas: *Technology/Internet*

The Old Farmer's Almanac **K-6**
URL: http://www.almanac.com/

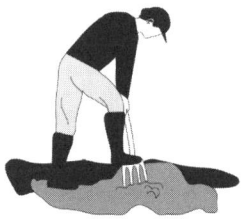

History relevant to the everyday can be found at this site just by clicking on the calendar's highlighted dates. The site is perfect for the K-3 classroom when teaching about the moon's phases or calendars. Listen to the almanac's audio or listen on the radio. This excellent site can be adapted to just about every subject and grade level.

Related Areas: *Social Studies; Science; Art & Music*

Teacher Resources

Pathways to School Improvement
URL: http://www.ncrel.org/ncrel/sdrs/pathwayg.htm

Here's a rich site for K-12 educators with a passion for school reform. Pathways to School Improvement addresses those issues and their connection to students, educators, content, methods, and environment. Each of these topics has a critical issues area with practical, action-oriented summaries of best practice and research, stories from schools successfully addressing the issues, and collections of materials to support change. Includes an outstanding white paper on how educational technology impacts education.

Photovault
URL: http://www.photovault.com/index.html

Photovault is a stock photo and assignment agency based in San Francisco. Their online index of images includes such subjects as aerospace, birds, cars, cities, fish, flowers, insects, mammals, nature, people, planets, reptiles, sports, and transportation.

Related Areas: *Art & Music; Health/PE; Language Arts/Languages; Science*

 Integration Idea

Volunteerism and activism are contributions often lost in the hustle and bustle of adult life, but they can be character-building activities for school students. Non-Profit Prophets has a unique way for your class to support nonprofit organizations and help solve problems world-wide. Promote interest in current events and global issues in your own students while raising public awareness through the creation of a Web site. Pathfinder has links to publications with articles that will help your class identify a problem they would like to help to solve.

Teacher Resources

Planet Innovation
URL: http://planet.rtec.org

This site provides tools that assist school administrators and teachers to successfully plan, implement, and evaluate technology innovations in the classroom. Best of all, Planet Innovation provides educators with the tools needed to appraise staff development while adapting to future technology growth!

Related Areas: *Technology/Internet*

Planet Zoom
URL: http://www.planetzoom.com

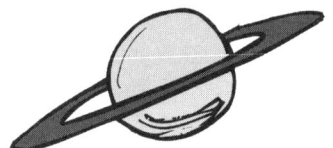

New on the Web, Planet Zoom is a Java-enhanced Web site for kids. While providing activities in science, reading, and social studies, the creators of "PZ" have kept one eye on education and the other on having fun. An excellent site for your young students!

Related Areas: *Science; Language Arts/Languages; Social Studies*

Portfolio Assessment Links
URL: http://www.magic.ca/~geofftay/portfolio.html

Does your school employ student portfolios as an assessment tool? If so, then be sure to consult this site to discover links to the latest information about this educational innovation. This site includes tips on "what to put in the box" to creating teaching portfolios and how to appraise other teacher efforts.

Private School Resource (PSR)
URL: http://www.ppusa.com/psrmagazine/index.htm

What Internet resource is not only free, but also earns money for private schools? It's the Private School Resource. PSR provides private schools with free access to the Internet, while at the same time offering these schools new fund-raising opportunities to pay for their technology needs.

Teacher Resources

Project Appleseed
URL: http://members.aol.com/pledgenow/appleseed/index.html

Ask most educators and they'll tell you that positive parental involvement is a vital ingredient to getting children interested in life long learning. Enter Project Appleseed, a nonprofit national campaign advocating improvement in public schools by increasing parental involvement in all 15,000 public school districts in the U.S. Their site on the World Wide Web contains valuable information on educational reports, workshops, governmental policies, and national updates, all designed to get parents involved in their children's education.

Project Maker
URL: http://edweb.sdsu.edu/edfirst/ProjectMaker.html

This is a Mac Hypercard program designed to answer the nagging question "What do I do now that my students have Internet access?" By having educators identify what problems they experience in the classroom, and what goals they'd like to set, the software allows users to jumpstart their project ideas. They can then create their own Web pages, complete with resources, links, and teaching tips.

Prufrock Press
URL: http://www.prufrock.com/index.html

Prufrock Press offers an award-winning line of books, magazines, and research journals supporting gifted education. Visit their Web site to read sample stories, search databases of past articles, and request free sample issues of *Gifted Child Today, Journal for the Education of the Gifted, Creative Kids,* and more.

⚠ Integration Idea

Using technology is a natural field of enrichment for gifted students. If you are seeking methods that will help your gifted students move beyond the curriculum to the higher level thinking skills of synthesis and evaluation, find Prufrock Press. This source will supply you with some basic material on which to build an Internet enrichment experience. Have the gifted children in your classroom get involved in an online project. Project Maker will provide the instructions you need to create an Internet project that exercises the critical thinking skills these talented students possess.

Teacher Resources

Ready Web
K-6
URL: http://ericps.ed.uiuc.edu/readyweb/readyweb.html

Teachers gearing up over the summer will find this Web site a potential godsend as it has devoted itself to providing a collection of resources on school readiness for educators and parents. The site is divided into two main sections: Helping Children Get Ready for School, and Helping Schools Get Ready for Children, each one chock full of information on curriculum, behavior, child development, fitness, and more.

Resources for Technology Coordinators
K-6
URL: http://www.wwu.edu/~kenr/TCsite/home.html

This is an excellent site custom-made for anyone who supports technology at their school or district level! This site includes links to discussion forums, software, Internet connectivity information, distance learning, acceptable use policies, grant resources, and more. A very rich, in-depth site that's sure to help technology staffers make the most of computer use in your district.

Related Areas: *Technology/Internet*

Rigby
K-6
URL: http://www.reedbooks.com.au/rigby/index.html

This Web site features many different subjects on primary education, library resources, foreign languages, and more. From here, students can find keypals to write to, examine an online atlas, get Internet help, or take part in a heated online discussion.

Related Areas: *Language Arts/Languages; Social Studies*

The Role of Technology in K–12 Schools: Scholastic Study
K-6
URL: http://place.scholastic.com/nwpromo/cast/execsum.htm

Presented by Scholastic, this Web page contains an in-depth summary of a recent study to assess the impact of communication technology and Internet access on K-12 schools. "It offers evidence that using . . . the Internet can help students become independent, critical thinkers, able to find information, organize and evaluate it, and then effectively express their new knowledge and ideas in compelling ways."

Related Areas: *Technology/Internet*

Teacher Resources

Schoolhouse Topics
URL: http://www.teacherpathfinder.org/School/school.html

Lesson plans and resources can be found at this site. Teachers will find lessons on art, health, physical education, and more. Links to other sites and assessment information are also available.

Related Areas: *Health/PE; Art & Music; Language Arts/Languages; Math; Science; Social Studies*

The School Page
URL: http://www.eyesoftime.com/teacher/index.html

Need help finding or developing lesson plans? Interested in a science newspaper for your classes? Need assistance evaluating your science curriculum? Looking for some interesting Web sites for you or your students to explore? Answers to these and many more questions can be found on this Web site, which lives up to its billing as "a place where we meet your needs and no concern is ignored."

Related Areas: *Science; Technology/Internet*

Science & Math Initiatives (SAMI)
URL: http://www.learner.org/content/k12/sami/

SAMI is a clearinghouse of resources, funding, and curriculum for rural math and science teachers. Includes areas devoted to math and science curriculum, lesson plans and projects, mini-grants, and "freebies." A unique teacher help service is available to aid educators in creating classroom lesson plans, activities, and projects using the Internet.

Related Areas: *Math; Science*

 Integration Idea

Are you looking for information to support making the Internet connection in your school? Anyone who questions the validity of integrating the Internet into the classroom need only visit The Role of Technology in K-12 Schools: Scholastic Study. Even young students gain from Web experiences. In fact, sites like Ready Web can even help you prepare children for school. Internet resources improve every day, and their impact on education will grow with the progress. Use these resources to encourage your school to "get connected"!

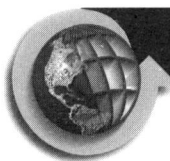

Teacher Resources

Smart Kid
URL: http://www.smartkid.com/

Having trouble looking for quality educational software? Looking for some books that your students can read during their free time? How about some good Web sites? This extensive online magazine attempts to provide parents and teachers with a guide to materials for young children available off- and online—and for the most part they succeed. You'll also find advice on dual language programs, worthwhile cultural events, fun fitness habits, and tips on how to turn a child's room into a palace.

Related Areas: *Technology/Internet; Art & Music; Health/PE; Language Arts/Languages; Science; Social Studies; Math*

StudyWeb
URL: http://www.the-acr.com/studyweb/studyweb.htm

StudyWeb is a free, online meta-encyclopedia of links to research quality sites, which were chosen to help students and teachers with their studies and professional development. The creators are even hiring high school students to assist in the development of the site!

Related Areas: *Technology/Internet*

SyllabusWeb
URL: http://www.syllabus.com

From the publishers of *Syllabus* magazine, *Syllabus Web* covers technologies of interest to educators in high schools, colleges, and universities. It contains news, case studies, product reviews and announcements, and feature articles on technology. Among the areas covered are: multimedia; graphics and visualization; quantitative tools; the Internet; telecommunications and networking; classroom products and technology infrastructure; personal computer and workstation technologies; and video and presentation technologies.

Teacher's Edition Online
URL: http://www.teachnet.com/

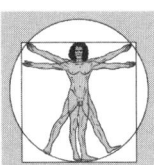

Everything you need for your class is here at this site! Lesson plans, classroom management ideas, classroom decor, organization ideas, articles, keypals, online discussions, and more! This is an excellent site for first-time teachers.

Related Areas: *Language Arts/Languages; Art & Music; Science; Social Studies; Technology/Internet; Math*

Teacher Resources

Teacher's Helper
URL: http://www.widomaker.com/~flowers/

Each month, a collection of lesson plans is posted to this site by the writers of popular children's books. The lessons focus on math, science, language arts, and the arts. Perfect for young students!

Related Areas: *Math; Language Arts/Languages; Art & Music; Social Studies; Science*

Teachers Helping Teachers
URL: http://www.pacificnet.net/~mandel/

The goal of this innovative online service is to provide basic teaching tips to inexperienced teachers that can be quickly and easily implemented in the classroom. There are also new ideas in teaching methodologies for all teachers, and a forum for experienced educators to share their expertise and thoughts with their colleagues from around the world.

The Teacher's Internet Pages (TIPS)
URL: http://www.iteachnet.com/

The Teacher's Internet Pages, or TIPS as they frequently call themselves, is a site for international—and internationally minded—teachers and administrators worldwide. Their mission is to help the international school community by providing them with a place to add their own ideas and experiences, and a forum in which to discuss it all. To that end, they have created a collection of department-oriented pages, each written by a master teacher and Web educator. You'll find articles with advice on everything from setting up local networks to HTML tutorials.

Related Areas: *Art & Music; Health/PE; Language Arts/Languages; Math; Science; Social Studies; Technology/Internet*

 Integration Idea

> Just about everything that an inexperienced teacher needs to know can be found at one of these excellent teacher resources. Teacher's Edition Online will help you get organized and make suggestions about how you can improve the look of your classroom. You will find lessons galore at Teacher's Helper. Where can new teachers get advice from others, especially teachers in their own department areas? The Teacher's Internet Pages is the place! Participate in a discussion, look for cross-curricular material, or visit a linked school. There are so many resources here, you won't know where to begin!

Teacher Resources

Teachers.Net
URL: http://www.teachers.net

Billed as an 'online consortium for teachers," Teachers.Net has put together a collection of materials that focus on helping educators learn how to incorporate the Internet into their classrooms. Have a question or an announcement you'd like to post? Check out its online bulletin board. Want to learn how to create your own Web pages? Check out the free Internet handbook, which covers the types of Web authoring tools available online.

Related Areas: *Technology/Internet*

Teacher Talk
URL: http://www.mightymedia.com/talk/

Teacher Talk is a public conferencing system for K-12 educators. This site provides an extremely easy-to-use conferencing system that allows educators to share ideas, engage in debate, or simply get to know fellow colleagues around the world.

Related Areas: *Technology/Internet*

Teaching Diversity Resources
URL: http://www.cob.ohio-state.edu/~diversity/

This site contains a wealth of information and links to online sites about teaching diversity in elementary, secondary, and postsecondary classrooms. You'll find hands-on teaching strategies, links to information about gender-specific issues, social classes, religions, and more. There's even an exhaustive listing of tips for teachers who want to practice what they preach.

Related Areas: *Social Studies; Language Arts/Languages*

Today's Fun Fact
URL: http://www.dreamsville.com/CSN/Wardo/fact.html

This Web site gives a daily tale of what event happened today in history. It serves both as a mailing list and a Web site. This site can be used in the classroom as the perfect warm-up activity for students of all ages!

Related Areas: *Social Studies; Science; Language Arts/Languages*

Teacher Resources

Turner Adventure Learning (TAL)
URL: http://learning.turner.com/

Turner Learning, Inc., is dedicated to enhancing education by making selected resources of Turner Broadcasting available to schools and libraries in the U.S., Canada, and abroad. Their Electronic Field Trips marry live cablecast and online computer technologies in one-of-a-kind, interactive events designed to give your students access to people, places, and experiences to which they might otherwise never be exposed. As participants in these field trips, your students "travel" across time and space to places of natural wonder, scientific inquiry, and historical meaning.

Related Areas: *Technology/Internet; Social Studies; Science; Language Arts/Languages; Art & Music*

The Ultimate Children's Internet Sites
URL: http://www.vividus.com/ucis.html

 This site offers great activities for students in grades K-8 including science, language arts, social studies, and other appropriate activities. Many of these activities you can print and use in your classroom.

Related Areas: *Art & Music; Language Arts/Languages; Social Studies; Science; Technology/Internet*

Understanding the Library
URL: http://www.hcc.hawaii.edu/education/hcc/library/understd.html

Have your students been studying library materials and their organization? Here they can learn the call numbers and why books are assigned to their place on the shelves. The Library of Congress Classification System is also included for subject reference.

Related Areas: *Language Arts/Languages*

 Integration Idea

> Many teachers use a calendar and discussion of the date to begin the school day, but why not use the Web to enhance the experience? Today's Fun Fact is the perfect way to set the tone of your classroom, and it will be a fun change from the norm. After you read the daily "Fun Fact," use skills from Understanding the Library to suggest methods of research to gather more information on the topic. You might want a student to visit the school library and test your class' ideas. This will help the students to see where to begin in researching a topic and how to organize their thoughts for a more effective search, and many of the research skills they will use apply to searches on the Net as well!

Teacher Resources

Urban Education Web
URL: http://eric-web.tc.columbia.edu/

This extraordinary Web site is dedicated to urban students, their families, and the educators who serve them. It offers manuals, brief articles, annotated bibliographies, and conference annoucements relating to urban education.

Related Areas: *Technology/Internet*

Urban Educator
URL: http://www.cgcs.org/newslett/

This Web-published monthly magazine contains urban education-related news from across the United States. Recent topics include urban school reform, enrollment issues, funding, class sizes, and school inequities.

Related Areas: *Technology/Internet*

U.S. Department of Education
URL: http://www.ed.gov

The aim for this award-winning Web site, which is hosted by the National Library of Education (NLE), is to provide visitors with information about the offices and programs of the U.S. Department of Education, education initiatives of the President and the Secretary, the full text of ED reports and publications, links to organizations they support, and more. This is an excellent resource for lesson plans and educational news.

Related Areas: *Technology/Internet; Art & Music; Health/PE; Language Arts/Languages; Math; Science; Social Studies*

Virtual School Floor Plan
URL: http://www.nhptv.org/floor.htm

Lessons plans, resources, links, and more are available at this site to be printed and used when you need them. Their are also virtual field trips, discussion groups, games, information on financial aid, and much more. This is a site that can be used by every grade.

Related Areas: *Art & Music; Language Arts/Languages; Technology/Internet; Social Studies; Science; Math*

Teacher Resources

Web 66: A K–12 World Wide Web Project
URL: http://web66.coled.umn.edu

Named after the well-known highway, Web 66 is designed to facilitate the introduction of technology into K-12 schools. Its goals are to help educators learn how to set up their own Internet sites, link servers, educators, and students at schools across the globe, and help find appropriate resources for educators on the World Wide Web.

Related Areas: *Technology/Internet*

WebGEMS: Librarian Subject Guide
URL: http://www.fpsol.com/gems/webgems.html

WebGEMS is a librarian's subject guide to Web sites which provide significant information useful to students at all levels, including short articles, longer texts, statistical data, dictionaries, directories, databases, maps, image archives, subject guides, and instructional resources. An excellent resource for media specialists and librarians in K-12 schools around the world.

Related Areas: *Social Studies; Science; Math; Language Arts/Languages*

What Parents Need To Know
URL: http://www.health.org/wpkit/efs6.htm

This site will give parents a guide to building self-esteem while also teaching communication about drug resistance and being a role model. This is an excellent resource for teaching students the statistics of kids and drug use.

Related Areas: *Science; Health/PE*

 Integration Idea

Are you a teacher of urban students? Urban Education Web and Urban Educator are two Web sources for you. At these sites you will discover articles and Internet links with information regarding all aspects of urban education. What are some of the related issues in teaching urban children? Parents and teachers will gain an understanding of many issues regarding urban education at What Parents Need to Know. Use the information found here to support your students in avoiding some of the pitfalls presented by urban life and boost their self-esteem with the positive rewards of making wise decisions.

Teacher Resources

World Wide Web Constructivist Project Design Guide

URL: http://www.ilt.columbia.edu/k12/livetext-nf/webcurr.html

You've managed to get access to the World Wide Web in your classroom and you want to create a problem-based, cooperative learning project, that provides relevant learning experiences through accessing and building communities on the Internet. Start by reading this well-organized hypertext document hosted by Teachers College at Columbia University which includes a constructivist approach to making Web pages.

Related Areas: *Technology/Internet*

World Wide Web Virtual Library: Educational Technology

URL: http://tecfa.unige.ch/info-edu-comp.html

This site is a meta-index of educational technology sites available worldwide via the Internet. More than two hundred site links can be found here. Updated monthly.

Related Areas: *Technology/Internet*

World Wide Web Virtual Library: Museums

URL: http://www.comlab.ox.ac.uk:80/archive/other/museums.html

This collection of Web pages provides visitors with an eclectic collection of WWW services connected with museums, galleries, and and other online collections and archives.

Related Areas: *Social Studies; Science; Language Arts/Languages; Art & Music*

Youth Central

URL: http://www.youthcentral.apple.com

This extremely child-friendly site created "by kids and teens for kids and teens," is a good place to take your young students when touring the Web for the first time. Visitors to the site can ask Louella for advice on day to day issues; share opinions on world issues at the Central Census page; download and share their favorite sounds, artwork, and stories; see photos from around the world; attend a live chat; or just try to find penpals. A free newsletter and calendar keeps kids informed about what's going on at the site.

Related Areas: *Art & Music; Language Arts/Languages; Math; Science; Social Studies*

Teacher Resources

Youth Net   K-6
URL: http://yn.la.ca.us/academy_one/special/menu.html

Here is a place where youth of all ages around the world can safely meet each other and participate in discussions, interactive learning projects, and activities that meet their needs.

Related Areas: *Health/PE; Language Arts/Languages; Math; Science; Social Studies*

 Integration Idea

Where can young children safely surf the Net and communicate with each other? At the Youth Central Web site. It is your one-stop spot for all of the interaction your young Web surfers can handle. You can also relate your students' Internet experience to other cultures by allowing them to visit Youth Net. This is another kid-safe site that permits them to communicate with children from other countries around the world. Both of these sites are perfect for locating keypals and sharing stories. Try having your students interview their keypals and create pictures of them based on their descriptions. They could even send their drawings to their keypals by email or regular snail mail!

YELLOW PAGES
TECHNOLOGY & INTERNET

Technology & Internet

Acceptable Use Policies
URL: gopher://ericir.syr.edu:70/11/Guides/Agreements

Acceptable Use Policies (AUPs) are crucial to the successful integration of the Internet into K-12 schools. Every school with Net access ought to at least consider creating an AUP, which outlines the rules and regulations of Internet use in the classroom. This is ERIC's collection of AUPs, available via gopher.

Related Areas: *Teacher Resources*

Ad Nauseum
URL: http://www.crl.com/~jnelson/nauseam/

A somewhat hip online e-zine containing helpful Web commentary, along with reviews of the latest hardware, software, and more.

Alta Vista
URL: http://www.altavista.digital.com

This search engine boasts one of the largest Internet indexes in existence and will help you search out the information you need on the Internet. You have access to 20 billion words found in over 41 million Web pages. A full-text index of thousands of Usenet newsgroups is also linked to this search engine.

America Online Access to FTP Mirror Sites
URL: ftp://mirrors.aol.com/pub/

This link connects you to a mirror site maintained by America Online. It contains archives of more than a dozen of the most popular ftp sites on the Internet, where you and your students can download educational shareware, graphics programs, and free word processors.

Technology & Internet

Audio Conferencing on the Internet
URL: http://www.classroom.net/voice-faq.htm

Thanks to some remarkable new software, K-12 students around the world are interacting with one other in real-time, using nothing more than their voices and a computer outfitted with a sound card, microphone, modem, and an inexpensive Internet connection. For an overview of the audio conferencing software now available on the Net, check out this Web site.

Related Areas: *Language Arts/Languages*

Background Colors
URL: http://colors.infi.net/colorindex.html

Here's an extensive list of all the "mysterious" HTML codes used to change the background, text, link, and visited link colors on Web pages enhanced for Netscape. A great help when building your own Web pages.

Back to School
URL: http://web.csd.sc.edu/bck2skol/bck2skol.html

School library/media specialists new to the Net should consider taking this online course for Internet newcomers. It consists of 30 individual, hands-on lessons distributed over a six-week period. All aspects of the Net are explained from the perspective of a librarian or media specialist. The class provides pointers to online information in eight academic areas.

Related Areas: *Teacher Resources*

 Integration Idea

Here you will find three activities that are perfect for the teacher who wants to be well-prepared! Although it was designed with school librarians in mind, Back to School is just right for any beginning Internet user. The online lessons located here will provide you with a basic understanding of the Internet. Use your new-found knowledge to create an AUP for your school with the help of Acceptable Use Policies. Then begin to use the resources of the Web by trying out the Alta Vista search engine. Your students will be impressed by your outstanding computer skills!

Technology & Internet

Ballad of an Email Terrorist
URL: http://www.gsn.org/gsn/articles/article.email.ballad.html

What do you do when your fourth grade student receives an obscene email message? How do you track down the offender and make sure that he or she doesn't become a re-occurring problem? Such an incident happened to a elementary school in New Jersey. This article from the Global SchoolNet Foundation tells the whole sordid story in detail and provides a practical guide on how to effectively handle this type of situation, as well as give a warning to older students about the potential consequences of abusing the Internet.

B.C. Ministry of Education—
The Technology and Distance Branch
URL: http://www.etc.bc.ca/home.html

The Ministry of Education in British Columbia, Canada, offers online access to a report about telecommunications in the classroom and a copy of their K-12 Education Plan.

Related Areas: *Teacher Resources; Social Studies*

A Beginner's Guide to Effective Email
URL: http://www.webfoot.com/advice/email.top.html?Yahoo

This is not a document on the mechanics of sending email, but instead focuses on the content of email: how to say what you need to say. For instance, if you're wondering why email is different than talking on the telephone or writing a regular letter, this is the place to get your answer.

Beginner's Guide to HTML
URL: http://www.ncsa.uiuc.edu/General/Internet/WWW/HTMLPrimer.html

```
<P>
</TD></TR>
</TD></TR>
</table>
<table width=550>
<TD align=left width=150><
<TD align=left width=185><
<TD align=center width=185
<TD align=right width=160>
</FONT></CENTER> </TD></TR
```

This online textbook is an excellent beginner's guide to learn the basics of the hypertext markup language (HTML) used to create World Wide Web pages. It's an introduction and does not offer instructions on every aspect of HTML. Still, if you're interested in finding out how to create your first Web page, this is the place to visit first.

Technology & Internet

Berit's Best Sites for Children
URL: http://db.cochran.com/db_HTML:theopage.db

Berit's Web site is another online directory of great sites for little hands. The page is organized into categories like animals or dinosaurs. Each site is rated based on five criteria, including content, ease of use, and suitability for a young audience.

Related Areas: *Teacher Resources; Art & Music; Health/PE; Language Arts/Languages; Math; Science; Social Studies*

CamCorner
URL: http://www.ovd.com:80/camcorner/

The Internet is home to hundreds of InternetCams — cameras and still cameras positioned around the world that feed live images of what they see to Web sites. This single site will link you to dozens of them—from a live image of Niagara Falls to the waves at North Beach in Hawaii. An interesting site that illustrates one of the incredible truths about the Internet — its immediacy.

Related Areas: *Social Studies*

Camp T-Equity
URL: http://www.wshs.fairfax.k12.va.us/tequity/

The primary goal of Camp T-Equity (tek-witty) is to help increase girls' participation in science and mathematics through technology (Internet) immersion in the earth and environmental sciences. Topics addressed include: high-speed computer networking via the Internet; Internet publishing using the World Wide Web; use of interactive multimedia authorware; and more. An important project that should be emulated by every school district!

Related Areas: *Science: Math*

 Integration Idea

> Email is an ideal way for students to communicate in a short period of time. There are, however, some precautions to be taken in this activity. You will discover how to use email effectively through A Beginner's Guide to Effective Email. The Ballad of an Email Terrorist article, meanwhile, describes the pitfalls of using email in the classroom. These sites will help you deal with the problems and find the rewards of email experiences. Encourage your students to correspond via email, but remind them to do it wisely.

Technology & Internet

CCC Net
URL: http://www.cccnet.com/

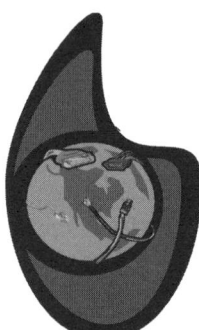

Computer Curriculum Corporation, an experienced multimedia publishing company involved in K-12 education, has created a unique Web site offering educators and students the chance to use the Internet to its full educational potential. Students surfing to the site will be able to post their art projects in "The Gallery," take part in a scavenger hunt at the "Travel Ship," or go on an online field trip with "SuccessMaker."

Related Areas: *Teacher Resources; Social Studies; Language Arts/Languages*

Censorship, Freedom of Speech, and Child Safety on the Internet
URL: http://www.voicenet.com/~cranmer/censorship.html

This site offers information on all of these issues, plus links to child-friendly resources on the Web.

Related Areas: *Teacher Resources*

Challenges and Strategies in Using Technology to Promote Education Reform
URL: http://www.ed.gov/pubs/EdReformStudies/EdTech/approaches.html

The vision for technology-supported, reform-oriented classrooms is one in which student groups work on long-term, multidisciplinary projects involving challenging content and using technology to collect, analyze, display, and communicate information. Making this vision a reality poses many challenges — which are outlined in this excellent document from the U.S. Department of Education.

Child Safety on the Information Highway
URL: http://www.larrysworld.com/child_safety.html

This online essay, written by columnist Larry Magid, is an excellent guide for parents and educators concerned about inappropriate material on the Internet, and children's access to it. The article covers the benefits of going online, the risks that might occur, how to take steps to reduce those risks, and some online safety rules that students can follow when on the computer.

Related Areas: *Teacher Resources*

Technology & Internet

Children's Shareware and More!
URL: http://www.gamesdomain.com/tigger/

In the past, searching for quality children's software on the Internet could often seem like a fruitless effort for parents as well as educators. That's no longer the case thanks to this incredible online storehouse of Mac and PC shareware! Arranged according to grade and age level, there are plenty of games and activities for grade-schoolers, preschoolers, parents, teachers, even babies! In addition, there are lots of cartoon icons to download, links to software reviews, and commercial software demos.

Related Areas: *Art & Music; Language Arts/Languages; Science; Math; Social Studies; Teacher Resources*

Classroom Without Walls
URL: http://www.tcimet.net/mmclass/

Billed as the first virtual K-12 school on the Web, Classroom Without Walls was designed by teachers, parents, children, and content experts worldwide. Site administrators are constructing a "core school" on the site, while students are building the rest of the school. Of interest to educators are a complete course on Teaching with Technology and information on a multimedia classroom project.

Related Areas: *Teacher Resources; Social Studies; Science; Math; Language Arts/Languages; Health/PE; Art & Music*

C/Net
URL: http://www.cnet.com

This online version of the popular Internet/computer cable television show contains regularly updated reviews of the latest software, Web sites, as well as in-depth features about various facets of the Net. This is the first place to come to when you want the latest Internet news.

 Integration Idea

> Educational sites which allow your students to add or submit their own material are unique in their dynamic nature. You may use these sites to show your class how they can get involved in the online world and change the information that they find on the Internet. Give your students the assignment of posting an art creation in the art gallery at CCC Net. Your class may read Web pages created by other students and learn something about creating their own Web pages at Classroom Without Walls.

Technology & Internet

The Computer Learning Foundation
URL: http://www.computerlearning.org/

The Computer Learning Foundation is an international nonprofit organization "dedicated to improving the quality of education and preparing youth for the work place through the use of technology." Its Web site serves as a year-round clearinghouse for parents and educators by providing copious amounts of information, not only on the company, but also on teacher materials, funding guides, student contests, and more!

Related Areas: *Teacher Resources*

Computer Virus Myths
URL: http://www.kumite.com/myths/home.htm

If you've been on the Internet for any length of time, chances are you received email about one or more email-based viruses. Your first reaction may be to panic! But before you do, load up your Internet browser and connect to this site. Here you'll learn about the myths, the hoaxes, the urban legends, and the implications of computer virus myths. You can also see a list of virus hoaxes from A to Z. So the next time you hear about a virus, check it out here first!

Computers in the Classroom
URL: http://seamonkey.ed.asu.edu/emc300/

Need to come up to speed on integrating the Internet into the curriculum, or on classroom management and other technology issues? Computers in the Classroom is a telecommunications course with six learning modules that prepare current and future teachers to use technology in the classroom. Created by Arizona State University, the course is especially helpful for educators new to the Net.

Related Areas: *Teacher Resources*

The Cross-Platform Page
URL: http://VTGinc.com/ebennett/xplat/

This site lists resources for reading and converting images, video, audio, and data compression/encoding file formats on most common computer systems.

Technology & Internet

CU-SeeMe Videoconferencing
URL: http://cu-seeme.cornell.edu

CU-SeeMe is a free program that allows you to link your students, by voice and video, to any Internet user or wired classroom, worldwide. It's available to anyone with a Macintosh or Windows PC, and a 28.8 or faster modem. Schools are just beginning to use this inexpensive, easy-to-set-up technology to meet with classrooms from around the world.

Related Areas: *Teacher Resources*

DejaNews
URL: http://dejanews.com

DejaNews is your gateway to a simple search engine for Usenet newsgroup postings. Enter your keywords in the box and DejaNews will search its mammoth database of past and present postings to the Net's 17,000+ topical bulletin boards in seconds. This site is very useful for educators and other school staffers.

Educator's Toolkit
URL: http://marlo.eagle.ca/~matink/

Unfortunately, a lot of online educational guides are little more than a poorly organized collection of 10 or 12 links. Not so this site, which has an enormous collection of links to good resources and has arranged them in useful categories that make it easy to find what you want. Each month a new "theme," such as insects or endangered animals, is added to the site. Of special note is *SafetyNet*, a free monthly guide to what's educational and what's interesting on the Internet. Each site is rated according to grade level and divided by subject matter.

Related Areas: *Teacher Resources; Art & Music; Health/PE; Language Arts/Languages; Math; Science; Social Studies*

 Integration Idea

> Integration is an idea that is great in theory but can be difficult in practice. The Educator's Toolkit is a terrific source for integration ideas. Their theme section will give you a selection of sites to incorporate into your theme-related lessons. Computers in the Classroom includes links to and ideas for Web pages that help you teach integrated units. Imagine creating your own resource Web page that your students will use as a part of their classroom experience! Integration is not always easy, but it is definitely rewarding!

# Technology & Internet

The Electric Library
URL: http://www3.elibrary.com/search.cgi

With an archive containing more than 1,000 publications, educators and students should head here for their research questions. Users can type in a complete question or keyword to retrieve photos, articles, reviews, and books on virtually any subject.

Related Areas: *Teacher Resources; Social Studies; Science; Math; Language Arts/Languages; Health/PE; Art & Music*

Email Discussion Groups
URL: http://www.nova.edu/Inter-Links/listserv.html

Wondering where to find a mailing list that matches your hobbies and interests? Looking for a good education discussion group? This site provides a complete guide to email discussion groups as well as help in understanding how to subscribe and unsubscribe from them.

Related Areas: *Teacher Resources*

Excite
URL: http://www.excite.com

Excite, a well-known Internet searching tool, employs a unique concept search technology to search and summarize more than 50 million Web pages and more than two weeks of Usenet newsgroup postings. Plus it includes over 61,000 reviews of Web sites written by professional journalists, and an hourly news update. It's one of the best ways for educators and students to navigate the Net.

Filamentality
URL: http://www.kn.pacbell.com/wired/fil

You say you want to create an educational Web page but just don't know how to go about doing it? No problem. Just head over to Filamentality, your online guide to brainstorming up a Web page. Whether you want to create a simple list of sites, an online scavenger hunt, or something more complex, this site will guide you through the basic steps you need to do all the hard computer work. All you need do is fill in the forms describing what you want on your page and voìla! With a click of the mouse your online contribution is ready for posting. If you can't think of a topic, they have a list of 50 to try out.

Related Areas: *Teacher Resources*

Technology & Internet

The Global Educator's Guide to the Internet K-6
URL: http://www.educ.uvic.ca/faculty/triecken/

A unique offering that puts a much-needed global slant on K–12 education. Includes an outline of the proper uses of the Internet in the classroom, links to relevant resources, and much more.

Related Areas: *Teacher Resources*

Grant Opportunity Resources K-6
URL: http://www.kn.pacbell.com/wired/grants/grant_res.html

This Web page contains links to more than three dozen of the better-known and most-reliable online resources for gaining the information and expertise needed for an intelligent pursuit of technology grant funding.

Related Areas: *Teacher Resources*

Heritage Online
URL: http://www.hol.edu/

Are you looking for a way to learn more about integrating the Internet without having to leave the comfort of your own home? If so, then you might want to take a look at the offerings of Heritage Online, a company specializing in Internet-assisted distance education for teachers. Choose from among 15 different online courses designed to help educators use the Internet in their classrooms, regardless of whether they're teaching math, science, art, or social studies. Each course has its own mailing list so participants can communicate with each other via email. Classes last for one full year.

Related Areas: *Teacher Resources*

 Integration Idea

Learning to search effectively is a key skill for all students to master. With the addition of the Internet, searching has become all the more essential. The Electric Library has abundant resources for your students to search for their next Internet project. One of the most well-established search engines, Excite is also a very helpful tool for anyone who wants to find something on the Net. Have your students use these searching agents to locate information and hone their searching skills. What can they do when a search has no results or yields results that do not suit the real concept? How can they modify a search among results to find the entries that will match their topic?

Technology & Internet

HotBot

URL: http://www.hotbot.com

HotBot is a relative newcomer to the Internet search engine race. However, this search tool boasts a 55+ million online document index to the Internet, which makes it the most comprehensive search tool currently available online. Easily searched via keywords. Sponsored by *Wired* magazine.

Hotlist Anywhere!

URL: http://myhotlist.com

Hotlist Anywhere! is a tool to let you access your hotlist from anywhere on the Web, from any type of computer, and from any browser. If you use the Web from home, school, on the road, or at your friend's house, Hotlist Anywhere! will save you time and effort. No more time wasted retracing your steps on Web searches. No more saying: "Can you spell out that URL for me again?" An excellent service for any Internet user looking to streamline their bookmark files!

How to Maintain a Healthy Computer

URL: http://pip.ehhs.cmich.edu/healthy/

If you're a newcomer to the world of computers, then this site will quickly become one of your favorites! Learn all the basics of your Macintosh of Windows PC, plus how to use your favorite programs. Also learn how to back up files, troubleshoot common problems, and keep your computer's hard drive free of clutter.

Related Areas: *Teacher Resources*

HTML Goodies

URL: http://www.htmlgoodies.com

This comprehensive site contains links to 50 HTML tutorials (beginner to advanced), information about Java with example scripts, HTML Primers, free Web images, and more. An easy-to-navigate site for use by any school staffer looking to make the most of HTML in the classroom!

Technology & Internet

InfoSeek

URL: http://www.infoseek.com

Billed as "proof of intelligent life on the Net" InfoSeek offers a searchable index to an impressive amount on online content—from Arts & Entertainment sites, to Politics, and beyond. You'll also find links to global directories, stock quotes, technology news, and more. Windows users will love QuickSeek software, which works directly with InfoSeek to track down Internet information for you.

Inquiry.Com

URL: http://www.inquiry.com

Have questions about setting up a school Intranet, Web site, or the features of the latest Internet browsers? Inquiry.com is a Q&A-style Web site that allows you to ask questions and get instant answers to your technology questions. This site includes "Ten-Minute Solutions" for a variety of needs, an Ask the Pros database containing advice, tips, and techniques from industry experts, and more.

InSite

URL: http://curry.edschool.Virginia.EDU/insite/

InSITE, the Information network of the Society for Information Technology and Teacher Education (SITE), is a World Wide Web resource dedicated to exploring ways in which the Internet can be used both to benefit teacher education programs at colleges and universities around the world, and to support K-12 staff development technology initiatives.

Related Areas: *Teacher Resources*

 Integration Idea

Anyone who uses the Internet frequently develops program preferences. What search engines do your students prefer? Why? Have them use the HotBot and InfoSeek search engines and determine which fits their needs more adequately. HotBot is a new search engine, while InfoSeek is a tad more experienced for its young field. Divide your class into groups and give them a list of questions to answer. Have them try to solve them using one of the two search engines. Now have them use the opposite search engine and solve new questions. Was HotBot or InfoSeek more effective in helping to find their answers? Why or why not?

Technology & Internet

Instructional Media: Web Style Manual
URL: http://info.med.yale.edu/caim/StyleManual_Top.HTML

Served up by the Yale Center for Advanced Instructional Design, this site contains all the information schools need to create robust, content-rich Web pages to further the educational process. Includes hands-on examples for creating Web-based courses, and how best to use the Web to create online curriculum materials.

Related Areas: *Teacher Resources*

Intel's 25th Anniversary of the Microprocessor
URL: http://www.intel.com/intel/museum/25anniv/shock/index.htm

This site takes full advantage of the latest multimedia technology to present information about the creation of the microprocessor at Intel in the late 1960s. Includes a compelling interactive section that allows students to join the founders of Intel in the '60s to discover what decisions they made when creating the first computer chip. Great content your students — technogeeks or not — will enjoy!

Related Areas: *Teacher Resources; Social Studies*

Inter-Links Internet Access
URL: http://www.nova.edu/Inter-Links/

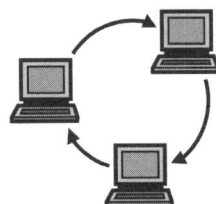

With an enormous amount of Internet links, this page would be useful enough for beginning surfers. What makes this page really valuable, though, are the links to Internet guides and tutorials that will help you and your students learn how to use the various Internet applications, such as email and gopher!

Interesting Places for Kids
URL: http://www.crc.ricoh.com/people/steve/kids.html

Internaut Stephen Savitzky put this Web site together for his ten-year-old daughter Katy. Here you'll find plenty of links to places on the Net that are just right for kids, including sites about crafts, hobbies, music, museums, games, and other material published by children on the Net.

Related Areas: *Teacher Resources; Social Studies; Science; Math; Language Arts/Languages; Health/PE; Art & Music*

Technology & Internet

Internet Browser Enhancements and Plug-ins

URL: http://www.netscape.com/comprod/mirror/navcomponents_download.html

Looking to turbo-charge your Internet browser? Look no further than Netscape's browser plug-in and helper applications home page. Here you'll find information on downloading the Net's hottest multimedia players that help make the Web a colorful, interactive place. Must downloads include: QuickTime, Real Audio, and ShockWave.

Internet for Minnesota Schools

URL: http://informns.k12.mn.us/

InforMNs (Internet for Minnesota Schools) is a joint project developed with the participation and support of various Minnesota educational groups. InforMNs is designed to provide Internet access to all K-12 public schools in Minnesota. Their primary goal, however, is to "help K-12 educators utilize the Internet and begin to realize the instructional potential" within a classroom setting.

Related Areas: *Teacher Resources*

Internet Learning Tours

URL: http://pavilion.baynetworks.com/pavilion/depot.html

Using a freight-train metaphor, this site guides you and your students through the basics of how the Internet works—from your computer, to switches, to routers, and all the rest. An interesting, rich site that is sure to answer any and all of your questions about how the Internet functions at a fundamental level.

Related Areas: *Teacher Resources*

 Integration Idea

> When you are ready to give yourself an Internet tutorial, these sites will be waiting! Internet Learning Tours will introduce you to the Net on a very basic level. Use the links you find at Inter-Links Internet Access to complete your Internet lesson. Internet for Minnesota Schools is designed to help you use the Internet effectively in your classroom. Once you fully understand what the Net has to offer and how you can use it, you will become an expert with using technology in instruction.

Technology & Internet

Internet Resources Newsletter from the U.K.
URL: http://www.hw.ac.uk/libWWW/irn/irn.html

Internet Resources is a monthly electronic newsletter, edited by Heriot-Watt University Library staff and published by the Heriot-Watt University Internet Resource Centre. The newsletter aims to raise awareness of new sources of online information to educators and students.

Related Areas: *Teacher Resources*

Internet Resources on the Web
URL: http://www.brandonu.ca/~ennsnr/Resources/resources.html

This page is a collection of resources that are useful to Internet trainers, as well as just about anyone else who is on the Net. Links to newsgroups, mailing lists, archives, and a variety of resources can be found here.

Internet Sleuth
URL: http://www.isleuth.com

Here you can peruse more than 900 searchable databases, directories, and search engines on the Internet — all from one site. This is a little slower than going to a search site direct, as it acts as a "middleman," but very useful nonetheless!

Internet Statistics
URL: http://k12.cnidr.org/janice_k12/states/summary.html

The Clearinghouse for Networked Information Discovery and Retrieval (CNIDR) has compiled an impressive array of statistics concerning Internet use by K-12 schools. There are stats on how many schools, districts, and administrative offices are connected to the Net, a 1993 census of K-12 user accounts by state, and more. The stats show that more than 150,000 U.S. students access the Web on a regular basis, and the numbers are climbing. This is great ammunition for teachers trying to convince administrators to bring the Net into the classroom.

Technology & Internet

Internet Tools for Educators
URL: http://tdi.uregina.ca/~itt/

A new guide for educators who are new to the Internet and looking for fresh ways to utilize it in the elementary school classroom. This site also includes hands-on ideas for using the Internet in virtually every curriculum area, links to practical ideas for its use, and much more.

Related Areas: *Teacher Resources*

Internet Trend Watch for Libraries
URL: http://www.leonline.com/itw/

The *Internet Trend Watch for Libraries* is an email newsletter highlighting innovative Internet applications in libraries. Its creators monitor current library and technology-related publications, mailing lists, Web sites, and other resources to keep subscribers up to date about the latest Internet news.

Related Areas: *Teacher Resources*

Internet Trends
URL: http://www.genmagic.com/Internet/Trends/

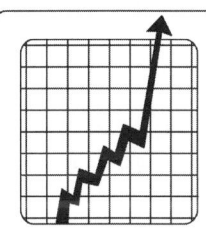

Wondering how many people are currently online? Or what the most popular tool of the Net is? Want to find out what the latest trends are? This site has complete abstracts and statistics of Internet usage.

Integration Idea

Have you wondered how many people use the Internet, who they are, and why they use it? These "trendy" sites will help you form a correct picture of Internet users. Internet Trends and Internet Trend Watch for Libraries will show you the current statistics relating to how many people are online and what resources they use. Internet Statistics has the complete information about schools on the Internet. One thing is certain; more and more users are finding useful information online than ever before!

 **Technology & Internet**

Internet Web Text: Index
URL: http://www.december.com/web/text/index.html

A fun, user-friendly orientation course on Internet basics. The site includes links to introductory Net documents and computer-generated maps of the Internet's cyberspace. Very easy and fun to navigate, this Web site is sure to keep you and your students informed and entertained for hours.

K–12 Acceptable Use Policies Page
URL: http://www.erehwon.com/k12aup/

This site, created by education technology consultant Nancy Willard, includes an extensive legal analysis of K-12 Acceptable Use Policies, including issues relating to due process, search and seizure, liability, copyright, and First Amendment rights. Also includes links to other AUP sites.

Related Areas: *Teacher Resources*

K–12 Technology Handbook
URL: http://pen1.pen.k12.va.us/go/techbook/toc.shtml

 The purpose of this online handbook is to provide schools in Virginia (and across the United States) with the best "electronic" resources available to assist in the technical aspects of incorporating voice, video, data, and computing resources into the K-12 classroom. An in-depth resource for educators and technology coordinators alike.

Related Areas: *Teacher Resources*

K–5 Cyber Trail
URL: http://www.wmht.org/trail/trail.htm

 This online presentation is a perfect introduction to the Internet for elementary educators. Follow resident expert, Syd the CyberGuide, as he shows you how innovative elementary schools around the globe are becoming a part of the World Wide Web. Syd will show you school home pages, student Web publishing, interactive Internet projects, and model sites for K-5 education.

Related Areas: *Teacher Resources*

Technology & Internet

KidsWeb: A Guide to Kids' Home Pages
URL: http://www.hooked.net/~leroyc/kidsweb/

Do you wonder if there are any other children out there with home pages on the World Wide Web? Would you like to see what kinds of things students are doing online during their free time? Then, by all means, head over to this site, an online collection of Web pages about or authored by kids. Arranged alphabetically, each link comes with a two-sentence review and explanation of what the site offers.

Kristy's Desktop Creations for Kids
URL: http://kwebdesign.com/kdesk/

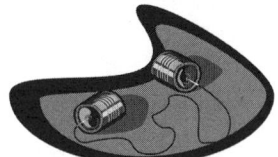 Dedicated for all the very young computer lovers, this site is chock-full of kid-oriented animated cursors, icons, wallpaper, desktop patterns, screensavers, and graphics. Have your students download these tools and then dress up their computer and Web pages!

Related Areas: *Art & Music*

Learn the Net
URL: http://www.learnthenet.com

The world's first online "field guide" to the Internet! Includes a comprehensive guide to the Net written in an easy-to-understand language that both teachers and students will appreciate. Modules include: Getting started, Internet basics, the World Wide Web, Email, and Multimedia. Contains a complete glossary of terms and educational games.

 Integration Idea

Even as babies, children love to watch each other, and kids never get enough of seeing other kids their age on the Internet. K-5 Cyber Trail will introduce your students to the many school and class Web pages currently online. KidWeb: A Guide to Kids' Home Pages will show your students Web pages created by other kids. After you have visited these sites, go to Kristy's Desktop Creations for Kids. Your students may download some of these "creations" and use them to personalize their own computers and Web pages. Wow!

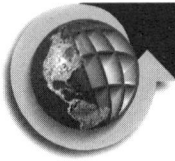

Technology & Internet

LETSNet
URL: http://commtechlab.msu.edu/Ameritech/

LETSNet (Learning Exchange for Teachers and Students) is a dynamic online environment where teachers can develop their understanding of the Web and find ways to effectively use it in their classrooms. To help teachers achieve these goals, the site's organizers have wrapped teaching resources around real-world classroom teacher stories, including lesson plans, curriculum standards and guides, pointers to mailing lists, and many other Internet and Web materials. The stories that have been collected to date center on teachers and their feelings about their successes, lessons learned, and plans for future Internet activities with their students.

Related Areas: *Teacher Resources; Social Studies; Science; Math; Language Arts/Languages*

Learning Resource Server
URL: http://www.ed.uiuc.edu

The LRS provides you with a "knowledge space" that links you to some of the most exciting uses of technologies for learning on the Internet. Using the LRS, you can link to real projects submitted by teachers and students, access the work of researchers who are articulating new visions of what learning can be, and learn how to create new knowledge yourself. The ultimate goal of this site is to help teachers move from being passive surfers of the Web to serving up information from their classrooms to the rest of the world!

Related Areas: *Teacher Resources*

Life on the Internet
URL: http://www.pbs.org/internet/

Educating students about the Internet has, for the most part, come from the grassroots up—not from the top down. Individual schools, educators, and parents who are not prepared to wait for the Internet to be taught in a traditional, widespread, and orderly manner have begun to teach students about the Internet in their own fashion. Check out the online transcript, hyperlinks, and live video stream of PBS's feature "Cyber Students" at their Life on the Internet Web site. Great content, and excellent examples of how the community is making the Internet an integral part of K-12 schools across the United States.

Related Areas: *Teacher Resources*

Little Fingers Software
URL: http://www.littlefingers.com/

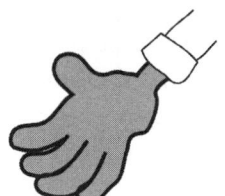

Little Fingers Software offers quality educational Macintosh and Windows shareware programs for children and adults. At this address you can download lots of fun, educational programs that are specifically designed for tiny hands.

Related Areas: *Teacher Resources; Art & Music; Health/PE; Language Arts/Languages; Math; Science; Social Studies*

LiveText
URL: http://www.ilt.columbia.edu/k12/livetext/index.html

LiveText is a comprehensive, annotated, structured index to online resources relating to network technologies and their use in K-12 schools. LiveText is being developed by the Institute for Learning Technologies at Columbia University, to support teachers and administrators in integrating technology into their curriculum and classroom.

Related Areas: *Teacher Resources*

Lycos
URL: http://www.lycos.com

Lycos is a diverse collection of Internet content. From a searchable index, to online sites organized by subject, to the latest national and international news, Lycos has something for everyone. Includes a comprehensive "City Guide" to the USA, featuring a clickable map of the country with links to nearly 8,000 online sites in 500 U.S. cities.

 Integration Idea

LetsNet and LiveText assist in integrating the Internet into the curriculum. Both sites include resources and/or lesson plans to print. Teachers who are not comfortable with using the Internet can gain information from the Learning Resource Server and then practice their newly acquired skills using the Lycos search engine.

Technology & Internet

Magellan Internet Guide
URL: http://www.mckinley.com

Magellan is an online directory of reviewed and rated Internet sites. Perform a search or explore Magellan topics and you'll instantly go to a list of sites in your area of interest. As the Internet expands, so does Magellan. Their writers review and rate thousands of new sites every month from every corner of the globe. Magellan's powerful search engine also categorizes and connects you with an ever-growing number of yet-to-be-reviewed sites. Magellan also allows you to search for "Green Light" sites, which have been found to be free of "adult" material.

Maggie's Guide To HTML Authoring Resources
URL: http://www.mindspring.com/~mconti/html.htm

A robust site with links to hundreds of other HTML-authoring resources on the Web, including how-to manuals; sound, image, and icon archives; browser and HTML editing software; and more.

Mailing List Directory
URL: http://k12.cnidr.org:90/lists.html

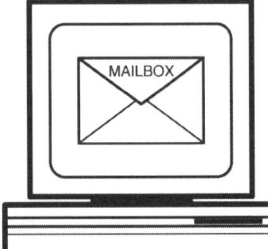

The Internet features thousands of email-based discussion lists on many topics, so that finding the one you want isn't always easy. This Web-based directory of educational discussion groups can help. Just click on the name of the list you'd like to subscribe to, fill in the appropriate information, click on the send button, and you're subscribed!

Related Areas: *Teacher Resources*

Microsoft Encarta Schoolhouse
http://encarta.msn.com/schoolhouse/

The Encarta site is an innovative, rich, online resource specially designed for educators worldwide. Every month the site features a timely curricular topic. Over the course of the month, the site's developers build a multidisciplinary collection of Microsoft Reference facts, Internet links, and learning activities related to that topic.

Related Areas: *Social Studies; Teacher Resources; Science*

 **Technology & Internet**

Multimedia Cross-Platform Page
URL: http://VTGinc.com/ebennett/

This single, simple Web page provides complete information on converting images, video clips, and audio bites across common computer platforms. That is, this site will help you convert that sound you recorded on your Macintosh into something you can play on your school's Windows 95 machine and vice versa. An important resource for educators involved with developing school Web sites or Web pages with their students.

Mustang
URL: http://mustang.coled.umn.edu/

Think of the University of Minnesota's Mustang Project as a new vehicle that enables educators to more efficiently cruise across the World Wide Web. The site gives you the tips and tricks you need to navigate the Web's offerings with the style of a '67 Mustang, helping you decide when to travel, which direction to take, and how far to go each time you surf. Using Mustang, teachers no longer have to worry about being overwhelmed by the vast amount of information on the Internet.

Related Areas: *Teacher Resources*

 Integration Idea

Teachers looking for random Internet help will find the Multimedia Cross-Platform site, Mailing List Directory, HTML Authoring Resources, and Magellan directory all very helpful in their searches. All these sites will assist teachers as well as student in increasing their Internet knowledge.

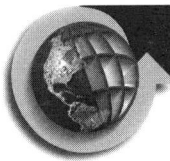

Technology & Internet

National Center for Technology Planning (NCTP)

URL: http://www.nctp.com

An in-depth site of interest to any school staffer involved in any aspect of technology planning! Includes professional articles about technology planning plus a sampling of state, district, business, and higher education planning guides from a well-known K-12 networking expert: Larry Anderson of Mississippi State University. Latest additions include real-time audio programs that help staffers develop tech plans, and new information on how to keep your technology plan up to date and relevant in today's fast-paced computer-centric world.

Net Beginners Central

URL: http://www.northernwebs.com/bc

If you're new to the Internet, head over to Beginners Central. Here you'll find an online Internet surfing tutorial that answers your burning questions about the Internet—from how to use email to retrieving the latest Internet browser software and plug-ins.

Networking for K-12 Schools

URL: http://falcon.jmu.edu/~ramseyil/network.htm

A beginner-level guide to creating local area networks (LANs) in K-12 schools. Includes links to a "computer jargon" dictionary, and more.

Related Areas: *Teacher Resources*

NYSERNet, Inc.

URL: http://nysernet.org

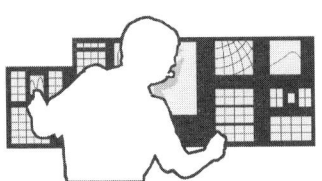

The New York State Education and Research Network (NYSERNet) provides high-speed Internet access to many of the state's K-12 schools, libraries, and museums. Their Web site provides information on their current educational projects, getting connected, and the latest networking technologies.

Related Areas: *Teacher Resources*

 **Technology & Internet**

On the Horizon
URL: http://sunsite.unc.edu/horizon/

No one knows for sure where the future will take us, especially in the world of education, where new technology is changing educators' methods of teaching day by day. The creators of On the Horizon, however, hope to lessen the shock of the new by keeping educators informed about the challenges that they will face in a changing world and the steps they can take to meet these challenges. The Web site itself holds a wealth of ideas and information for teachers to access. Their bimonthly publication covers national programs and in school issues, while their mailing list gives teachers the chance to share their own concerns and comments about changes in the world of education.

Related Areas: *Teacher Resources*

Online Faculty Lounge
URL: http://www.naples.net/media/wsfp/lounge.htm

Take a break from your hectic day and visit this friendly, online faculty lounge. You'll find a handy, straight-forward set of links to online magazines and newspapers, the latest information about distance learning and using the Net in schools, helpful hints about designing Web pages, and information about finding outside sources of funds for technology integration.

Related Areas: *Teacher Resources*

 Integration Idea

Combine the information about networking with technology planning and the Online Faculty Lounge, and you are ready to move your school into the computer age! Allow your students to work their way through the networking site until they have mastered the concept and then have them help set up the schools network system (assuming, of course, that you are creating a rather simple school network!).

Technology & Internet

Online Internet Institute
URL: http://oii.org

Wired educators know that the Net holds virtually unlimited potential for transforming education, but how do you apply its vast resources to your specific curriculum? The Online Internet Institute (OII) provides educators with a learning environment to support integrating the Internet into their individual teaching styles. OII offers a combination of online and onsite collaborations in which participants develop projects to use in their classrooms.

Related Areas: *Teacher Resources*

OWLink Distance Education Site
URL: http://www.rice.edu/armadillo/Owlink

The OWLink Project currently connects five schools in Texas via an interactive computer network. The site contains lesson plans that integrate the Internet into classroom activities, training materials for the teachers, online resources, and network plans for educators. Think of OWLink as a template for other states and countries to follow when creating large-scale computer networks for student and teacher use!

Peter Milbury's School Librarian Web Pages
URL: http://wombat.cusd.chico.k12.ca.us/~pmilbury/lib.html

An extensive guide to Web pages either created or maintained by school librarians for entire schools or just for themselves. Links to professional associations and creating Web sites are also here.

Related Areas: *Teacher Resources*

Plugged-In
URL: http://www.pluggedin.org/

This Web site is from Plugged-In, a nonprofit group that brings technology to low income families in Palo Alto, California. Here, you can browse through dozens of past or present projects to generate ideas for designing technology-based student projects at your school. There are great examples of computer learning activities that develop students' creative talents.

Related Areas: *Teacher Resources*

Technology & Internet

Point Review
URL: http://www.pointcom.com

PointCom Review is much more than an ordinary directory. Its creators have reviewed more than a million Web sites, and offer a searchable database of their reviews at this site! After reading the review, you can click on the name of the site and link right to it. No doubt you've seen sites with a "Top 5% of All Web Sites" award — this is the place where all of these great sites have been indexed.

Preservice Teacher Education: Technology
URL: http://www.coe.uh.edu/insite/elec_pub/html1996/06preser.htm

This incredible site was created by a trio of staffers from the University of South Florida. It's a synopsis of a presentation given by the team, which contains mountains of hands-on information to help preservice teachers get up to speed with technology and the Internet quickly and painlessly. The material also contains information to help link preservice educators to currently available technology field experiences. If you're a new teacher, or about to graduate, this is a must!

Related Areas: *Teacher Resources*

Quality Education Data (QED)
URL: http://www.infomall.org:80/Showcase/QED/

QED has tracked technology deployment and in public schools since 1981. The QED National Education Database is the source for the graphs contained in this presentation. Here are results of annual surveys of virtually all public schools in the U.S. (more than 80 percent) for technology usage.

Related Areas: *Teacher Resources*

Integration Idea

Is your classroom not quite as familiar with the Net as you'd like? Plugged-In has lessons that can be adapted and used in a classroom setting to help familiarize your students with the Internet. Add School Library Web Pages and Point Review for a listing of extra resources to assist students in their searches for online information.

Technology & Internet

Research-It
URL: http://www.iTools.com/research-it/research-it.html

Where can you find an online dictionary, thesaurus, quotation finder, foreign language dictionaries, maps, telephone numbers, and various library, financial, and mailing tools all at once? Why at the Research-It Web page, of course! Think of this as a *SavvySearch* for hurried educators. Using this page prevents you from having to go hopping around the Net from address to address while doing work. Here you can check the day's stock quotes, track FedEx packages, look up area codes, search through the King James Bible, and conjugate your French.

Related Areas: *Teacher Resources; Language Arts/Languages*

SafeSurf
URL: http://www.safesurf.com/

Here you'll find information about a rating system for the World Wide Web, a parent-child AUP, and instructions on how to block access to America Online chat rooms.

Related Areas: *Teacher Resources*

SavvySearch
URL: http://guaraldi.cs.colostate.edu:2000/form

Savvy Search links to more than a dozen Internet search engines, which are searched in real-time directly through this service. Enter your keywords, and Savvy Search sends them to all of the engines at the same time! Watch out, though; this is a very popular service, so it may take some time for the results to return to you.

SchoolWrite Students Software
URL: http://www.ozemail.com.au/~dbates/free.htm

This free software, which runs under DOS, was specifically designed for teachers and school administrators. Use it to maintain academic records, and provide a centralized database for all students—from the start of kindergarten through graduation.

Related Areas: *Teacher Resources*

Technology & Internet

SCOTT's Guide to Web Databases
URL: http://users.why.net/redbear/scott/

SCOTT is designed to help newcomers to the Internet use online search tools to find the information they need. First, access SCOTT with a search topic in mind. SCOTT knows that there is no one tool that is perfect for hunting down all of the information online. As a result, SCOTT asks you several questions about your information quest, and then suggests which tool is best for your search.

The Scout Report
URL: http://wwwscout.cs.wisc.edu/scout/report/

The Scout Report is published weekly by Inter NIC Information services, and contains links to the latest and greatest Internet sites to come online!

Search Engine Tutorial for *School Webmasters*
URL: http://www.northernwebs.com/set

The Search Engine Tutorial for *Web Designers* explains how to design your Web site with the search engines in mind, and why it is necessary to do so. Knowledge is a powerful weapon and having knowledge of what a search engine is going to do with your pages allows you to build a page that's guaranteed to be picked up and properly indexed by every search tool on the Internet.

 Integration Idea

These various sites assist in many ways in connecting you to an appropriate search engine. The search engine tutorial helps Webmasters in designing their sites and in deciding how to choose the best search engines for their site. School Webmasters should also consider integrating the Net into keeping track of student grades. The Schoolwrite site, for example, has free downloads of computerized report cards.

Technology & Internet

Steve and Ruth Bennett's Family Surfboard
URL: http://www.familysurf.com/

The Bennett family put together this award-winning Web site "to help parents enjoy fun and educational computing with their children." It includes information about great sites for kids and suggestions for online activities that help them explore the Net in a safe, purposeful manner.

Related Areas: *Teacher Resources; Social Studies; Science; Math; Language Arts/Languages; Art & Music*

Switched-On Classroom
URL: http://www.swcouncil.org/switch2.html

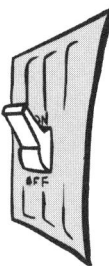

This site offers an online, hyperlinked book outlining a 12-step technology planning and implementation process for public schools. It contains instructive narratives, case studies of successful technology implementation, and an extensive listing of resources that will assist schools in their strategic planning efforts.

Related Areas: *Teacher Resources*

TalkCity EduCenter
URL: http://www.talkcity.com/educenter/

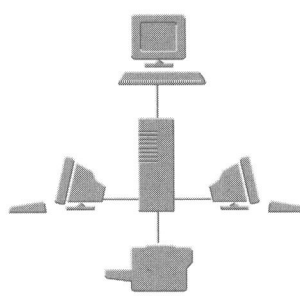

This Web Chat center, designed to allow educators to post their questions and comments, is divided into three general auditoriums. One for teachers, one for parents, and one for students. Each auditorium is then divided up into other rooms according to discussion topics. These topics include arts in the schools, classroom management, football coaching, and teaching students with special needs. There's also a special online journal offering news on upcoming conferences, resources, and projects.

Related Areas: *Teacher Resources*

Tammy's Technology Tips for Teachers
URL: http://www.sv400.k12.ks.us/tips/

Written by an educator for educators, this is a home-grown site that provides hands-on information to teachers who don't have time to learn all there is to know about technology in the classroom. There are tips to help educators at all levels use computers and the Internet in the classroom. An excellent offering!

Related Areas: *Teacher Resources*

Technology & Internet

Teaching Critical Evaluation Skills for the World Wide Web

URL: http://www.science.widener.edu/~withers/webeval.htm

The need for evaluating Internet resources, and particularly for evaluating World Wide Web resources, is increasing as more and more people are using the Web for research. This site provides materials to assist educators in teaching how to evaluate the informational content of Web sites by focusing on teaching how to develop critical thinking skills. A number of different checklists are available for printing, each one designed for a specific type of site (i.e., personal home pages, business pages, informational pages).

Related Areas: *Teacher Resources*

Teaching with Electronic Technology

URL: http://www.wam.umd.edu/~mlhall/teaching.html

Thousands of K-12 schools worldwide make it a priority to offer Internet access to their students and staff. But the question remains: How can educators integrate this wondrous resource into their curriculum, and then measure its effect on learning? This Web page is your link to the answers, with information about more than two dozen K-12 schools and institutions of higher learning already making the grade using the Internet in the classroom. In addition to links to online courses offered by five innovative schools, you'll find hyperlinks to pedagogical resources for "wired" teachers on virtually any subject, an online teaching demonstration using the Internet, and learning measurement tools.

Related Areas: *Teacher Resources*

 Integration Idea

Just because it's on the Internet doesn't mean it's always true. Use the critical evaluation site to gain information on how to evaluate a Web site and then instruct your students on this skill. Then have them visit Steve and Ruth's Family Surfboard to practice their evaluation of real sites. They can also discuss their favorite sites and the importance of judging information found online by chatting at the TalkCity Web site.

 **Technology & Internet**

Tech Corps
URL: http://www.ustc.org

Tech Corps is a national nonprofit organization that brings volunteers with technical expertise into schools to assist with local technology initiatives and projects. School districts connect with the group through their state Tech Corps chapter which can be located on the Tech Corps home page. Volunteers provide technical assistance and advice, staff training, mentoring, and assistance with classroom instruction.

Technology and Education Reform
URL: http://www.ed.gov/pubs/EdReformStudies/EdTech/welcome.shtml

This Web site is the result of a research project done by the U.S. Department of Education and SRI International. A team of researchers looked at nine school sites where school staff were active participants in incorporating technology in ways that support education reform. "These pages report on the experiences of the teachers and students at these schools."

Technology Coordinator's Home Page
URL: http://www.wwu.edu/~kenr/TCsite/home.html

 Your "official" job title may not be technology coordinator, but if you play a role in integrating technology in your school or district, then this site should be of interest to you. While most of the resources and references cited here are paper-based publications, there are also hypertext links to information on networking, administrative management, support, and general planning.

Related Areas: *Teacher Resources*

Technology Skills: Staff Assessment Survey
URL: http://www.mccsc.edu/survey.html

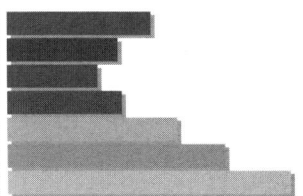 This Web page provides an excellent template for a staff survey which can be used to assess staff development needs, personnel expertise, curriculum integration levels, equipment standards, and maintenance scheduling. If your school is looking to make technology a solid, long-term part of the education process, then this assessment survey will help you get a handle on current and future needs.

Related Areas: *Teacher Resources*

Technology & Internet

TeleEducation NB: Learning on the Web   K-6
URL:http://teleeducation.nb.ca/lotw/

Learning on the Web: An Instructor's Manual helps teachers learn, adapt, and develop their own courses for delivery using the World Wide Web. With so many schools (elementary, secondary, university) beginning to offer courses via the Web, this is an important, one-stop source of information about developing online courses at your school at any level.

Related Areas: *Teacher Resources*

Using the Internet as a Telephone   K-6
URL: http://www.northcoast.com/savetz/voice-faq.html

Can you really use the Net as a telephone? According to this online document you can! Complete information on how to use the Internet to participate in live Internet chats. Perfect for use by students and educators! Includes links to free versions of the software that makes it all possible.

Using the WWW in Education   K-6
URL: http://wwwtools.cityu.edu.hk

This site is designed to help K-12 educators use the World Wide Web to deliver classroom content to their students. It provides links to the latest tools for teaching via the Web — including free software! An interesting site that looks to the future for schools around the world.

 Integration Idea

Wondering what, if anything, you can get for free on the Internet? Check out the Using the Internet as a Telephone and the WWW in Education Web sites. There you'll find free software that can be downloaded for use in your classroom. These sites are also a great way to get other teachers interested in using the Internet in their curriculum. Lastly, send your colleagues to the various technology sites listed here, and assist them in expanding their knowledge of the Internet.

Technology & Internet

Virtual Curriculum Coordinator (VCC)
URL: http://www.kuvcc.org

While there is a wealth of educational materials on the Web, the problem is knowing where to find them. Locating useful resources within the maze of information can be a sometimes daunting task. That's where VCC comes in, helping "wired" teachers and students make the most of their time online! This site is designed to assist teachers and students in locating and accessing the vast educational resources of the Web.

Related Areas: *Teacher Resources*

Way Cool Software Reviews
URL: http://www.ucc.uconn.edu/~wwwpcse/wcool.html

Do your students have a favorite CD-ROM or software that they'd like to share with other students and teachers? Do you? If so, this is the place to go. Students (and other interested people too) send in reviews of software they have at home or school that they think of as "way cool." While any software can be reviewed, the moderators are especially interested in software that is appropriate for students with disabilities.

Related Areas: *Teacher Resources; Language Arts/Languages*

Web21 Hot Sites
URL: http://www.web21.com/services/hot100/index.html

Looking to visit the latest and greatest Web sites to hit the Net this week? Look no further than the Web21 sites. It contains links to the most popular new Web sites, and excludes links to "inappropriate" material, colleges, Internet Service Providers, and Internet browsers.

Related Areas: *Teacher Resources*

Web Color Maker
URL: http://www.missouri.edu/~wwwtools/colormaker/

Want to spruce up your Web pages with color? Let this handy site help you color your text, backgrounds, links, and more. Advice on making tables and frames is also here. A must visit for every educator who encourages students to create Web pages!

Technology & Internet

The Web Developer's Virtual Library
URL: http://www.stars.com

Schools around the world are creating innovative, content-rich Web sites. Web-savvy educators and students who are looking for the latest information about online publishing now have a one-stop source of Web development information. This site contains the world's first online Webmasters' Encyclopedia. Over 500 pages and thousands of references are provided, all written in a fresh, conversational style. An immensely popular and respected resource for online developers and publishers—including K-12 schools!

WebCrawler
URL: http://www.webcrawler.com

The WebCrawler search engine is all about search and discovery. WebCrawler is a powerful, online searching service that helps you find personally relevant information in the sea of Web content. In addition, you'll find WebCrawler Select reviews and Special features to make WebCrawler the place to go when you're seeking some of the latest education-related sites or just want to see what's out there. WebCrawler is limited by the size of its index to Internet content, which is far smaller than its larger search rivals (HotBot and Alta Vista).

Webmaster Reference Library (WRL)
URL: http://www.webreference.com

School Web authors and Web masters will find the Webmaster Reference Library to be an invaluable tool to creating successful school Web sites. With over 700 carefully selected and annotated Web sites plus original articles, the WRL is a comprehensive Web developer's resource.

Related Areas: *Teacher Resources*

 Integration Idea

> Aid your students in creating wonderful colorful Web pages by using the Webmaster Reference Library, Web Developer's Virtual Library, and the Web Color Maker sites. All three of these will give you and your students hints and directions on how to make your school Web pages not only attractive, but eye-catching!

Technology & Internet

When the Book? When the Net?
URL: http://www.ilt.columbia.edu/k12/livetext/docs/netbook.html

When is a book the best place to turn? When is the Net the best source? When will a CD-ROM encyclopedia or periodical collection outperform them both? This informative article will help you ponder these questions as your school rushes onto the Information Superhighway.

The Well-Connected Educator
URL: http://www.gsh.org/wce/

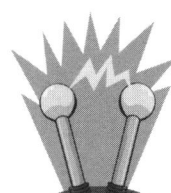

Do you consider yourself a well-connected educator? Would you like to be one? Then by all means, head over to this comprehensive site, a collaborative effort between the National Science Foundation, Microsoft, Compaq, and the Global Schoolhouse. This site is *the* online publishing center for the education community. It creates an arena for educators to publish; provides a forum to discuss educational technology issues; and promotes thinking about education reform and the impact of technology on learning.

Related Areas: *Teacher Resources*

The World Kids Network (WKN)
URL: http://worldkids.net/

Wow, what a massive site! WKN is a Web site for kids, run by kids from the ages of three to infinity. There are currently more than 500 children from every corner of the globe involved in this project, aimed at getting students educated and involved in their community, both online and off. Follow tour guides Gorf, Empress Zhimera, Robotica, and Duke "Nuke" Narley as they take you through such fanciful child-created sites as *G.I.R.L.*, *Rainbow Road*, *Critters*, and *Care Quest*.

Related Areas: *Art & Music; Language Arts/Languages; Social Studies*

World Wide Web FAQ
URL: http://www.shu.edu/about/WWWFaq/

A complete guide to the World Wide Web, from its historical origins to how to create your own Web content. Answers the most frequently asked questions of both neophyte and expert Web surfers. Sample questions include: What is the Web?, What is a URL?, Can I catch a virus from a Web site?, and Where can I obtain Web browser software?

Technology & Internet

Writing for the Web: A Primer for Librarians
URL: http://bones.med.ohio-state.edu/eric/papers/primer/webdocs.html

The most time consuming aspect of setting up a K-12 library/media center World Wide Web service is creating and maintaining the documents which make up the site. Save time by getting all the tips you need to set up your school's Web site right here!

Related Areas: *Teacher Resources*

Writing Web Pages with Wesley
URL: http://wtvi.com/html/

Learn the basics of creating Web pages with this in-service guide created for K-12 educators in Texas. The class is designed for Internet surfers with little or no experience creating Web pages. Via this material you'll learn how to put text and graphics on the Internet, link to other Internet resources, and more. Participants will depart this online class with a functional school Web page "skeleton" and the skills to further develop it.

WWWEDU Mailing List Home Page
URL: http://k12.cnidr.org:90/wwwedu.html

Introducing WWWEDU, an unmoderated mailing list dedicated to the use of the World Wide Web in education. WWWEDU is sponsored by The Center for Networked Information Discovery and Retrieval (CNIDR) and The Corporation for Public Broadcasting. The purpose of WWWEDU is to offer educators, school Webmasters, and policy makers a continuous discussion on the potential of World Wide Web use in education and K-12 schools around the world.

Related Areas: *Teacher Resources*

Integration Idea

Give your students practice in reading an informative and challenging article dealing with research materials and the information highway using the When the Book? When the Net? site. Then, encourage your students to visit World Kids Network and examine and discuss the different sites located there. Categorize them by subjects and rate them as being a useful or not useful site.

Technology & Internet

The WWW Virtual Library
URL: http://www.w3.org/pub/DataSources/bySubject/Overview.html

 Virtually every subject matter, from Aboriginal Studies to Zoology, is indexed and listed here at this very thorough guide of the different subjects and sources of information that exist online.

Yahoo!
URL: http://www.yahoo.com

An easy-to-use, graphical "subject tree" of World Wide Web sites geared to educators and older students alike. If you've got some extra time to search the Internet for educational information, Yahoo! is certain to contain enough links to relevant information to get you started. Major subject headings include: education, arts and humanities, news and media, reference, regional, government, social science, science, health, and society and culture.

Yahooligans!
URL: http://www.yahooligans.com

 Yahooligans! is a Web guide made specifically for students in grades K-6. It contains solid resources that are safe for searching and viewing by young students. Kid-friendly links include: world cultures, art soup, school bell, homework help, computers online, sports and recreation, science, entertainment, and news. Yahooligans! is the sister site to Yahoo!, an equally excellent starting point for adult Internet surfers who are new to the Net.

Favorite Sites

SITE:
URL:

NOTES:

SITE:
URL:

NOTES:

SITE:
URL:

NOTES:

SITE:
URL:

NOTES:

SITE:
URL:

NOTES:

SITE:
URL:

NOTES:

Favorite Sites

SITE:
URL:
NOTES:

SITE:
URL:
NOTES:

SITE:
URL:
NOTES:

SITE:
URL:
NOTES:

SITE:
URL:
NOTES:

SITE:
URL:
NOTES:

Favorite Sites

SITE:
URL:

NOTES:

SITE:
URL:

NOTES:

SITE:
URL:

NOTES:

SITE:
URL:

NOTES:

SITE:
URL:

NOTES:

SITE:
URL:

NOTES:

Favorite Sites

SITE:
URL:

NOTES:

SITE:
URL:

NOTES:

SITE:
URL:

NOTES:

SITE:
URL:

NOTES:

SITE:
URL:

NOTES:

SITE:
URL:

NOTES:

Now for...
Macintosh
PowerMac
& Windows!

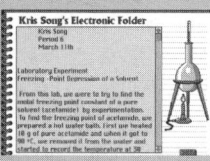

With HyperStudio YOU can:
- Create your own CD-style projects!
- Add multimedia elements in 60 seconds or less!
- Move Projects between Windows & Mac!
- Capture elements from the Internet, laser disc, CD-ROM, & Photo-CDs!
- Be successful from the very first time you use it!

Does your family have the software they need for our mediacentric world?

HyperStudio

As communicating ideas in visual form becomes increasingly important in this Age of CD-ROM and Internet, simple tools to create your own interactive presentations are a necessity! HyperStudio lets you successfully combine information, graphics, movies, and sound into exciting projects. Your family can now use one program, HyperStudio, to communicate in this new style of expression! From interactive reports for history, writing, and science, to executive-level business preparations, HyperStudio is being used by more families than all the other multimedia authoring programs combined!

Beyond bringing together text, sound, graphics, and video, only HyperStudio provides its own innovative approach to multimedia communication: Mac-Windows project compatibility, the ability to create & edit QuickTime™ movies, access data on the Internet, built-in capture of images with AV Macs or the QuickTake™ camera, and the widest range of file-type compatibility for graphics and sounds.

There isn't a typical age group or user for HyperStudio any more than there is for a pencil! Regardless of one's learning style, mode of expression, or grade level, HyperStudio makes it possible for non-technical users to create interactive multimedia projects with the look and feel of CDs.

FREE Preview CD!
Call us today and mention *Classroom Connect!*

For your FREE HyperStudio CD, call:
1-800-HYPERSTUDIO
1-800-497-3778

Roger Wagner PUBLISHING, INC.

HyperStudio is available from these dealers:
MacZone 1-800-248-000
MacWarehouse 1-800-255-6227

The way you do research.™
http://www.k12.elibrary.com/classroom

◆ A complete online research library.
◆ Deep and broad consumer reference product.
◆ The best way for students and families to do research.
◆ Content is as safe as local public library.
◆ Accessible via the Internet.
◆ Updated daily via satellite.

Using The Electric Library, a student can pose a question in plain English and launch a comprehensive and simultaneous search through more than 150 full-text newspapers, over 900 full-text magazines, two international newswires, two thousand classic books, hundreds of maps, thousands of photographs as well as major works of literature and art.

In a matter of seconds, query results are returned to a user ranked in relevancy order, displaying reference data, file size, and grade reading level. With this easy-to-use product a researcher need only click on the document or image of interest and it is automatically downloaded. The materials can also be copied and saved into a word processing document with bibliographic information automatically transferred.

Included in The Electric Library database are materials from world renowned publishers such as Reuters, Simon and Schuster, Gannett, World Almanac, Times Mirror, and Compton's New Media. The Electric Library also incorporates a host of local, ethnic, and special interest publications.

All retrieved information can be downloaded and saved or transferred to a word processor in real time, and used for educational purposes. This includes both the text and images from The Electric Library's databases.

PARTIAL LIST OF ELECTRIC LIBRARY CONTENT

Magazines/Journals	Books/Reference Works	Newspapers/Newswires
Art Journal	3,000 Great Works of Literature	Baseball Weekly
The Economist	Monarch Notes	Jerusalem Post
Editor & Publisher	The Complete Works of Shakespeare	La Prensa
Inc.		Los Angeles Times
Lancet	The World's Best Poetry	Magill's Survey of Cinema
Maclean's	Compton's Encyclopedia	Newsbytes News Service
Mother Jones	King James Bible	News India
National Review	Thematic Dictionary	New York Newsday
New Republic	Webster's Dictionary	Reuters
World Press Review	World Fact Book	USA Today

PRICING
Individual User: $9.95 per month
School Site License: $2,000 per year

(800) 638-1639

i! infonautics

Infonautics Corporation
900 W. Valley Rd., Suite 1000
Wayne, PA 19087-1830
Voice: (800) 304-3542
Fax: (610) 971-8859
Email: k12@infonautics.com

Making the most of *Classroom Connect*, online!!
How to take full advantage of our free Net services

For more than three years, *Classroom Connect* has offered top-of-the-line materials to wired educators who want to successfully integrate the Internet into their classrooms. In addition to our popular line of supplementary materials for online educators, we also offer an abundance of free online resources which are available 24 hours a day, seven days a week!

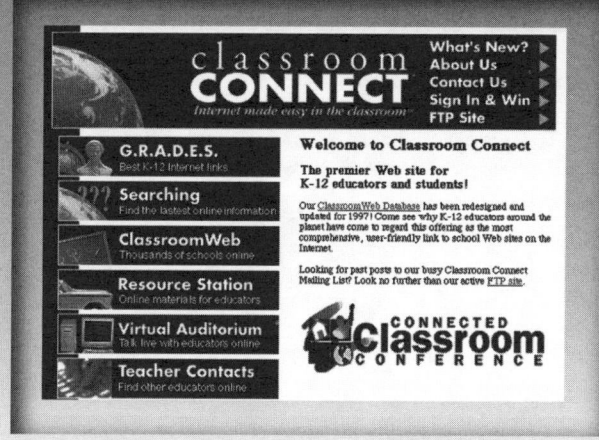

Classroom Connect Web Site
URL: http://www.classroom.net

Our free Web site is your link to the hottest educational Web links and in-depth information about using the Internet in the K-12 classroom worldwide. The staff of *Classroom Connect* has designed this site with three things in mind.
1. Our GRADES database and Searching Page help educators around the world locate and use the best K-12 educational resources the Internet has to offer. You'll find these links right on our home page.
2. Our Teacher Contact Database offers access to other wired teachers, lesson plans, projects, and keypals. Wired educators now have an easy way to find other teachers who are interested in doing keypal exchanges, projects, and more. Take a few minutes to fill out a Teacher Contact form. When you'd like to find other educators for online projects, keypal exchanges, etc., simply connect to our site and search through our database. We also offer a school Web site database (ClassWeb) where you can mount your school Web pages for free.
3. Discover how the *Classroom Connect* newsletter and our entire family of K-12 Internet products can save you precious time and help you to accomplish learning goals through the use of online technology. Our products area is your link to more information about our newest books, CD ROMs, conferences, seminars, and more. You can even place an order online.

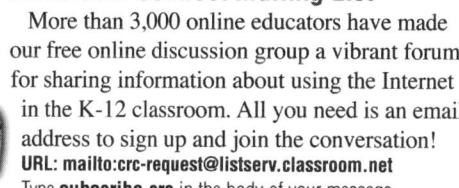

Classroom Connect Mailing List
More than 3,000 online educators have made our free online discussion group a vibrant forum for sharing information about using the Internet in the K-12 classroom. All you need is an email address to sign up and join the conversation!
URL: mailto:crc-request@listserv.classroom.net
Type **subscribe crc** in the body of your message.

A digest of past postings and more information about our list can be found on our Web site.
URL: http://www.classroom.net/classroom/maillist.html

Classroom Connect FTP site
Looking for teaching software, lesson plans, or the latest Internet navigation tools for your Macintosh or Windows PC? Our file transfer (ftp) site is up 24 hours a day, seven days a week to fill your needs. Access this URL with your Web browser to access our ftp site any time.
URL: ftp://ftp.classroom.net/